Bilingual Children: from Birth to Teens

Bilingual Children: from Birth to Teens

George Saunders

MULTILINGUAL MATTERS LTD
Clevedon · Philadelphia

P
115.2
.S28
1988

Library of Congress Cataloging in Publication Data

Saunders, George, 1948–
  Bilingual children.
  Bibliography: p.
  Includes index.
  1. Bilingualism in children. 2. Communication in the family.
I. Title.
P115.2.S28   1988   404'.2   88-5249

British Library Cataloguing in Publication Data

Saunders, George, *1948-*
  Bilingual children : from birth to teens.
  — 2nd ed. (Multilingual matters).
  1. Children. Bilingualism
I. Title   II. Series
404.2'088054

ISBN 1-85359-009-6 Pbk
ISBN 1-85359-010-X Hbk

Multilingual Matters Ltd
Bank House, 8a Hill Road   &   242 Cherry Street,
Clevedon, Avon BS21 7HH,   Philadelphia, PA 19106-1906,
England.   USA.

Typeset by Wayside Books, Clevedon, Avon BS21 7JG
Printed and bound in Great Britain by Short Run Press, Exeter
EX2 7LW

Contents

Preface

This book is based on and is a sequel to my book *Bilingual Children: Guidance for the Family* which was written in 1981 and published in November 1982. That work was based on a study of eight years of bilingualism in my family, a period extending from the birth of my eldest child, Thomas, through to his eighth birthday. The present book adds to this considerably, by describing as well developments which have occurred in the children's bilingualism during the subsequent five years, until Thomas enters his teenage years. This second book is about three children, rather than two as was the first. When the first book was written, my daughter Katrina had not yet begun to speak, but she is now a fluent young lady of six years. Her bilingual development is thus also described and compared with that of her two brothers. Since 1982 quite a number of publications have appeared which deal with various aspects of bilingualism, and in the present book I have added references to those which are relevant. Sections of my first book do also appear in this volume, where they are still applicable, but usually in a condensed or modified form in order to make room for new material. Many speech samples have been replaced by others, new speech samples have been added, some sections are completely new, e.g. a chapter on the children's experiences during their first ever visit to Germany. I hope, therefore, that readers familiar with my first book will find that this second volume answers their questions about what has happened in the intervening years, and also that new readers will find the present account complete in its own right.

Many friends and colleagues have helped me over the years with their continued interest in my research, with their encouragement, with fruitful discussions, suggestions, etc. I would particularly like to express my gratitude to the following, although the list is by no means exhaustive: Marjukka and Mike Grover, the enthusiastic publishers of Multilingual Matters; Jim Hunt of the University of Tasmania; Michael Clyne, Anne Pauwels, Susanne Döpke and Monty Wilkinson of Monash University; Manfred Pienemann of the University of Sydney; Bruno di Biase of the Macarthur Institute of Higher Education; Jürgen Meisel, Günter Radden and Jochen Rehbein of the University of Hamburg; Annick De Houwer of the Free University of Brussels.

Many other friends, relatives and acquaintances, too numerous to mention by name, also deserve thanks for assisting in various ways, e.g. by accepting and in some cases actively supporting the family's desire and efforts to bring up the children speaking two languages; without this acceptance and support, the task would undoubtedly have been much more difficult. I am particularly grateful to my parents, Kate and Tas Saunders, who, although themselves monolingual, have always encouraged me in my linguistic pursuits and have good-humouredly accepted the use of German between their son and his children.

My wife, Wendy, deserves a special word of thanks. She has helped in many ways, not only in the production of this book (e.g. by reading drafts and offering valuable suggestions on content and clarity), but also in the task of raising our children as bilinguals, by showing an unflagging conviction that this was not only possible but also a beneficial and enriching experience for the whole family.

Last, but definitely not least, to the three subjects of this study, Thomas, Frank and Katrina, for many pleasurable hours of conversation and play, for the many insights into bilingualism they have given me, as well as for their cheerful willingness to be recorded and written about, I would once more like to say simply, but very sincerely: "Danke schön".

George Saunders
Scamander, July 1987

Glossary

Ambilingual: Equilingual (see).

Balanced bilingual: Someone who is approximately equally skilled in two languages (but not necessarily passing for a native speaker in both, or even in one of them).

Bilingual: Able to use two languages (for some or all of the skills of speaking, listening, reading and writing).

Biliteracy: The ability to read and write in two languages.

Code switching: Switching from one language (or variety of a language) to another for part of a sentence or conversation (because of triggering [see], situation, stylistic reasons, etc.).

Cognate: A word in one language which is historically related to a word in another language and which in the present form of the language may still have basically the same meaning, e.g. German *Mutter* (= mother) and English *mother,* or a somewhat different meaning, e.g. German *Baum* (= tree) and English *beam.*

Dominance: The degree to which a bilingual is more proficient in one language than the other; the language in which there is greater proficiency is said to be his or her "dominant language".

Equilingual: Having an exactly equal command of two languages, usually with the added implication that native speakers of both languages would assume that one was a fellow native speaker.

Homophonous diamorph: A word having the same meaning and sounding the same or similar in another language, e.g. German *Bier* and English *beer.*

Intelligence quotient (IQ): A ratio of mental age to chronological age. A child with a mental age of 6 years and an actual age of 5 years has an IQ of 1.2, usually expressed as 120.

Interference: Transference (see).

Interlocutor: A person taking part in a conversation.

Language maintenance: Continuing to use a language in the face of competition from another language.

Language shift: Giving up using one language in favour of another (the opposite of language maintenance).

Lexical transference: The use of words from one language in another but which are not normally considered part of the other, e.g. "I'll meet you at the *Bahnhof.*" (German for "station".)

Linguistic: Of or relating to language or linguistics (see).

Linguistics: The scientific study of language. A person engaged in such study is a linguist.

Loanword: A word which originally belonged to one language but which is now also considered part of another, e.g. English has *Kindergarten* from German, *spaghetti* from Italian, *Kangaroo* from Guugu Yimidhirr, and so on. (In many cases loanwords started out as lexical transfers [see] but have now gained acceptance in the language.)

Mental age: The degree of mental development or intelligence of an individual in comparison with the average intelligence of normal children at different ages.

Monoglot: Monolingual (see).

Monolingual: Having only one language.

Multilingual: As for bilingual, but involving more than two languages.

Phonological transference: A sound in one language is identified with and pronounced like the closest available sound in another language, e.g. a German, lacking the /ð/ sound of "*that*" in his native language, may, when speaking English, substitute /d/ for it, thus "*dat*"; the result of phonological transference is perceivable as a foreign accent.

Polyglot: Multilingual (see).

Quotational switching: Leaving quotations in their original language while speaking another language, e.g. "and Dad said, '*Paß auf!*'" (German for "Watch out!").

Receiving bilingual: A person who understands two languages but who can speak only one.

Receptive vocabulary: One's hearing or "passive" vocabulary, i.e. the amount of words one understands (but does not necessarily actively use, e.g. one might *understand* the word "gargantuan" but never *use* it oneself).

Semantic transference: Either (a) the transference of the sense of a word in one language to a word in another language which is sometimes an equivalent (e.g. a German-English bilingual using "card" in English instead of "ticket", because German *Karte* means not only "card", but "map" and "ticket" as well), or (b) the transference of the sense of a word in one language to a word in another language which sounds similar but never has the same meaning (e.g. a German-English bilingual using *Rente* in German in the sense of "rent", whereas the German word means only "pension"). Included in semantic transference are also literal translations of words and idioms in another language (e.g. a German-English bilingual using "washbear", a literal translation of German *Waschbär,* instead of the normal English "racoon").

Syntactic tranference: The use in one language of sentence patterns and/or system of inflections belonging to another, e.g. a German-English bilingual's "I had my school jumper all day *on"* (which has the word order of the corresponding German sentence).

Switching: Code switching (see).

Transference: the use by bilinguals of any elements of one language in another (also referred to in the literature as "interference").

Transfer: Any example of transference (see).

Triggering: A switch from one language to another in a sentence or a conversation, brought about by a trigger word (see), a quotation said or heard in the other language, or the context of the situation.

Trigger word: A word which, because of its similarity in both languages, causes a bilingual to forget which language he is speaking and to switch from one language to the other, e.g.

This is called *edelweiss* — das ist eine kleine Blume . . .
(trigger word) (German: *that's a little flower . . .*)

Trilingual: As for bilingual, but involving *three* languages.

Unilingual: Monolingual (see).

1 Bilingualism

Introduction

This book has been written for all those interested in bilingualism, particularly in the bilingual upbringing of children in the home. It is directed not only at the reader with some background in linguistics, but also, and especially, at the non-specialist reader. Consequently, care has been taken to explain terminology and procedures in terms, which, it is hoped, will make them easily understood by the general reader. Explanations of the more technical terms are also listed in a glossary for easy reference. An English translation is provided for any material quoted in other languages.

Readers wishing to consult the works of authors mentioned in this book will find these acknowledged in the conventional way, e.g. Einar Haugen (1953:65) refers to page 65 of a work written by Einar Haugen and published in 1953; full publication details can be easily found by looking up HAUGEN 1953 in the bibliography at the end of the book.

Bilingual families are by no means a rarity in today's world. Indeed, bilingualism is a far more common phenomenon than the predominantly monolingual native speakers of a world language such as English might realize. In fact, bilinguals outnumber monolinguals. According to Joshua Fishman (1967), a prolific writer on bilingual matters, more than half of the world's population today uses more than one language while engaging in the activities basic to human needs. In many societies (e.g. in Papua and New Guinea, Africa, South America, India and South-East Asia, etc.) bilingualism has long been considered the norm rather than the exception. In Aboriginal Australian communities, for instance, as Bob Dixon (1980:32,69) points out in his book *The Languages of Australia*, there has always been a great deal of bilingualism "due to intermarriage, meetings at intertribal gatherings, and simply interest in acquiring new languages. Most people will speak at least two languages (and probably understand one or two others), while some may speak six or seven ... A child will often have parents speaking different languages." With the arrival of European settlers in 1788, "Aboriginal Australians — naturally multilingual in their traditional society — found no difficulty in learning to understand and speak good English" — a marked contrast to the predominantly

1

monolingual English-speaking settlers, few of whom ever learned to communicate with the original inhabitants in their own languages.

In this century many people have, for various reasons, left their homelands to settle or work in other countries where they have, of necessity, had to acquire some knowledge of the local language, thus becoming to varying degrees bilingual. In Australia, for instance, the 1976 Census (Clyne, 1979, 1980, 1982) revealed that 12.3% of the Australian population over the age of five regularly used a language other than English, compared with 1.4% who did not use English and 86.3% who used only English. (The actual percentage of bilinguals would undoubtedly be somewhat greater if account were taken of [i] people who know, but do not *regularly* use a language other than English; [ii] people who know more than one language but do not know or regularly use English.)

Parents who speak a language other than the officially recognized language of a country and who wish their own language to be retained in the home both by themselves and by their children, often do not succeed in achieving this. For example, the 1976 Australian Census showed that 44% of Dutch immigrants, 31% of Maltese immigrants, 28% of German immigrants, 20% of Polish immigrants, 10% of Yugoslav immigrants, 6% of Italian immigrants and 3% of Greek immigrants had shifted to using English only. In most cases this means that these immigrants will not pass, or will not have passed, the language on to their children. Indeed, in the second generation, the Australian-born children of immigrants, the shift to the use of English only is even more striking. If we take Maltese immigrants as an example, we find that about 31% of them have shifted to the use of English only; yet about 57% of second generation Australian of Maltese parents have shifted to using English only, this rising dramatically to about 97% where only one parent is Maltese.

Various reasons can be put forward to explain why such language shift takes place and why some individuals and groups are more successful than others at maintaining their language in another country. A factor favouring language maintenance is an immigrant's settling in an area of his new country where there is already a considerable number of people who speak his language — he then may have greater opportunities to use the language frequently in a number of domains, e.g. in shops, clubs, church, cinemas, perhaps even in employment; this in turn increases the likelihood that the language will continue to be used in the home and be passed on to the children. A family settling in a neighbourhood where their language is spoken by very few people has a much more difficult task in retaining their language. Yet such a situation may be looked on as a challenge and definite language maintenance efforts be undertaken. Other factors may also (as pointed out by Heinz Kloss (1966)) either aid or work against the retention of a minority language, for example, the attitude of the majority group in the society towards the minority language. A hostile attitude towards, or even attempts at suppression of, the minority language may cause its speakers to shift quickly to using only the majority language. On the other hand, such hostility may cause the minority language speakers to fight determinedly to retain their language.

The same applies if the majority group is tolerant of the minority language. Such tolerance can give minority language speakers, especially children, confidence in using their language. In some cases, however, lack of opposition to a minority language may lead to complacency among its speakers and result in no particular effort or interest being shown in retaining it or passing it on to the children.

Even when parents themselves retain their own language in a new country, why is it that so many fail to pass it on to their children? In some cases they simply do not try to do so; they see little point in their children speaking any language other than the language of the new country, since that is where they will be living and growing up. They are often reinforced in their attitude by the popular view, called by the Australian linguist Michael Clyne (1974:65) a "prize fallacy", that the children of immigrants will learn the majority language better if they forget their home language and if only the majority language is spoken in the home. (This is discussed further in chapter 2 in the section entitled "Infant bilingualism".)

In other cases parents do wish to pass their language on to their children, but are discouraged by the seeming impossibility of doing so. The views of Margret Hofmann (1957) a German immigrant in the U.S.A., are typical in this respect. She answers the question asked in the title of her article, "Can the mother tongue be retained for children of German immigrants?", in the negative:

> I believe that Americans will not have much success in their efforts to raise their children in the German language or bilingually... The quickly established rule, 'At home we will talk only German' can be followed for a very short time at best.

Referring to her experiences with her own child, she writes:

> ...we were enthusiastic, and with the little one, as well as in his presence, we talked German. But, perforce *(sic)*, our enthusiasm waned soon. After all, we were not the only ones who talked to him. All our guests, of course, spoke English. Whenever he visited he heard English ... For each item he had to learn two words: one German and one English, and that took him too long. As a result he began to stutter ...

She pessimistically concludes that the best that can be hoped to be done under such circumstances as far as the language is concerned is to get children "to practise typically German sounds frequently", so that they can learn the language more easily later on on a visit to Germany.

This book looks at the possibilities of bilingualism in the home much more optimistically, yet realistically. It aims to show that whilst difficulties will arise, as they do in most aspects of life, they are by no means insurmountable, and that parents *can* achieve a reasonable standard of bilingualism for their children. This is a view shared by, among others, readers who responded to the article by Margret Hofmann, e.g. Thomas Brandt (1957):

> I believe that the answer to the question raised depends a great deal upon the manner and method of approach, upon genuine interest, and circumstances of the project discussed. If German immigrants preserve their native tongue as a living thing without allowing it to disinte-grate..., if they are careful not to have it compete with the American language, and if they provide for a natural setting within their family, children will offer no resistance to speaking, reading or even writing it.

To which can be added the words of Henriette Vent (1957):

> Even if children do not learn all the German words and even if their speech may sometimes be halting, it is, in my opinion, far better to teach them to know and speak some German than to drop it altogether for fear of achieving mediocre results. I do not think that in bringing up nor-mally intelligent children bilingually, there is any danger that their English will suffer and turn into a hodgepodge. Their schooling, as well as the fact that most of their day is spent speaking English outside the home should prevent that.

A country's stock of languages can be seen as an important and valuable national resource, and the loss of any of them is to be regretted. After all, the ability to speak a language other than the majority language is seen as a desirable educational attainment in most societies, with one or more foreign language usually forming part of the school curriculum. Yet, paradoxically, often little is done in many societies to encourage the preservation of languages already spoken by many children at home. As the Australian sociologist, J. J. (George) Smolicz (1979:132) succinctly puts it:

> It is a curious fact that bilingualism in 'migrant' children is often discouraged, while the same phenomenon is favoured for the élite of the dominant group through the painful process of the acquisition of a second language at school.

Moreover, the number of children, at least in English-speaking countries, who persist long enough with a school language program to acquire a good level of competency in a foreign language is not great.

However, even when educational authorities show a more enlightened attitude and make provision for children from certain minority language groups to have some of their schooling in those languages as well as in the majority language, for many children this is already too late for them to benefit from it, since their competency in the minority language is by school age already minimal or non-existent. There is a need for information and encouragement to be given to families in which one or more parents speak a language other than the dominant language of the community and who wish their children to acquire that language, but are unsure how to go about it, and perhaps apprehensive about the possible consequences.

This book looks closely at how one Australian family has gone about raising its children bilingually over a period of thirteen years. It is hoped that by documenting in some detail what has happened, and is still happening, in one family, as well as drawing on other relevant research, other parents who are contemplating raising their children bilingually can be shown that whilst such an endeavour is not all plain sailing and does require some effort, it *is* possible and can be a rewarding experience for both parents and children. Much of the book consists of short anecdotes and incidents taken from tapes of the children's conversations; these have been chosen not only to illustrate various aspects of bilingualism in what, it is hoped, is an interesting and informative way, but also in the hope that they will reveal an actual normal family living its everyday life, a family in which two languages co-exist more or less harmoniously. The family is, however, not a model to be followed unswervingly. Obviously each family is unique, with its own particular set of circumstances. Readers will quickly realize whether certain things will work in quite the same way in their family and make appropriate modifications. It is hoped that this family's experiences will also show that it is possible for fluent non-native speakers of a minority language to create a bilingual home environment from which their children can derive considerable benefit.

Whilst the book does contain many anecdotes, it is by no means just impressionistic. The anecdotes are based on careful observation and are illustrated with actual dialogue, taken in most cases directly from over 600 hours of tape recordings made at regular intervals over the years. Moreover, the children's performance and progress in their two languages are analyzed not only interpretatively but also using objective measurements.

During the course of the book an attempt is made to give or suggest answers to many of the questions people raise concerning bilingualism in young children. Among the typical questions asked are:

— Should a child be exposed to two languages simultaneously or should one be established before the other is introduced? (See pp. 33–56.)

— Won't acquiring two languages simultaneously place too great a mental burden on a young child? (See particularly p. 21f., 33–49.)

— Will a child spoken to in two languages from birth begin to speak later than a child spoken to in only one language? (See p. 51.)

— Is the developmental sequence followed by a child acquiring two languages simultaneously the same as that followed by children acquiring only one? (See pp. 50–56.)

— What influence will one language have on the other? Will a child be able to keep his or her two languages separate? (See pp. 33–56 and chapter 7.)

— Will bilingualism retard a child's progress in the majority language of the community? (See pp. 33–56 and chapter 7.)

— Won't the effort of becoming bilingual retard a child's intellectual development? (See pp. 14–25 and chapter 7.)

— Will children simply acquire the home language if the parent(s) use(s) it to communicate with them or do they have to be formally taught the language? (See especially pp. 33–56.)

— Will family harmony be jeopardized if each parent speaks a different language with the children? (See particularly chapters 2–5.)

— What happens in such a case if a child wishes to address both parents at the same time? (See pp. 57–59.)

— Will bilingualism be effective with young children in a two language household if the parent who is to pass on the minority language has reduced contact with the children because of employment? (See particularly pp. 50–56 and chapter 6.)

— Won't the use of a minority language cause friction with acquaintances, friends and relatives who do not understand the language? (See chapter 5.)

— Won't being required to speak two languages cause young children to have difficulty expressing themselves or to stutter? (See especially pp. 100–105.)

— Won't children's desire to conform to their peers cause them to reject the home language when they start kindergarten or school? What can be done if children refuse to speak the language? (See particularly p. 109–114 and pp. 118–122.)

— Should dialect speaking parents who are bringing up their children bilingually in a foreign environment speak to them in the dialect or in the standard language? (See p. 219.)

— Won't attempting to teach children to read and write the minority language interfere with and impede their progress in reading and writing in the majority language at school? (See chapter 8.)

The suggested answers to these and other questions are based both on careful observation and evaluation of one family and on evidence from other studies of bilingual children.

What is bilingualism?

The word "bilingual" has different connotations for different people. To some people, bilingualism means "native-like control of two languages", a definition put forward by the American linguist Leonard Bloomfield (1933:56). However, such a definition leaves many speakers of more than one language unaccounted for, people who do not have "native-like control" of one (or even, in some cases, both) of their languages. Some writers refer to the type of bilingualism as defined by Bloomfield above as "true" bilingualism, and some are even more demanding in their definition than his "native-*like* control". Christopher Thiéry (1976), for example, calls a "true" bilingual someone who would at all times be taken for a native by native speakers of both languages concerned. He justifiably refers to this definition as restrictive and as representing the highest degree of bilingualism. Such bilingualism represents an ideal which is very rarely attained and which is perhaps best referred to by the less emotive term *equilingual* (also known as *ambilingual*), although a more precise description would probably be "dually monolingual", since a person at this level of bilingualism would in effect be able to function as if he or she were two monolinguals.

Some writers, unfortunately, use the term bilingualism without defining precisely what they mean. Ilsa Andrews (1980:273) in an article on bilingualism, for example, dismisses out of hand Werner Leopold's (1939–49) classic study of his daughter Hildegard's acquisition of bilingualism, *The Speech Development of a Bilingual Child: A Linguist's Record* (which is referred to often in this book), with the words:

> Looking for literature on bilingualism..., I discovered that this field of inquiry had had a very slow start in the 1930s, and that the early studies yield but little insight. Leopold's frequently quoted study of his daughter Hildegard turned out to be especially disappointing because *it does not deal with bilingualism, its title notwithstanding.* (This writer's emphasis.)

However, she offers no explanation as to why Hildegard should not be considered as a bilingual. Presumably she does so because Hildegard's ability in German was considerably less than in English. Contrast this with Leopold's (1949b:139) own assessment of Hildegard at age six years, two months:

Hildegard is now, for all practical purposes, bilingual. She understands in both languages everything within her range of comprehension and is capable of expressing her thoughts, feelings and wishes in both. The expression is, however, much more restricted and halting in German.

Andrews' judgement of Leopold's work is surprising, since none of the bilinguals mentioned in her article are equally proficient in both their languages. Moreover, to show that motivated adults can become bilingual, she quotes and lends credence to the far-fetched claims of a nineteenth century German, Heinrich Schliemann (1881:9) who wrote:

> ... I succeeded in acquiring in half a year a thorough knowledge of the English language. I then applied the same method to the study of French, the difficulties of which I overcame likewise in another six months ... This unremitting study had in the course of a single year strengthened my memory to such a degree that the study of Dutch, Spanish, Italian and Portuguese appeared very easy, and it did not take me more than six weeks (*sic*) to write and speak each of these languages fluently.

It is extremely doubtful if Schliemann's knowledge of English and French after six months of study, let alone his knowledge of the other languages he learned in six weeks, would match Hildegard Leopold's knowledge of German acquired over a period of many years.

How proficient does a person have to be, then, to be classed as a bilingual? Einar Haugen (1953:7), an American linguist who has worked extensively in the field of bilingualism, suggests that bilingualism begins "at the point where a speaker of one language can produce complete, meaningful utterances in the other language". Diebold (1961) considers that a type of bilingualism has even commenced when a person begins to *understand* utterances in a second language without being able to utter anything him- or herself.

Bilingualism, therefore, simply means having two languages (and bilingualism is often used in the literature to mean the same as multilingualism, that is, having more than two languages). Bilinguals can be ranged along a continuum from the rare equilingual who is indistinguishable from a native speaker in both languages at one end to the person who has just begun to acquire a second language at the other end. They are all bilinguals, but possessing different *degrees* of bilingualism. A monolingual (also called a unilingual or monoglot) is thus someone who knows only one language. (In this book monolingual is used, for the sake of convenience, to refer also to persons near the extremity of the bilingualism continuum, namely to persons who are minimally bilingual, that is, who have very little proficiency in more than one language.)

A bilingual's degree of bilingualism can be assessed in the four skills of listening comprehension, speaking, reading comprehension and writing. There are many possible combinations of abilities in these skills. Many children of immigrants, for instance, possess all four skills solely in the official language of their country of residence (e.g. English in Australia), whilst they may be able to understand only the spoken form of their parents' language (e.g. Italian) and barely be able to speak it. Mari Haas (1953) would class such children as "receiving oral bilinguals", since they are bilingual only in receiving the spoken form of two languages, in listening comprehension. Someone who is bilingual in all four skills would, using this system, be classified as a "receiving sending oral visual bilingual". Again, within each skill there could be differing abilities in each language, e.g. an English-Chinese bilingual educated through English could be much more proficient at writing English than Chinese, whereas his spoken Chinese could be better than his spoken English, and so on.

The term "balanced bilingual" is frequently encountered in the literature on bilingualism. Whilst some writers (e.g. Haugen, 1973:508) use it as a synonym of equilingual, most researchers use "balanced bilingualism" in a different sense which does not imply perfect mastery of both languages (e.g. Peal & Lambert, 1962:8). Balanced bilinguals in this sense are bilinguals who are roughly equally skilled in their two languages, i.e. a balance exists between the two.

This means that someone who could pass for a native in both languages would be considered a balanced bilingual, but so too would someone whose performance in one (or both) of his languages was less than perfect, as long as his ability in both was roughly equal. Much of the recent research comparing bilingual and monolingual children has been done with balanced bilinguals. Various tests are used to determine which bilinguals are balanced. For example, Doyle *et al.* (1978:16) used the Peabody Picture Vocabulary Test (see chapter 7 for further details of this test), and called those children balanced bilinguals who had a discrepancy of 20 IQ points or less between the French and English forms of the test. One of the tests used by Peal and Lambert was a word association test in which children had to write down in 60 seconds as many words as they could think of in the same language as particular stimulus words. A child who overall scored 20 words in French and 20 in English was obviously classed as balanced on this test, but so too was someone scoring 20 words in French and over 11 in English (or vice versa). A similar leniency of assessment is shown by other researchers (e.g. Louis Balkan, 1970).

Even balanced bilinguals are therefore usually "dominant", that is, more proficient, in one of their two languages, although they may not be dominant in the same language in all areas. There may be domains or situations in which bilinguals usually use only one of their two languages, e.g. an Australian child may use only English at school but speak only Greek with his or her mother at home; consequently he or she may have a greater English school vocabulary and be better able to talk about events at school in English, yet be better able to talk about, say, cooking in Greek. A number of tests can be administered to determine language dominance in various domains or contexts (see the final section in chapter 7 for discussion and examples).

The term "dominant" is also used (e.g. by John Macnamara, 1967), to describe two other aspects of bilingualism. Firstly, for one language to be used when, from the point of view of speaker, topic, situation and so on, the two languages are equally suitable, e.g. a German-English bilingual might keep a diary in English, when he or she could equally well use German; such a preference when there is a choice could be taken as an indication that his or her dominant language is English. Secondly, "dominant" is used with reference to the tendency for a bilingual's two languages to have some influence on each other, that is, for what Weinreich calls "interference" to take place between the two languages. In his book *Languages in Contact*, Uriel Weinreich (1953:1) defines interference as:

> Those instances of deviation from the norms of either language which occur in the speech of bilinguals as a result of their familiarity with more than one language.

Michael Clyne (1967) in his work *Transference and Triggering*, a perceptive study of the language of German-speaking immigrants in Australia, prefers the term "transference" to refer to this transferring of elements of one language into another, and this is also the term which will be used in this book. Transference may be of various types, as shown in the following examples from the speech of English-German bilinguals (more detailed explanations of the terminology with illustrative examples are given in the section beginning on p. 92): *lexical*, e.g. Katrina (2;4,10) (= age two years; four months, ten days; all ages will be given in this form): A gorilla's *wie* a big monkey (from German *wie* = "like"); *semantic*, e.g. Thomas (6;7,8): *Before* two weeks Craig's dog had pups (from German *vor* = "before", "in front of", "*ago*"); *syntactic*, e.g. Frank (5;9,29): And then we'll walk the hill *up* (from the German sentence pattern where "up" [*rauf*] would occur at the end: Und dann gehen wir den Hügel *rauf*); *phonological* (using sounds from the other language, resulting in a foreign accent); etc. Transference can occur in both directions, that is, from language A to language B as well as from language B to language A. The language in which transfers (instances of transference) occur least is thought to be a bilingual's dominant language.

But, as has been seen above, there are also various other factors which may be taken into consideration when determining a bilingual's dominant language, and for some bilinguals it may be difficult to decide with any precision which language could, overall, be considered dominant. Although very few bilinguals manage to avoid interference or transference altogether, they usually have one language in which it is reduced to a minimum (as in the English of the children in this study; see, for example, chapter 7).

As will be seen, the type of bilingualism attained by the children in this book falls within the definition of balanced bilingualism given above. An effort is made to achieve some sort of balance between the two languages in all domains. A realistic achievement to be aimed at would seem to be what Anastasi & Cordova (1953:32) call "bilingual parallelism", that is, a type of bilingualism where the individual learns to express himself in *all* types of situations *in at least one language*. The other language "provides a parallel means of expression in some *or* all situations, depending on the thoroughness of its mastery."

In an article entitled "The bilingual as a competent but specific speaker-hearer" François Grosjean (1985:471) makes a strong plea for what he calls the bilingual (or wholistic) view of bilingualism in any consideration of bilinguals. This is in contrast to the monolingual (or fractional) view, which always compares the linguistic ability of bilinguals with that of monolingual speakers of the languages concerned, and which has for so long dominated the thinking of researchers, educators and laypeople. Taking the wholistic view, a bilingual should *not* be considered as the sum of two complete or incomplete monolinguals, since the bilingual has a unique and specific language configuration:

> The coexistence and constant interaction of the two languages in the bilingual has produced a different but complete language system. An analogy comes from the domain of athletics. The high hurdler blends two types of competencies: that of high jumping and that of sprinting. When compared individually with the sprinter or the high jumper, the hurdler meets neither level of competence, and yet when taken as a whole, the hurdler is an athlete in his or her own right. No expert in track and field would ever compare a high hurdler to a sprinter or to a high jumper, even though the former blends certain characteristics of the latter two. ... In many ways the bilingual is like the high hurdler: an integrated whole, a unique and specific speaker-hearer, and not the sum of two complete or incomplete monolinguals.

An important aspect of bilingualism is *code switching*. Code switching, or switching from one language to the other, in the course of a conversation, even in mid-sentence, is usually carried out by bilinguals without any significant pause in the flow of speech. (Speakers of only one language also switch in a similar fashion between varieties of that language, e.g. between an English dialect and Standard English.)

Switching may be due to a number of factors, both linguistic and extralinguistic. Among the extralinguistic factors the following are the most common. Firstly, the person being spoken to is obviously an important consideration. A monolingual speaker of either of a bilingual's languages will clearly be addressed in the language which he or she can understand, e.g. the children in this study, if speaking German to their father, will switch to English to address people who understand only English. But what if both speakers know both languages? Often one of the two languages becomes established as the one mostly used. This is the case in families where communication between certain members of the family may take place in one language, between other members in another, e.g. in this study communication between children and father is in German, between children and mother in English, so that in a family conversation the children switch frequently from one language to the other depending on which parent they are addressing, e.g.:

> **Frank** (5;6,0) (to father): Das war Klasse (*That was terrific*), wasn't it, Mum?

Young children quickly become very skilled at this type of switching, switching automatically and seemingly effortlessly whenever required to do so.

Some bilinguals may switch languages according to domain, e.g. in some Australian families children speak a non-English language in the home to certain members of the family, but the moment they leave the home domain and go out into the community they switch to English to speak to the very same people.

Amongst themselves bilinguals may also switch languages for stylistic reasons, e.g. according to topic; they could be discussing school or work in one language, yet switch to another to talk about sport (perhaps because each topic is strongly associated with a particular language). Similarly, while speaking one language to each other, bilinguals may switch to their other language to quote something written or something said in that language, in much the same way as a speaker of Australian English might attempt a British English accent when quoting an Englishman (see the section on quotational switching in chapter 4). In discussions and arguments between bilinguals a speaker may switch to a language in which he feels he can make his point more forcefully or eloquently.

Much depends on the attitude of bilinguals towards language switching as to how much switching actually takes place in any interaction. Some bilinguals like it to be kept to a minimum, preferring one language or the other to be used, whilst other bilinguals are quite happy to switch languages constantly according to topic, etc. In the home children are, with regard to switching, guided to a large extent by their parents' preferences and example.

Another kind of switching is what Michael Clyne (1972:24) calls "internally conditioned switching", that is, switching caused by linguistic factors. The occurrence of a word which belongs to, or at least appears to belong to both languages (e.g. a proper noun such as Canberra) causes a speaker to forget momentarily which language he or she is speaking, and he or she continues in the other language, until it is realized what has happened. Clyne (1967) calls such words "trigger words", since they trigger a more or less unconscious switch from one language to another. The switch may be made just before trigger words ("anticipational switching") or, more commonly, immediately following them ("consequential switching"), e.g.:

Frank (5;5,3): Mum, what can I have to drink?
Mother: Do you want some Prima?
Frank: Ja, bitte, (*Yes, please.*) (PRIMA, which is an Australian brand of orange juice but also a German word meaning "terrific", has triggered a switch from English to German.)

Although some involuntary switching and transference do occur between a bilingual's two languages, albeit to different degrees in different individuals, bilinguals are usually remarkably adept at keeping the two functionally separate when speaking. (For remarks on very young bilingual children see chapter 3.)

Einar Haugen (1956:72) points out that a crucial factor in the kind and extent of a person's bilingualism is the age at which the two languages are acquired, because the aptitudes, opportunities and motivations for learning are so different at various ages. He thus refers to *infant, child, adolescent* and *adult* bilingualism.

Infant bilingualism is the type under close scrutiny in this study, although the other types, particularly child bilingualism, are also referred to. Infant bilingualism is the *simultaneous* acquisition of two languages from birth (see the section entitled "Infant bilingualism" in chapter 2 for further details). Child bilingualism implies *successive* acquisition of two languages, that is, a child acquires first one language within the family and then acquires a second language through kindergarten and/or the early school years. The distinction between infant and child bilingualism is in some cases difficult to draw. For example, a child may be exposed to only one language in the home but have some informal contact with speakers of the other language right from the beginning. Infant and child bilinguals usually acquire both their languages with a native or native-like pronunciation, whereas adolescent bilinguals (who become bilingual after puberty) and adult bilinguals (who acquire their second language when adults) usually speak their second language with a non-native accent (see the section entitled "Phonological transference" in chapter 7 for further discussion of this phenomenon).

Louis Balkan's (1970) major study of Swiss 11–16-year-old bilinguals suggests that infant and early child bilingualism could have certain advantages over later child bilingualism. Balkan first compared all his bilinguals with monolinguals, with whom they were matched for non-verbal intelligence and socio-economic status. The bilinguals scored at a significantly higher level on tests of numerical aptitude, verbal flexibility, perceptual flexibility and general reasoning. Balkan then divided the bilingual group into two: those who had become bilingual *before*

the age of 4 and those who had become bilingual *after* the age of 4. He found that
the early bilinguals were not only markedly superior to the monolinguals but also
significantly superior to the later bilinguals.

Is bilingualism an advantage or a disadvantage?

For many of the world's bilinguals this question is purely academic: they
have no choice but to be bilingual. But for parents who are in a position to decide
whether they are to raise their children bilingually or not, the arguments for and
against bilingualism are an important consideration in making that decision.

Much controversy has surrounded the question of whether a person's,
particularly a child's, bilingualism can be considered an advantage or a disadvantage. Much of the writing on the subject during the first half of this century
concentrated on what were seen as the detrimental effects of bilingualism. In 1922,
for instance, Otto Jespersen wrote in his book *Language. Its Nature, Development
and Origin*:

> It is, of course, an advantage for a child to be familiar with two
> languages, but without doubt the advantage may be, and generally is,
> purchased too dear. First of all the child in question hardly learns either
> of the two languages as perfectly as he would have done if he had
> limited himself to one... Secondly, the brain effort required to master
> two languages instead of one certainly diminishes the child's power of
> learning other things which might and ought to be learnt. Schuchardt
> rightly remarks that if a bilingual man has two strings to his bow, both
> are rather slack... (p.148)

Bilingualism has been seen as something unnatural. In 1933, Leo Weisgerber
a German linguist, believed that bilingualism could impair the intelligence of a
whole ethnic group. Thirty-three years later, Weisgerber still believed that any
possible advantages of bilingualism were outweighed by what he saw as "the
certain detrimental effects", that by nature man was basically monolingual, and that
being bilingual was like trying to belong to two different religions at the same time.

In an article published in Switzerland in 1928, de Reynold expressed the
opinion that bilingualism leads to language mixing and language confusion which
in turn results in a reduction in the ability to think and act precisely, a decrease in
intelligence, an increase in mental lethargy and reduced self-discipline.

Besides such evidence against bilingualism based on personal intuition,
many studies also seemed to indicate that bilingualism had a negative effect on in-

tellectual development. In 1923, Saer, for instance, studied 1,400 7–14-year-old Welsh-English bilingual children in five rural and two urban districts of Wales, and concluded that bilingualism results in lower intelligence. However, Saer failed to consider social differences between the bilinguals and monolinguals. Even so, it was only in the rural districts that the bilinguals were found to score lower on intelligence tests; in the urban districts the bilinguals' average IQ was slightly higher than that of the monolinguals:

TABLE 1

	Average IQ	
	Urban districts	Rural districts
Monolingual children	99	96
Bilingual children	100	86

It seems that the urban bilingual children had much more contact with their second language before beginning school and then outside school hours than did their rural counterparts. There would thus be much more balance between the urban bilinguals' two languages than would be the case with the rural bilinguals, and this would allow them to complete on a more equal footing with monolinguals in verbal intelligence tests. Subsequent research in Wales (e.g. by Morrison in 1958) shows also that if the occupational status of parents is taken into consideration when comparing rural and urban children no differences are found.

Caution must be exercised when comparing monolinguals and bilinguals on tests of intelligence, particularly on tests of verbal intelligence, and particularly if, as often happens, the bilinguals are tested in only _one_ of their languages, perhaps their "weaker" language (see the first part of chapter 7 for further discussion).

In 1956, Einar Haugen, in a review of studies conducted in America to that time, concluded that knowing two languages did not appear to affect non-verbal intelligence. He noted further that the verbal intelligence of bilinguals was retarded at most by two years at any point, and that this difference disappeared by the time bilinguals reached college age.

However, even these conclusions have been convincingly challenged by research carried out since the early 1960s which shows bilingualism in a very favourable light. In 1962 Elizabeth Peal and Wallace Lambert, for example, studied the effects of bilingualism on the intellectual functioning of ten-year-old children from six Montreal French schools. The bilingual children, who were selected for being balanced bilinguals, were matched for socio-economic class, sex and age. At the start of their study, Peal & Lambert predicted that their findings would be similar to those of previous investigations, i.e. that whilst non-verbal IQ tests would reveal little difference between the bilinguals and monolinguals, the monolinguals would perform significantly better than the bilinguals on verbal tests of intelligence.

However, both of these predictions proved to be wrong. Not only did the bilinguals perform *significantly better* than the monolinguals on the *nonverbal* IQ tests, but also scored significantly higher on all the tests of *verbal* IQ. Moreover, the bilingual children were found to be in a higher grade at school than the monolingual children of the same age, and also to achieve better results in their schoolwork than the monolingual children in the same grade. Peal & Lambert (1962:15) thus concluded: "... it appears that our bilinguals, instead of suffering from 'mental confusion' or a 'language handicap' are profiting from a 'language asset'." These findings seriously question the not uncommon belief, such as expressed by Andrew Wilkinson (1970:100) in his book *The Foundations of Language*, that "learning a second language imposes a burden on development in both languages and on educational attainment."

Peal & Lambert (1962:20) sum up their research as follows:

Intellectually [the bilingual's] experience with two language systems seems to have left him with a mental flexibility, a superiority in concept formation, and a more diversified set of mental abilities, in the sense that the patterns of abilities developed by bilinguals were more hetero-geneous. It is not possible to state from the present study whether the more intelligent child became bilingual or whether bilingualism aided his intellectual development, but there is no question about the fact that he is superior intellectually. In contrast, the monolingual appears to have a more unitary structure of intelligence which he must use for all types of intellectual tasks.

These results were criticized (e.g. by John Macnamara, 1966) on the grounds that the bilingual students were chosen for the study if their English vocabulary was comparable to their vocabulary in their mother tongue, French; since there is generally a relationship between vocabulary and intelligence — the greater the vocabulary the higher the intelligence — it seemed probable that only the intellec-tually brighter children were chosen for the bilingual group. Wallace Lambert and Elizabeth Anisfield (née Peal) (1969) convincingly refuted this objection: the important criterion for selecting the bilingual children was that they had to approach a balance of skills in their two languages, i.e. they had to be approximately equally good *or poor* in both languages.

A large scale follow-up study by Anisfield (1964) confirmed the conclusions reached in the 1962 investigation: groups of immigrant children who, because of their circumstances, had no choice but to be bilingual, were found to score better on intelligence tests than monolingual control groups.

Other studies also indicate that bilingualism can have a positive effect on intelligence and can give a child certain cognitive advantages over his or her mono-

lingual peers. Norman Segalowitz (1977), for example, states that "the bilingual's
verbal and cultural background is inherently richer because of its bilinguality, and
thus produces an earlier occurrence of certain experiences critical to intellectual development". Some of these cognitive advantages can be summarized as follows:

(a) Earlier and greater awareness of the arbitrariness of language

Anita Ianco-Worrall's (1972) study of Afrikaans-English 4–9 year-old bilingual children in South Africa showed that bilingual children analyse language more
intensively than do monolinguals and are better able to analyse language as an
abstract system. The bilingual children become conscious at a much earlier age of
the fact that names are arbitrarily assigned to objects and are subject to change. That
is, that there is no intrinsic connection, for example, between the word *dog* and the
animal it symbolizes. A word is just what people use it to mean; it is not an attribute
of the thing it names.

The bilingual and monolingual children in Ianco-Worrall's study were asked
questions such as: "If you were making up names for things, could you call a dog
'cow' and a cow 'dog'?" The great majority of the monolingual children replied
that the names of objects could *not* be changed, whilst the majority of the bilingual
children agreed that in principle this could be done.

Feldman & Shen's (1971) study of 4–6-year-old Spanish-English bilingual
American Headstart children and Jim Cummins's (1978) study of grade 3 and grade
6 Irish-English bilingual children confirmed Anita Ianco-Worrall's findings: 68.8%
of the Spanish-English bilinguals and 70% of the Irish-English bilinguals, compared with only 31.1% and 27.5% respectively of the children in the monolingual
control groups, asserted that the names of things could be interchanged. It would
seem that the experience which bilingual children have in acquiring their languages, part of which is an early realization that most things are referred to in at least
two ways, not just one (e.g. dog/*Hund*), promotes this sort of awareness.

(b) Earlier separation of meaning from sound

The ability to separate the *meaning* of a word from its *sound* is, as Jim
Cummins (1976:33) points out, "necessary if a child is to use language effectively
as a tool for thinking". The available evidence suggests that bilingualism can give
children a head start here. Ianco-Worrall (1972) for example, found that the
bilingual children in her study were capable of separating the meaning of a word
from its sound at a much earlier age, in fact some two to three years earlier, than their
monolingual peers. The children were given 8 sets of 3 words, such as *cap, can* and
hat, and asked, "which is more like *cap — can* or *hat?*" 54% of the 4–6-year-old

bilinguals consistently interpreted similarity between words in terms of *meaning* rather than their sound, whereas almost none of the monolingual children did this. Thus, monolinguals chose *can* as being more like *cap*, because of the similarity in sound, whilst the majority of bilinguals chose *hat* because of its similarity in meaning to *cap*.

These findings are confirmed by Sandra Ben-Zeev's (1972) study of Hebrew-English bilingual children and offer support for Leopold's (1949a:188) claim that:

A bilingual, who constantly hears two words for one thing, is compelled to pay more attention to the meaning expressed than the word used to express it, whereas the monolingual is often satisfied with a hazy definition of a word and will use it without understanding it fully.

(c) Greater adeptness at evaluating non-empirical contradictory statements

Jim Cummins (1978) found that grade 3 and grade 6 bilingual children (whose home language was English but who at school were being taught through Irish) were better able to evaluate non-empirical contradictory statements than monolingual children with whom they were matched on IQ, socio-economic status and age. This type of statement takes the form: "The counter in my hand is blue and it is not blue." The children had to answer true, false, or whether it was not possible to know, and then had to justify their responses.

(d) Greater adeptness at divergent thinking

Scott (1973) carried out a seven-year-study of a group of English-Canadian children who were given the opportunity to become bilingual by doing most of their schooling in French. He found that these bilingual children performed better than monolingual peers on divergent thinking tasks. Divergent thinking is a special type of cognitive flexibility which some researchers see as an index of creativity while others look on it more cautiously, for example Wallace Lambert (1977:17) who calls it "a distinctive cognitive style reflecting a rich imagination and an ability to scan rapidly a host of possible solutions". Measures of divergent thinking provide a person with a starting point for thought and ask him or her to produce a whole series of permissible solutions, such as "Think of a paper clip and tell me all the things you could do with it."

(e) Greater adeptness at creative thinking

Carringer (1974) measured the creative thinking ability of 15-year-old "balanced" Spanish-English bilingual children and compared it with that of monolinguals. The bilinguals scored higher than the monolingual control group in all respects (verbal and figural fluency, flexibility and originality). In his discussion of these results, Carringer says:

> Although only exploratory, this study suggests that bilingualism does promote creative thinking abilities and at least in part serves to free the mind from the tyranny of words. Since the bilingual has two terms for one referent, his attention is focused on ideas and not words, on content rather than form, on meaning rather than symbol, and this is very important in the intellectual process as it permits greater cognitive flexibility.

(f) Greater linguistic and cognitive creativity

Carolyn Kessler & Mary Quinn (1987) have carried out a number of empirical investigations of the effects of bilingualism on the linguistic and cognitive creativity of children. Their research both confirms what has been said above in (d) about bilingual children's superiority in divergent thinking and also reveals other intellectual advantages which appear to be the result of bilingualism. In one study (1987:177), very low socio-economic grade 6 Spanish-English bilingual children in the USA were compared with upper socio-economic grade 6 English-speaking monolingual children on their ability to solve science problems and to write scientific hypotheses after a 5-week science inquiry program. The bilinguals consistently outperformed the monolinguals on both the quality and linguistic complexity of their hypotheses.

In another study (1987:178) with similar groups of 11-year-old, grade 6 children, it was found that even though the upper socio-economic monolingual English-speaking children performed better than the very low socio-economic Spanish-English bilingual children on a standardized test of reading in English, the bilinguals generated over three times as many high quality scientific hypotheses (divergent thinking) and used more complex language to do so than the monolinguals. In addition, the bilingual children demonstrated a much higher level of *convergent thinking* by making much greater use of metaphors — over twice as many as their monolingual peers. Whereas *divergent* thinking entails generating a large number of possible solutions to a problem, *convergent* thinking involves, as the name implies, zeroing in "on disparate objects and ideas, relating them to each other to find a commonality. A metaphor points up a surprising similarity between apparently unlike things in the process of creating and transferring meaning from one universe of knowledge to another" (Kessler & Quinn, 1987:181). "Metaphors are taken as indicators of the cognitively creative ability to utilize data in making generalizations and manipulating variables. In both aspects of creativity, linguistic and cognitive, the bilinguals appear to excel" (Kessler & Quinn, 1987:180).

(g) Greater social sensitivity

There is some evidence indicating that having two languages can give children a greater social sensitivity than monolingual children. For example, Genesee, Tucker & Lambert (1975) found that English-speaking children in French school immersion programs (i.e. receiving most of their instruction through French) proved to be more sensitive to the communication needs of blindfolded listeners than other children.

Sandra Ben-Zeev (1977b:41) found that bilingual children tended to be more sensitive to cues, being more open to correction and guidance than monolinguals.

(h) Greater facility at concept formation

The experiments of Liedtke & Nelson (1968), using a Concepts of Linear Measurement Test with 6-year-old monolinguals and children exposed to two languages in the home, confirmed Peal & Lambert's (1962) conclusion that bilinguals were significantly better at concept formation, which is a major part of intellectual development. They surmise that this is because the bilingual child, by virtue of his or her two languages, is exposed to a more complex environment and to a greater amount of social interaction compared to a child acquiring only one language.

These studies certainly give a brighter picture of the effects of bilingualism on children's intellectual development. However, it should be noted that the bilingual children in these studies were chosen because they showed no great differences between their two languages, that is, they were all types of "balanced" bilinguals (although they were by no means equally proficient in their two languages). Also, in some cases other tests were conducted in which there was no significant difference in results between the bilinguals and the monolinguals, e.g. the bilinguals' performance on empirical questions (e.g. "The counter in my hand is yellow and it is not green. True or false?") in Jim Cummins's (1978) study was not significantly better than that of monolinguals.

Jim Cummins (1976:23) hypothesizes that "those aspects of bilingualism which might accelerate cognitive growth seem unlikely to come into effect until the child has attained a certain minimum or *threshold level of competence* in his second language". However, it would seem that this threshold is well within reach: the children in the studies just mentioned who were, according to fairly lenient assessment criteria, considered balanced bilinguals, had clearly reached this hypothesized threshold level of competence.

A very interesting investigation carried out by Carolyn Kessler & Mary Quinn (1982) indicates that bilingualism increases adeptness at divergent thinking even in the case of children who are *not* fully proficient in their two languages, i.e. who are not balanced bilinguals. The bilinguals investigated were fourteen 6th grade 11-year-olds in Pennsylvania who were dominant in English and used Italian only in the home and neighbourhood. They were compared with 14 English mono-linguals, with whom they were matched for IQ, grade-point average and reading ability. The bilingual children were better at generating hypotheses than the mono-linguals.

Various researchers, such as Anna-Beth Doyle *et al.* (1978) and Sandra Ben-Zeev (1977a), have found that there is one type of test in which bilinguals frequently perform worse than monolinguals, namely in tests of vocabulary. The reason for this would seem to be that bilingual children have to learn two different labels for everything, one for each language. This reduces the frequency with which they will hear a particular word in either language. In other cases particular words may be associated with certain situations in which only one language is regularly used and the corresponding names in the other language may not (yet) be known (see the section "Receptive Vocabulary" in chapter 7 for further discussion). And since bilingual children are usually tested on their knowledge of vocabulary in only one language, or if in both, in each language separately, it is possible that they will perform less well than similarly aged monolingual speakers of either of their languages. However, this does not mean that they know fewer *concepts* than the monolingual children. If the bilingual children's *two* languages are taken into account, their overall performance will usually improve significantly and they may then equal (as found, for example, by Bergan & Parra, 1979), or even outperform monolingual children (see the first part of chapter 7 for elaboration of this point).

From the evidence, therefore, it appears that if bilingual children have a reasonable degree of balance between their two languages, their overall intellectual development is not hindered and is, in fact, in many ways enhanced.

One type of child bilingualism needs to be included in our discussion here, for it has raised questions in a number of countries about the possible detrimental effects of bilingualism on children's intellectual development and academic prog-ress. It occurs when bilingual children's *weaker* language is also the language of the school and the native language of their monolingual classmates and teachers.These children are in a "sink-or-swim" situation, this is submersion in the second language. Such bilingualism is often referred to as "subtractive" bilingual-ism, since in many cases the children's first language (the home language) skills are being replaced, or "subtracted" in the process of acquiring the second language (the language of the school). Such children's proficiency in the school language may appear quite good on the surface and indeed be adequate for everyday face-to-face communication and, as a consequence, their teachers may assume that if they cannot keep up academically with their monolingual peers the reason is not linguistic but lack of intelligence. However, as Jim Cummins (1984b:9) points out, to keep pace with their peers and to cope with more complex linguistic situations and to process and understand more complex subject matter, the bilingual children need also to acquire *academic* skills in the language of the school, and it can take some time to attain such a level of competence. Ideally, such children should also receive assistance with their school work in their stronger language.

Michael Weigt (1985), for example, shows in a study carried out in Hamburg, that many Turkish-German bilingual children from Turkish-speaking homes there have been wrongly assigned to schools for children with learning difficulties (*Schulen für Lernbehinderte*) because their difficulties have not been recognized as being basically linguistic. These children *seem* to have a reasonable command of German, but this command is deceptive and superficial, being satisfactory only for simple, everyday conversation. When even quite limited use of Turkish was made in class by a Turkish speaking aide, the children showed a marked improvement in comprehension of lessons and increased their active participation in class discussions *in German*, their weaker language. Similarly, research by Jochen Rehbein (1985), a professor in German linguistics at the University of Hamburg, has shown that 10–14-year-old Turkish language dominant children in German schools had considerable difficulties in retelling in German a story which they had heard in German; although superficially their command of German appeared reasonable, they could reproduce only fragments of the story. However, if the children heard the story in *Turkish*, their home language, they were then able to retell the story quite satisfactorily *in German*, their weaker language. These findings demonstrate clearly that these children are in no way cognitively deficient — their problem is clearly linguistic. For children such as these, their bilingualism is a disadvantage because it is not (yet) sufficiently balanced and because the school system often makes little effort to understand and/or help them to overcome their linguistic difficulties. (See also the section "Ethnic schools and playgroups" in chapter 11 for further discussion of this point.) As will be discussed further in chapter 2, the best way for parents to help children in such a position is *not* by giving up speaking their own language to them and attempting to use the language of the school in the home, but to do their best to ensure that they provide them with as much input as possible in the home language.

As far as the bilingual's brain is concerned, Norman Segalowitz (1977:31), in a review of research on neurological aspects of bilingualism, concludes that:

> ...there does not seem to be strong neurological evidence indicating a basic difference in the way language is represented in the monolingual and bilingual brain. ...the evidence presently available does not indicate that a bilingual brain suffers some neurological burden that a monolingual brain escapes. From the strictly neurological point of view, a brain can handle two languages just as easily as one.

With regard to memory, there is no evidence to indicate that it is impaired in any way by bilingualism. One theory regarding the structure of memory in bilinguals is that they have two separate memory stores, one for each language, with information presented in one language not being readily available in the other (a view put forward, for example, by John Macnamara in 1967 and also in 1971). However, evidence from many studies (reviewed, for example, by Norman Segalowitz (1977) and Barry McLaughlin (1978)) suggests that concepts are not segregated in the brain according to the language with which they are associated; bilinguals store words in memory in terms of meaning, i.e. there is one semantic system underlying the two languages. Items are then in some way "tagged" with the right language at the time of speaking. This means that bilinguals who hear information first in one language and then repeated in their other language will retain the information just as well as if they had been given the same information twice in the same language. Paul Kolers (1968:83) gives a concrete example of this in an article published in the *Scientific American*:

> ... suppose one wanted to give a student two lessons in geography. If the student knew two languages, he would retain as much geography from one lesson in each language as from two lessons in one of them. Moreover, he would be able to talk about geography readily in both languages.

There is also much evidence from bilinguals' accounts of their experiences that information is stored by the brain according to content and meaning and not according to language (and can, therefore, be recalled in either language). Tove Skutnabb-Kangas (1984:108), a well-known researcher in the field of bilingualism, who grew up with two mother tongues, Finnish and Swedish, says:

> ... it has often happened that I have had no idea afterwards which language I was using in a conversation with someone as bilingual as I am, and with whom for various reasons I sometimes use one language, sometimes the other.

The only real problem bilinguals may encounter when required to recall and then report in one language on information obtained only in another (and understood), is not usually with the content (provided they have understood the content, of course!), but perhaps with vocabulary, especially specialized terminology, which at that moment may be known only in the language in which the information was received. For example, Thomas, one of the children reported on in this book, was able to explain at age 13 very well to his father *in German* all that he had learnt *in English* about rainfall in a geography lesson at school ; his only difficulty in doing this was with a few specialized terms, such as "orographic rainfall", for which he did not know the German but whose meaning he could easily explain, e.g.:

Thomas: ... Und dann gibt es auch *"orographic rainfall"* — die Wolken sind in die Nähe von einem Berg, und ein Wind kommt und bläst sie, und sie gehen höher und höher, weil sie können nicht durch den Berg gehen, und dann wird es sehr, sehr kühl, und — ah—, sie —, die Wolken werden zu Wasser. *(And then there's also "orographic rainfall" — the clouds are near a mountain and a wind comes and blows them, and they go higher and higher, because they can't go through the mountain, and then it becomes very, very cool, and — ah—, they —, the clouds turn into water.)*

This is clearly not a problem with retrieving information from memory, but rather a vocabulary problem (which, if desired, can usually be rectified by seeking out the appropriate terminology in the other language).

François Grosjean (1985) raises an interesting point with regard to the continual comparisons which are made between monolinguals and bilinguals. He says that the effects of bilingualism have been so closely scrutinized because the monolingual viewpoint regards bilingualism as the exception, whereas, as he rightly points out, at least half of the world's population is *bilingual:*

As a bilingual myself, I have often wondered why the cognitive consequences of *monolingualism* have not been investigated with the same care!

Unfortunately, this negative monolingual view of bilingualism may also influence some bilinguals, causing them to downgrade their own language competence if they are not just about perfect in each of their languages, or, if they have managed to reach this sort of standard, to be critical of those who have not. A consequence of this for bilingual families could, of course, be that parents may have unduly high expectations of the level of bilingualism which their children should attain. Unrealistic perfectionism on the part of parents can represent a danger to the survival of bilingualism in a family: parents' desire for their children to speak both languages perfectly can cause them to abandon the attempt to raise their children bilingually when they realize that such perfection is an almost unattainable goal. This does not, however, mean that parents should not do their best to help their children to reach a high standard of bilingualism. But at the same time they should not forget that most bilingual children simply do not have equal exposure to both their languages, so that usually one language will be "weaker" in some way. However, just because it is "weaker" does not mean that it cannot be an effective and natural means of communication between children and parents. This is surely a commendable achievement in itself and something worthy of being fostered.

Most of the problems associated with bilingualism are really social or cultural problems, that is, problems brought about by a hostile or discriminatory attitude of the majority group in a society, or sections of it, towards the presence of other languages and cultures, as well as the conflict faced by children expected to live in one culture at home and in another in the world outside. These factors can, of course, adversely affect a person's bilingualism: a child who wishes to conform to the majority group in society may reject the culture and language of the home. Much depends on an understanding and supportive home environment if this is to be avoided. If children's bilingualism (and biculturalism) were viewed favourably both by their families and by the population in general, few problems would exist.

Within the family itself, particularly where each parent speaks a different language to the children, it is probably advisable, to avoid problems, that each parent understand the other's language to a certain extent, and that the parents co-operate and be supportive of each other's efforts to transmit his or her language to the children. Such co-operation may mean, for example, giving preferential treatment to the language which is in the weakest position. These questions are discussed further throughout this book.

2 Establishing bilingualism in the family

The family

This study looks closely at my three Australian-born children's acquisition of bilingualism in English and German. The children, Thomas, Frank and Katrina, were born on 9 November 1973, 1 October 1975 and 13 February 1981 respectively. They have spent most of their life in Australia, the only exception to date being when they lived in Hamburg in the Federal Republic of Germany from July to December 1984. From birth, the children have been addressed by their mother and most other people in English, whilst I have always spoken to them in German. This situation differs from most of those reported in the literature on bilingual families in that not only is English the dominant and official language of the community in which the family lives and the native language of the mother, but it is also the native language of the *father*. Such a situation makes possible the observation of many factors affecting the fostering, maintenance and nurturing of a minority language, and, since the father is not a native speaker of German, it also affords some insight into difficulties experienced by parents who, by choice or necessity, communicate with their children in a second language.

Both my wife, Wendy, and I were born in Tasmania, Australia's island state. We both come from monolingual English-speaking families and speak General Australian English as our native language. As far as can be ascertained, both sides of the family have consisted of only English-speakers for at least six generations. My great-great-grandfather, for example, was born in England in 1814 and, like the forefathers of most Australians, arrived in Australia as an immigrant, albeit not a voluntary one. He ran foul of the harsh penal system of the time, being sentenced in Nottingham at the ripe old age of thirteen to transportation for life to Van Diemen's Land (present-day Tasmania) for the obviously serious offence of misappropriating a brace-and-bit.

Both Wendy and I had our first contact with foreign languages in high school, an experience which had not been available to our parents. Wendy learnt French for four years and did moderately well at it, but she did not like the subject particularly, finding the pronunciation of the language strange and difficult.

I studied both French and German for five years at high school, where, encouraged by enthusiastic and skilful language teachers, the two languages quickly became my favourite and best subjects. This interest continued on to university, where I studied French for a further three years and German for another four years as major subjects in a Bachelor of Arts honours degree at the University of Tasmania. I attained the degree with First Class Honours in German. This was followed by four years working on a doctoral dissertation in German linguistics. Fourteen months of this time were spent studying German linguistics and Dutch and carrying out linguistic field-work at a university in Germany. Since completing my doctorate I have taught languages at a high school, institutes of higher education and a university. Because of my occupation, and also because of my interest in shortwave broadcasts, particularly those in German, I have been able to maintain a high degree of competence in the language. My German could not be called perfect in the English sense of the word, i.e. not entirely flawless, although errors in grammar and pronunciation are rare. Native speakers of German have referred to my German as *perfekt* which, in its German sense, means "excellent". Some native speakers of German, particularly those not from North Germany or those who have lived in Australia for a number of years, have on occasion even mistaken me for a native speaker of the language. I feel confident about using German in most situations, although I am aware that my command of the language is not equal to that of my native language, English. (See the end of chapter 7 for details of my language dominance, and chapter 6 for references to my accuracy.)

Wendy's motivation to learn German came shortly after her marriage at the age of twenty-one. There was a distinct possibility, which later eventuated, that I would receive a travelling scholarship from the German Academic Exchange Service which, together with an Australian Government Postgraduate scholarship I already held, would enable me to conduct research for my doctorate in Germany the following year. Since she wished to continue practising her profession of nursing sister while in Germany, and since her return fare to Australia would have to be earned in this way, motivation to learn some German was, understandably, strong. After eleven months of tuition from me she had acquired a rudimentary knowledge of German grammar, a vocabulary of about 1,500 words, and a reasonably accurate pronunciation, which enabled her to participate somewhat hesitantly in simple conversations. She took care to learn carefully the medical terminology she thought she would need in a German hospital.

Even so, her minimal competence was not to be enough to shield her from a number of rather traumatic linguistic experiences, experiences most likely encountered by many an immigrant, guest-worker or simply traveller abroad. On arrival in Germany, Wendy took up employment firstly as a nursing aide, and then, when her qualifications were finally recognized, as a sister on a private ward of a large hospital where the medical personnel and cleaning staff were predominantly mono-lingual speakers of German. Recourse to English when faced with a linguistic predicament was therefore not possible. Aided only by a small pocket dictionary, she had to cope with being in sole charge of the ward three hours a day, answering the telephone, dealing with emergencies, and so on. Whilst this experience was initially rather nerve-racking and stressful, it did bring about a dramatic improve-ment in her comprehension of and fluency in German.

On her return to Australia, she decided to consolidate the knowledge of German she had already acquired by studying it more formally as a subject for the Tasmanian Higher School Certificate (HSC). This year of study proved very beneficial in increasing her proficiency in German grammar and giving her much practice in writing the language. During the year she won first prize in a German essay competition run by the German Australian Club in Tasmania, and in the end-of-year HSC exam gained 166/200, the second highest mark awarded that year. Since then she has maintained her German mainly through reading, watching German films on Australia's multilingual television network, and, of course, through being consistently exposed to the language in the home. She still speaks it fluently, although not with complete grammatical accuracy, and her level of comprehension is very high. During a six month stay in Hamburg in 1984 she had no difficulty in communicating in German in a wide range of situations, ranging from everyday chit-chat to quite complex and formal transactions in banks, travel bureaux, etc. Only occasionally, in certain types of discussions (e.g. about politics), does she feel a little frustrated because she cannot express her point of view as spontaneously or as aptly as she can in English.

Wendy's experience with German aroused her interest in other languages and cultures, and as a hobby, she and I studied Indonesian together at HSC level, both reaching a good level of competence. I also sat, for interest's sake, the HSC Dutch exam and obtained a good mark. In addition I have acquired a good reading knowledge of the closely related Afrikaans.

It needs to be pointed out that in this study the children usually address their father as Bert (pronounced as in German, the "er" part of the word being said like the English word "air"), and that in German Thomas is often addressed and referred to as Ernie (also pronounced in the German way). These are nicknames which date from when Thomas was aged 4;9 and was fascinated by the television show *Sesame Street* and by German comic books (*Sesamstraße*) which I had about the same show. Thomas subsequently assigned each family member the name of a character from *Sesame Street*, and these two names have persisted and become the usual forms of address in German, although since his eleventh birthday Thomas has increasingly been called Tom. Although the children call me Bert in German, they have always referred to me as Dad(dy) when talking about me in English; for this reason, in the English translations of German conversations given in this book, Bert is translated as Dad(dy).

At this point, a few words are needed about studying the language development of one's own children, since such studies are not without their critics. Personally, I think that studies by parents are virtually indispensable in any thorough investigation of children's language development (Saunders, 1982a). Only parents, in their unique position of being in continual close contact with their children, can ensure a reasonably accurate picture of their language, particularly in the period before they start school. Mike Byram (1981), however, sees dangers in such studies, such as "the possible effects on family relationships and the upbringing of the child which constant observations and note-taking by a parent might have". The apprehension here would, I feel, only be justified if the observations and note-taking were carried out in an obtrusive and insensitive way. In my family, "observation" of the children has been kept pretty low-key; it is a *by-product*, not the purpose, of the parents' normal interactions. When the children were young, tape-recordings were made as discreetly as possible; usually they were aware that they were being taped and normally this did not concern them, as long as it did not interrupt their play. As the children got older, tapes were made with their full knowledge and agreement, and at times which they considered convenient. Their reaction to my note-taking and recording is little different from that which they and probably most children have to being photographed — they object only if they see it as interfering with what they are doing at the time.

Some parents may also find it questionable that my children are clearly identified. I do not see anything wrong with this, since it is possible, without detracting from the accuracy or the representativeness of the study, to omit from publication anything which might offend or embarrass the children (or adults mentioned) if it were made public knowledge. When in doubt about this, I have checked. At age 13, for instance, Thomas browsed through the whole of this book in draft form and, after suggesting some minor changes, gave it his seal of approval; his brother and sister were less interested, but expressed no misgivings about being written about.

Another question which such studies raise is whether parents can really give an objective appraisal of their own children's language development. Of course, as any parent knows, it is difficult to remain completely objective, but at the same time one does have a much deeper knowledge of the children than any outsider ever would. In this book I have made every effort to give an honest picture of my children's bilingual development, recording the problems and failures along with the benefits and successes. Fortunately, as will be seen, the successes have outweighed the failures by a considerable margin.

Motives for creating bilingualism in the family

In this case there were several motives for Wendy's and my decision to raise our children bilingually. Firstly, we both believed in the intrinsic value of a knowledge of more than one language, providing as it does an awareness and appreciation of another culture and its way of thinking. We ourselves had gained much pleasure and insight from our acquaintance with other languages and wished to share this with our children, just as music-loving parents might encourage their children to appreciate music and perhaps even to play a musical instrument.

Secondly, on a more practical level, due to my profession and interests, it was probable that our family would at some time in the future be visiting or living temporarily in a German-speaking country. In view of the difficulties encountered by Wendy during her stay in Germany, we were both convinced that, if the children were fluent in German, the time needed to adjust to the new environment would be significantly reduced and such a stay would consequently be much more enjoyable for both children and parents, particularly if the children had to attend school while there. Observations of difficulties encountered by the children of guest-workers in Germany and by recently arrived immigrant children in Australia reinforced this conviction.

Thirdly, we were curious about the difficulties seemingly associated with attempts to maintain a language other than English in the Australian setting. We knew of many parents who had as their native language a language other than English and who had not succeeded in passing it on to their children. This seemed to be particularly so when one marriage partner was Australian-born. Michael Clyne's (1979,1980,1982:36ff) analysis of the 1976 Australian Census shows, to take one example, that 27.8% of Australian residents born in Germany no longer regularly use German. The shift to exclusive use of English among Australian-born children of two German-born parents is just over double this figure: 59% of them use English only. The chances of languages other than English being passed on diminish even more in mixed marriages, that is, marriages where one spouse is born overseas, the other in Australia. For example, if we look at marriages in Australia in which one parent is German-born, the other born in Australia, Britain or Eire, we find that only 4.4% of children with a German mother and 3.6% with a German father speak German. Moreover, such mixed marriages are by no means unusual in Australia: for the period 1969-1973, for instance, 38% of males and 24% of females from twelve different groups of immigrants born in non-English-speaking countries married Australian-born persons (Price, 1977:345).

Fourthly, I was also interested in the problems faced by parents who, by choice or necessity, use a language which is not their native language to communicate with their children, a situation also by no means unusual in immigrant families in Australia where English has in many cases become the language of the family.

Fifthly, I myself felt a need for a regular conversation partner willing to talk only German with me at all times and on all topics. I had, it is true, in my work and in various organizations I belonged to, some opportunities for speaking German on a reasonably regular basis. However, by their nature, such conversations tended to be rather formal and technical. Informal conversations about ordinary, everyday, even mundane matters rarely took place. I could have used German in the home with Wendy for such conversations, which we indeed did do occasionally for practice, but these interchanges, whilst enjoyable and helpful, did have an air of artificiality about them. In addition, I had discovered that many German-speaking immigrants who had lived for some time in Australia were, unfortunately, often more interested in demonstrating their knowledge of English, even if it was poor, than conversing in German, even among themselves. It was felt (and hoped) that a child would have no inhibitions about speaking German to his father and would regard it as natural to use it at all times with him. As will be seen, this feeling proved in large part to be justified.

The "experiment" was begun not without a certain amount of apprehension as to its possible outcome. At that stage, we had not consulted the literature on the subject extensively, and we relied heavily on accounts from immigrant families; most were pessimistic, forecasting failure at various stages in the children's development: before kindergarten age, on beginning kindergarten, at the start of school, etc. Other people expressed fears that the children would become confused. However, we had fortunately also encountered some children, and read of others, who seemed to be coping happily with two, or even more languages. In particular, a visit one year before the birth of our first child to friends in Sarawak (East Malaysia) had impressed us with the feasibility and advantages, not to mention the pleasures of family bilingualism. Danny, our friends' three-year-old son, chattered happily with us in English, with the maid in Hokkien (a Chinese language), with his parents in Hokkien and English, with his paternal grandparents in Hokkien, and with his maternal grandparents in Malay. Of course, the conditions prevailing in the city of Kuching were very favourable to some form of bi- or trilingualism: Hokkien (together with the closely related Teochew and Hakka) was the language of the large Chinese population, English was the main language of a largely overseas-educated administration, and Malay, as the national language of Malaysia and long a lingua franca in the region, was steadily gaining in importance. Hobart, Tasmania, on the other hand, was a predominantly monolingual city where support outside the home for the speaking of a language other than English would be minimal. An indication of the position is given by the 1976 Census which reveals that only 4% of Tasmania's population over five years of age regularly uses a language other than English. Of these languages other than English, German is, admittedly, the one most widely used in Tasmania, but by only about 1% of a total population of just over 400,000.

Of course, not all parents will have the same motives for wishing to raise their children as bilinguals. The native language of the parents (or one of them) may, for example, be different from that of the society in which they live and their native language may represent their most effective means of communication. This language may also be the only language of relatives and friends in the country of origin. To *not* pass the language on to the children could be seen by the parents, and later perhaps also by the children (as found by Anne Pauwels (1980:177) in her questioning of children of Dutch-Dutch marriages in Australia), as reducing the effectiveness of communication in the family, perhaps drastically, and as depriving both children and monolingual relatives of the means of unhindered communication, and cutting them off from part of their cultural heritage. Velta Rūķe-Draviņa (1967:100), a Latvian-born linguist, considers that it may have a lifelong effect on children if they do not acquire the language of their parents, as they are then cut off from the family's circle of relatives and friends.

Some writers (e.g. Michael Clyne (1985:44) and Lenore Arnberg (1987:43)) have expressed doubts about whether the results obtained in "middle class" families, such as the one in this book, where one of the parents is a linguist or someone with a professional interest in language(s), can be achieved in families without this sort of background. Michael Clyne (1985:43), in a review of my first book (Saunders, 1982c), remarks:

> ... one does gain the impression that the Saunders family... revolves around the bilingual language acquisition "experiment", that discussions of language ... are central to their family life.

It is probably true that it is usually only this sort of parent who, because of a professional interest, keeps a detailed record of and eventually writes about his or her children's bilingualism. However, being a linguist is certainly not a prerequisite for, nor a guarantee of, successfully bringing up children as bilinguals, just as it is not necessary for children to have middle class parents with a degree in child psychology if they are to grow up well-adjusted and normal, although such parents may have certain advantages in that they (should) have an awareness of what is possible and what is normal.

Still, it is my impression, from talking to numerous parents, that language teachers, linguists, and the like, are no more or no less successful in bringing up their children bilingually than other parents. For instance, the French linguist François Grosjean (1982:106,175 and 1985),whose wife Lysiane is also French, has described how his sons Marc and Eric became monolingual in English in the USA. (A stay in Switzerland later on turned them back into bilinguals, but that is another story.) Parents,with or without such a professional background, who are keen to help their children to become and stay bilingual, and who are prepared to put in some effort to achieve this goal, *can* and *do* succeed. I have, for example, reported elsewhere on a Turkish labourer with only primary school education who successfully raised his two daughters in Australia as competent Turkish/English bilinguals (Saunders, 1984b). The key to success is not really high academic qualifications or socio-economic status, but a reasonable amount of motivation and commitment. Most of the hints and techniques suggested in this book for raising children in two languages are applicable to almost any family, with slight modifications to allow for particular family circumstances.

With regard to "middle class", in their book *The Bilingual Family,* Edith Harding & Philip Riley (1986:24) stress that whilst many middle class families may be relatively privileged in comparison with most migrant communities, it is neither helpful nor accurate "to talk about them as if they were rich, with the implication that their riches can automatically solve their linguistic problems." They add: "We keep meeting a great variety of couples who would certainly be labelled 'middleclass' in sociological surveys, but who are at a complete loss as to how to go about maintaining two languages in their family." It should also not be forgotten that the term "middle class" can cover a wide spectrum of the population. Recent research in Australia by Craig McGregor (1987), for instance, indicates that at least 60% of the population consider that they belong to the middle class.

Nor does all family life have to revolve around the acquisition of bilingualism, which is an impression readers may gain (as did Michael Clyne, just quoted above) from reading about my family's experiences. This is in fact not the case, although it is probably natural that in bilingual families language-related matters assume more prominence than in monolingual families (just as a family of musicians would obviously talk much more about music than a non-musical family). And it is only natural in a book on bilingualism to focus on linguistic aspects of family life, rather than on other aspects, such as the children's hobbies, sports, etc. So, whilst there is no denying that bilingualism is an important part of my family's life, it is not something pursued fanatically, at all costs. It is simply a part of everyday living.

Infant bilingualism

As already mentioned in chapter one, infant bilingualism is the term often used by linguists (e.g. by Einar Haugen, 1956:72) to describe the type of bilingualism resulting from a child's being exposed simultaneously to more than one language from birth. Other terms are also used to refer to this type of bilingualism; for example, Merrill Swain (1972) calls it "bilingualism as a first language",

Henning Wode (1978) "first language bilingualism", Ana Huerta (1977) "native acquisition of two languages", and Jürgen Meisel (1986) "simultaneous acquisition of two first languages".

The child has, therefore, as these terms suggest, from the beginning two (or more) languages, although this does not imply that he or she will have equal command of both. Circumstances rarely ensure that a child will have even approximately equal contact with both languages in all situations. Consequently, it is highly likely that one language will predominate and be spoken more fluently, more accurately, or with a greater range of vocabulary. If circumstances change, for example when the child begins school, a shift in language dominance may occur. This is perfectly natural and should not cause parents undue concern or discourage them. Perfect balance between the two languages is an ideal, an ideal which is hardly ever realized by children, or for that matter by adults. In fact, I personally have never met an adult whose ability in two languages was equal in *every* respect. This does not mean that a very high standard cannot be attained in both languages. Unfortunately, some parents who are attempting to pass on their native language to their children in an environment in which the dominant language of the community is another language, become upset and despair because their children's ability in the language is not on a par with that of monolingual children in the parents' homeland. Because of this, some parents have even come to regard the attempt as a failure and to consider it a waste of time to continue. This is a tragic loss both to the family and to the country as a whole. For, as Werner Leopold (1957) points out, children *can* acquire a serviceable knowledge of their parents' language, being able to communicate with relative ease at a level appropriate to their age and experience, even if perhaps not with grammatical exactitude, while at the same time acquiring a perfect knowledge of the dominant language of the community. This would seem to be a perfectly reasonable and worthwhile accomplishment. In any case, the children's ability in a language acquired naturally through interaction with their parents in the home will usually be far superior to any ability they may acquire later through studying it as a foreign language at school, particularly as far as a native-sounding pronunciation is concerned. And if children do wish to study their parents' language formally at a later stage, they can already have a solid foundation on which to build. Instead of laboriously learning a second language, they will then be consolidating and developing one of their first languages.

Of course, not all children who are bilingual have been exposed to their two languages from the beginning. Studies of bilingual children generally distinguish between infant bilingualism, as outlined above, and the successive acquisition of two languages in childhood (called by Einar Haugen (1956:72) "child bilingualism" and by Hugo Baetens Beardsmore (1982:25) "consecutive bilingualism"), in which the child has reached an age (an arbitrary cut-off point of three years being suggested by Barry McLaughlin (1978:99)), where one language has become relatively well established before exposure to the second language occurs (e.g. as with the children mentioned in Velta Rūķe-Draviņa's (1967) study). This is a situation many immigrant children find themselves in, the second language being acquired in many cases in a natural environment, that is, through contact with playmates etc., but without any systematic formal instruction. In many respects the problems facing such children and their parents, as they strive to acquire the language of the community and continue to use their own language in the home, will be similar to those encountered by families attempting to establish infant bilingualism.

Many immigrant parents believe, or are led to believe by their children's teachers, that they will best serve their children's interests if they attempt to speak only the dominant language of the community in the home. The assumption is that the more of this language the children hear, the sooner they will become competent in it; speaking another language in the home would only reduce exposure to and hinder acquisition of the dominant language. Such an assumption seems to imply that by subtracting one of a bilingual's languages his or her other must necessarily improve. Indeed, that is the belief of quite a number of (monolingual) Australian teachers, including teachers of English as a second language, with whom this writer has spoken and who are working in schools with a high percentage of children from a non-English-speaking background. However, this assumption fails to consider some important factors. Firstly, the parents' command of the dominant language of the community may be defective or even very meagre. For them to attempt to speak this language exclusively to their children may mean that communication between parents and children is far from spontaneous or efficient. Moreover, the children are being presented with an imperfect model of the dominant language of the community, perhaps with faulty pronunciation and deviant grammar, which is scarcely going to improve their proficiency in the language. The children may even come to look down on their parents' deviant variety of the language. Rūķe-Draviņa (1967:91), writing on her observations of Latvian children in Sweden, supports this view:

> Those Latvian children who spoke their mother tongue at home had, as a rule, greater success in Swedish, the language of the school, than those bilinguals who spoke mainly Swedish with their parents ... An explanation for this apparent contradiction is that the children who had spoken Swedish at home with their non-Swedish parents had learnt it with a poor pronunciation and faulty expression, which meant a much worse start for Swedish instruction at school than the other alternative, namely to speak the mother tongue at home and to learn the second language outside the home from a good 'pure' source, that is, from its native speakers.
> (Translated from the German)

Els Oksaar (quoted by Toll, 1977) noted much the same for Estonian children in Stockholm. Similarly, Michael Clyne (1967:116), in his investigation of two hundred German-English bilinguals in Australia, concluded that maintaining a good standard of German did *not* go hand in hand with inferior English. Jim Cummins (1984b) states that there is considerable evidence that for minority children who are academically at risk, strong promotion of proficiency in their home language represents an effective way of developing a conceptual and academic foundation for acquiring proficiency and literacy in the language of the school. Thus, even parents with little proficiency in the language of the school can assist their children academically by providing them with as much input as possible *in their own native language.*

Using the parents' native language within the family, a language in which the parents most probably feel more at ease and are more proficient, would also have the advantage of improving the children's esteem for them.

Another aspect worthy of consideration is that discarding the parents' language can mean problems for children of those immigrant families which decide to return to live in their original homeland. Stephanie Thompson (1980:205), in her study of 138 settlers who returned from Australia to Italy, describes how many children (who were either Australian-born or had arrived in Australia when very young) had to repeat years of study in Italian schools because of difficulties with language:

Often (the children) were more proficient in English than in Italian, particularly in the written language; and even in their homes in Australia some of them had insisted on speaking only English. As a result, most of the school-age children had language difficulties to overcome following their return to Italy.

Even in cases where there is no permanent return to the original homeland, loss of the language by the children cuts them off from close contact with grandparents, etc., still living there. Even if the grandparents migrate with the family and manage to acquire a reasonable knowledge of the language of the new country, it would still seem advisable for the grandchildren to acquire or retain competence in the home language, since there is evidence (e.g. from research by Michael Clyne, 1977a) that migrants over 60 revert more and more to their first language, this reversion being accompanied by a clear decline in ability in their second language; communication between the elderly and their family is hindered if the children and grandchildren have lost the ability to speak the home language — this is a common complaint emerging from Susan Hearst's (1981) study of immigrant elderly from eighteen different ethnic communities in Australia.

Whilst the number of possible kinds of infant bilingualism is, in theory, and no doubt also in practice, quite large, published research reports mainly on the following types:

1. The two parents have different native languages, one of which is the dominant language of the community (indicated in bold print). Each parent uses his/her language to the child from birth. Each parent has some degree of competency in the other's native language, e.g. Ronjat (1913) (mother German, father **French**); Leopold (1939–49) (mother **English,** father German); von Raffler-Engel (1970) (mother **Italian**, father English); Taeschner (1982) (mother German, father **Italian**); Kielhöfer & Jonekeit (1983) (mother French, father **German**); Porsché (1983) (mother **German**, father English); De Houwer (1984a,b) (mother English, father **Flemish**).

2. The child is exposed from the beginning to two languages, but has minimal contact with the second language until kindergarten. In such cases, the two parents may have different native languages, one of which is the dominant language of the community, but it is the language which is not the dominant language of the community that is used by both parents to the child, e.g. Fantini (1985) (mother's native language Spanish, father's English, residing in the USA, Spanish used to the children), Zierer (1977) (mother's native language Spanish, father's German, residing in Peru, German used to child), Vihman (1985) (mother's native language English, father's Estonian, residing in the USA, Estonian used to the children).

3. The parents may share a common native language which is different from the dominant community language and which they use to the child, e.g. Haugen (1972:10) (Norwegian in the USA), Bubenik (1978) (Czech in Canada), Oksaar (1971, 1977) (Estonian in Sweden and Germany), Rūķe-Draviņa (1967) (Latvian in Sweden). Haugen was born in America of Norwegian parents, with whom he always spoke Norwegian, whilst he spoke English with most people outside the home: "Thanks to my parents' adamant insistence on my speaking their native language at home, the threshold of the home became the cue to my code switch."

4. The parents may have different native languages, both of which differ from the dominant language of the community, and use one of them to the child, e.g. Elwert (1959) whose parents, a German and an English-woman residing in Italy, spoke to him only in English. From most other people he heard Standard Italian or the local Italian dialect. In some

cases where the parents have different native languages, both of which differ from the language of the community, each may use his/her native language to the children, with the children acquiring the language of the community outside the home, i.e. becoming *trilingual*, e.g. Charlotte Hoffmann (1985), who lives in England and herself grew up as a German/Danish bilingual, speaks German to her children, whilst her husband speaks to them in his native Spanish.

However, reports on cases of infant bilingualism where one of the languages acquired by the child is not the native language of either parent, nor the dominant language of the community, are rare: apart from my own research (Saunders, 1979 etc.), I know of only a few: Past (1976), Dimitrijevic (1965), Stephens (1952), Corsetti (1986) and Brennan (1987), and Facey (1986).

Al Past reports on his daughter Mariana's acquisition of English and Spanish in Texas. Both he and his wife are native speakers of English, and both also speak Spanish, although far from perfectly. On a Foreign Service Institute type language proficiency test, where a score of 0 represents a complete lack of communicative ability and a score of 5 indicates the ability of an educated native speaker, Past and his wife scored 2[+] and 3[+] respectively.

The Past family's situation differs in several ways from the present study, the principal difference being that the parents attempted to spend 60–90 minutes a day talking only Spanish to each other and to their daughter. That is, in the home there was no clear division of languages according to interlocutor. Instead, Mariana was encouraged to speak Spanish, and not English, to both parents at certain times of the day. To increase her exposure to spoken Spanish, her parents encouraged her to watch bilingual television programs, gave her opportunities to play with Spanish-speaking children, and at age 5;0 enrolled her in a bilingual kindergarten. As another means of exposing Mariana to native quality Spanish, her parents began to teach her to read the language, along with English, when she was only one year eleven months old and just learning to speak.

And what were the results of this experiment? Although Mariana preferred to speak English whenever she had a choice, and although her speech was not as rapid in Spanish as in English and she occasionally had to grope for a Spanish expression, she could communicate well in Spanish if she wanted to. The Oral Language Dominance Measure administered at the start of school showed her English to be only slightly superior to her Spanish and she was rated as a balanced bilingual capable of receiving instruction in either language. Her reading ability was assessed as a second grade level in both languages (see chapter 8 for further comments on biliteracy). Her experience with speaking and reading the two languages resulted in practically no confusion and she enjoyed normal relations with her peers.

Dimitrijevic (1965) gives an unfortunately very brief report on a case which seems very similar to that described in the present study. Although not stated specifically in the article, Dimitrijevic and his wife are apparently both native speakers of Serbian living in Yugoslavia, yet Rayko, their son, is spoken to in English by his father and Serbian by all others. Rayko's two languages seemed to develop equally well until he started to have Serbian playmates, at which point he began to show a preference for Serbian and his English lagged behind. Nevertheless, although his father did not insist on it, Rayko still continued to use some English with him when there was no urgency involved and they were alone together.

Stephens (1952), in an even briefer and more unusual report, writes that he spoke to his four-year-old son exclusively in Esperanto (the artificial language invented in 1887 by Zamenhof), while his wife always used English, making the child undoubtedly one of the very few native speakers of Esperanto! Stephens states that his son spoke both languages equally well and that his English was at least of the same standard as that of a monolingual child of the same age.

Renato Corsetti & Traute Taeschner (1986), and Anna Brennan (1987), report on an another interesting case involving Esperanto, but in this case it is one of *three* languages being acquired by two children. Renato Corsetti, a native speaker of Italian, and his wife, Anna Brennan, whose native language is English, have a good knowledge of each other's native language, but speak Esperanto to each other. Renato also speaks Esperanto with their two children, Gabriel and Fabiano, whilst Anna speaks English to them. Since the family lives in Rome, the children also have contact with and are acquiring Italian. Renato Corsetti (personal communication, 1987) estimates that there may be about 200 other families in the world in which Esperanto is being spoken to and by the children. He himself knows more than ten people of different nationalities who speak a good Esperanto which they learned from their parents.

Andrea Facey (1986) describes how she and her husband, Graham, Australians living in Sydney, both speak only German to their two children, Nicole (born 1980) and Patrick (born 1982).They also speak German to each other in the presence of the children, although "we revert to English once the children are in bed!" Both Andrea, a language teacher, and Graham, an electrical engineer, are native speakers of English and did not learn German until they were at university. As a result of their own experiences with language learning they were convinced that a child exposed to a second language from the start would acquire it much more effortlessly and naturally than an adult, a conviction which motivated them to attempt to give their own children this opportunity. Although Andrea and Graham are more proficient in their native language, they have lived for some time in Germany and do speak German fluently. In 1983 Graham's proficiency in German was rewarded when his firm sent him to Stuttgart for 18 months and his wife and children were able to accompany him. As the children already knew German, they were able to participate without difficulty in German life from the moment they arrived in Germany. Since the family's return to Australia in 1985 German has remained the language used between the children and their parents. The children can also function in English as well as their peers who speak only English.

This type of bilingualism is not without its critics. In their book *Zweisprachige Kindererziehung* (= Raising Children Bilingually), for example, Bernd Kielhöfer & Sylvie Jonekeit (1983: 15, 95) refer to it as "artificial bilingualism", presumably because a parent is passing on a non-native rather than a native language to his or her children. In fact, these authors explicitly warn parents not to attempt such "artificial bilingualism", stating rather ominously that all such cases that they know of have failed.

There are, of course, many parents in the world who speak to their children in a language which is not their native language, but usually this occurs when immigrants use the language of their new country to their children rather than the language they brought with them. Such situations would, however, seem to fall outside Kielhöfer's & Jonekeit's concept of artificial bilingualism, since here monolingualism in one language is simply being replaced by monolingualism in another. There are also parents whose native language is the language of the community but who have learnt their spouse's native language and have chosen to speak to their children in that language (e.g. Alvino Fantini (1985), the son of Italian immigrant parents in the USA speaks Spanish, his wife's native language, with her and his two children). Such a family situation would also probably not be classed as "artificial", since one parent is a native speaker of the home language and the children are acquiring the other language from native speakers in the community outside the home.

There are also quite a few examples of "artificial" bilingualism. Indeed, some countries have relied on large numbers of their citizens speaking a non-native language to their children to enable the creation of a national language. A good example of this is the revival of Hebrew as a spoken language with native speakers using it in all aspects of life. For many centuries it had not been spoken as a native language, its use having been reduced to a language used by Jews for public and private readings of religious writings and for prayers. Its revival as a native language meant that many parents spoke to their children not in their own native languages but in Hebrew, a language they knew only from books and religious activities. And it worked. Their children grew up speaking Hebrew as their native language, and now there are several million native speakers of the language. Some other languages which are at present in danger of dying out (e.g. Scottish Gaelic, Irish) will also probably have to rely to some extent on the assistance of non-native speakers who have, or acquire, a good command of the languages and then consciously pass them on to their children, if the languages are to be conserved or revived.

There seems to be adequate evidence that "artificial" bilingualism *can* be successful, the family in the present study being a case in point. It should also be be noted that by no means every attempt at "natural" bilingualism proves successful. Many of the problems faced in both kinds of bilingualism are similar. The parent who speaks a non-native language to his or her children will need to have a good command of the language so that he or she can converse easily about most everyday matters with the children. Such parents may have some gaps in their vocabulary, may not be grammatically perfect, and may speak the language with an accent influenced by their native language. This may cause them doubts because they are not passing on a "genuine" version of the language. They may also be criticized by native speakers of the language for what they are doing. However, it is revealing to observe the linguistic behaviour of immigrants who speak their native language to their children in a foreign environment. It has been well documented that the language of such immigrants is fairly quickly influenced by the language of the new country so that it begins to diverge from the variety spoken in the linguistic homeland: words may be adopted from the language of the new country to refer to new concepts, when a word in the home language is momentarily forgotten, for expressiveness, etc. Thus the language which the children of immigrants acquire from their parents is somewhat different from the same language spoken by their peers in their parents' country of origin. And if these children in turn pass the language on to their children the differences will be even more noticeable. The non-native speaker speaking the language to his or her children has much in common with the immigrant and with the immigrant's offspring.

The term "artificial" bilingualism is a little unfortunate, since "artificial" can have negative connotations, implying unnaturalness, lack of genuineness. However, it is artificial really only in the sense that one of the languages being passed on is being passed on by a non-native speaker of the language. But if that particular parent speaks the language fluently and confidently, and does so with the children right from the start, the situation will very quickly not seem artificial to the parent, and certainly not appear artificial to the children. After all, that is the language they have heard from their parent as long as they can remember. Even if the parent speaks it with a non-native sounding accent or intonation, initially the children will not be aware of this or, if they are, it will not concern them unduly: the important thing is that the parent speaks to them in this language, it is the language of intimacy between them and the parent. As far as they are concerned, it *is their* language! Such a situation appears "artificial" only to the outsider who is convinced that a parent must be a native speaker of a language to be able or entitled to transmit it to his or her children.

What such children experience could be called a "home language immersion program", since in many ways it parallels the experience of children in so-called immersion programs which in recent years have proven to be popular and particularly effective in schools in Canada and the USA. Of course, children in a bilingual home obviously begin their "immersion" at a much earlier age than the children in these school programs. In these programs, children from English-speaking homes are, from the start of schooling, "immersed" in French or Spanish, that is, receive all or a significant part of their instruction in these languages (although, unlike the situation for most immigrant children — which could be called "submersion" — these children have classmates with the same home language and with the same level of proficiency in the school language and as well bilingual teachers who can understand their home language if need be). The children receive some instruction in English language as a subject and outside school hours use mainly English, the dominant language of the society in which they live. Careful evaluation of such language immersion programs (e.g. by Merrill Swain *et al.* (1981), Sharon Lapkin *et al.* (1983), Elaine Day & Stan Shapson (1987)) has revealed how very effective they are. At first the children show some retardation in English compared with their peers being instructed in English, but this rapidly disappears. At the same time, however, they acquire a knowledge of their second language which in many ways approximates that of native speakers. Moreover, their performance in subjects such as mathematics and science is on a par with that of children being instructed in English. Even below average students progress as well in the immersion program as they would in a regular English program and, in addition, acquire functional competence in speaking and understanding French, something which such children rarely acquire if learning French as a traditional school subject.

Method employed

In the literature, a number of methods are advocated for fostering and maintaining bilingualism in the family. The method employed in this study is similar to that followed by the French linguist Jules Ronjat (1913) who wrote one of the first detailed case studies of infant bilingualism. Ronjat's native language was French, his wife's German. They lived predominantly in France, but had frequent contacts with German speakers. When their son, Louis, was born in 1908, Ronjat received a letter from the linguist Grammont, in which he offered the following advice for raising the child bilingually:

> There is nothing to teach him. It is sufficient that when something is said to him it be said in one of the languages you want him to know. But the important thing is that each language be represented by a different person; that you, for example, always speak French to him, his mother

German. Never reverse these roles. In this way, when he begins to speak, he will speak the two languages without being conscious of doing so and without having made any special effort to learn them. (Translated from the French)

Ronjat and his wife followed this advice closely. They consciously created a one-language–one-parent home environment. To their son they always spoke their respective native languages, whilst to each other they spoke German, unless a monolingual French speaker was present. Whilst not discounting the possibility that infant bilingualism could be achieved by other methods, Ronjat (1913:106) was convinced, as a result of observing his own son and other children, that this one-person–one-language method not only offered the surest guarantee of success but also required the least mental exertion on the part of the child.Until the age of five, at least (where Ronjat's account unfortunately finishes), Louis's progress under this method was impressive. He acquired both French and German with a native pronunciation and there was little evidence of the vocabulary or syntax of one language influencing the other. Louis was able to express himself fluently and appropriately in either language.

The German-born US linguist, Werner Leopold, whose four-volume study, published between 1939 and 1949, gives perhaps the most detailed account of the acquisition of infant bilingualism, followed this method with his daughter Hildegard. Hildegard was usually addressed in English by her mother, a native speaker of that language. The family lived in America, except for a summer holiday in Germany when she was five. Leopold's wife, a third-generation German-American, could understand German and express herself in it faultily, but fluently. During courting they had spoken English to one another, but after marriage, Leopold (1957:5) reports, "... I was obstinate enough to speak German to her regularly ... She usually answered me in English." When Hildegard was born, this well-established practice was simply continued, the mother speaking to her in English, the father in German, but with the expectation that, unlike in interactions with the mother, he would receive German in return from his daughter.

Leopold did not apply the formula of "one person, one language" as rigidly as did Ronjat. Leopold, for instance, addressed Hildegard in English when monolingual English speaking playmates or visitors were present. There was also some indecision in the family regarding the mother's choice of language when speaking to Hildegard. During their six month stay in Germany in 1935 the mother began speaking only German to Hildegard (Leopold, 1949b:95).

Since she was practically her daughter's only contact with English there, Hildegard's use of that language declined rapidly. Wishing his daughter to retain her English, Leopold persuaded his wife to revert to speaking it to her. This she did, but a month later Leopold (1949b:107) had second thoughts: "I am now in favour of [her mother using] German in order to reinforce the position of German to induce Hildegard to speak only German at home after her return to America." However, this resolve was forgotten until the family returned to the USA at the beginning of 1936, but even then it was not put into effective practice: "Her mother is by no means consistent in carrying out the principle of 'German at home'. She accepts Hildegard's English." (1949b:125). The situation was, therefore, as Leopold (1957:5) himself readily admits, far from ideal, since he represented Hildegard's only real contact with German in America. When Hildegard was aged 6;2,2, Leopold (1949b:135) summarized her linguistic progress to that point as follows:

> At the moment ... I can state that she speaks both English and German fluently. Both languages are fully formed. There are no significant gaps in the grammar. The vocabulary is large in both languages, but it is more complete and ready at hand in English ... she often hesitates [i.e. when speaking German], which shows that English expressions come to her mind first.

Two years later, just after Hildegard's eighth birthday, he (1949b:146) wrote:–

> Hildegard keeps on speaking German to me. In longer narrations she has considerable difficulty in expressing herself, but eventually, halt-ingly, she can say everything.

Hildegard's use of German had no adverse effect on her English. At an early age (4;2,13) she was judged to be far ahead of her age with regard to purity of pro-nunciation and vocabulary (1949b:58-9). Her ability in English and generally at school was considered above average (1949b:143). At high school and college Hil-degard studied German and achieved her best results in it. In 1950, then aged 20, she went to Germany for the summer to help with postwar reconstruction. She spent ten days in France en route, where "she struggled with her meager college French. She breathed a sigh of relief when she entered Germany and people really under-stood her" (1956:6).

This result might not be ideal, but it is surely a very satisfactory achievement in the circumstances.

Werner Leopold's experience with his second child, Karla, born six years after Hildegard, is perhaps even more interesting in that it shows that even when an attempt at raising a child bilingually seems to have achieved little success, the child may be unconsciously absorbing the language and establishing a foundation on which he or she can later build. Leopold and his wife followed the same procedures with Karla as they did with Hildegard. Hildegard herself announced her intention of speaking German to her little sister so that she would learn it, but this did not eventuate, mainly because their mother was nearly always present speaking English (1949b:102). Leopold always addressed Karla in German but, whilst she understood almost everything he said, she rarely answered him in German. In other words, she was basically a receiving bilingual. Commenting on her speech to him at age 5;0,1, Leopold (1949b:159) writes:

> Her German is extremely limited. She ... scatters some German words over her English sentences when she speaks to me, as a sort of concession to my way of speaking. Her German is restricted to such fragments, words and brief sentences.

However, she accepted that her father spoke only German, and at age 5;9,10 even objected when he addressed her in English because the maid was present and involved in the topic: "Don't talk to me in English" (1949b:160).

Karla's exposure to German did not impair her knowledge of English. Leopold (1949b:164) writes, for instance, that when she was in fourth grade her teacher drew attention to the fact that she had "a remarkable flair for English writing". Like her sister, she took German at high school and it was also her best subject. At the age of nineteen she visited Germany where, as Leopold (1957:6) reports, she was able to activate her dormant German:

> For the first few days there she did not try to speak German because her parents were along and did the talking. Then she opened up and spoke German fluently and with surprising correctness. In view of the lack of practice in speaking, I had not expected her to be able to converse so well; but the long, deeply embedded preparation, although passive in her case, asserted itself amazingly.

Since the studies by Ronjat and Leopold are perhaps the best known in the field of infant bilingualism, they will be referred to frequently in the following pages and comparisons will be drawn between their observations and those made by other researchers, including the present writer.

Not all researchers agree that this type of one-person–one-language approach to achieving infant bilingualism is advisable. The most forceful objections are perhaps those presented by Ernesto Zierer (1977). Zierer, a native speaker of German residing in Peru, and his wife, a native speaker of Spanish (each having a good knowledge of the other's native language), decided to raise their son bilingually. However, they decided to make German the language of the home and not to expose him to Spanish until he had first become reasonably proficient in German, because they believed that:

1. Simultaneous acquisition of Spanish and German would "produce pertur-bations in the child's cognitive and affective control" and "would undoubt-edly constitute very considerable mental exertion for the child".

2. "Considering the powerful unifying force that a language exercises on its speakers, the integration of the family would have been affected if the child had spoken to his mother in one language and to his father in another."

These assumptions are not supported by the evidence presented by Ronjat and Leopold, or, by many other studies, including, as will be seen, the present study, and would seem to underestimate the young child's ability and adaptability. There is at times undoubtedly some mental exertion involved for the child who is simul-taneously acquiring two languages, but whether delaying exposure to one of the languages would lessen any such exertion would be difficult to refute or confirm. The assumption of a danger to the integration of the family would probably only be valid if one marriage partner did not have a good understanding of the other's language. This could have a detrimental effect on relationships within the family, since the parent not understanding one of the languages might resent not being able to understand conversations between spouse and child. However, even in such a situation, friction could possibly be avoided if the child and parent used the language only when the monolingual parent was absent or, more practicably, by providing him or her with a running summary in translation, which is, in any case, often done by young bilingual children before they realize that both parents understand both languages; Harrison & Piette (1980:220) mention an apparently successful example of the first type of arrangement in a family in which the mother and the two children speak Welsh to each other except when the monolingual English-speaking father is present, in which case they all use English in order to accommodate him. I myself am familiar with examples of the second type of arrangement which seem to function successfully, e.g. an Italian father in Australia has always spoken to his 20-year-old daughter, Lisa, in Italian, although the girl's English-speaking mother knew no Italian at the time of Lisa's birth and even today has only a smattering of the language ; the most important factors contributing to their and others' success is undoubtedly a positive and accepting attitude on the part of the monolingual parent towards what his or her partner is doing and a little effort by the bilingual parent and the children to ensure that the monolingual parent is catered for in some way and does not feel left out of family conversations. Gail Schaefer Fu (1986), an American who lives in Hong Kong and is married to a Chinese, gives a moving account of this in an article entitled "In defence of the monolingual mother". Despite much effort, she has acquired only an elementary knowledge of Chinese and has always spoken English to her daughters, Laura (16) and Erica (10), while her husband has always spoken Cantonese to them. Describ-ing some of the difficulties and rewards of such a situation, she writes:

And how do I feel about all of this? To be the only member of the family who is not fluently bilingual? Well, there is a whole gauntlet of feelings, of course. I have felt humble when asking a six year old to relay a telephone message that was linguistically too difficult for me to handle; ... I have felt isolated, attending dinner parties where I had only a meagre idea of what was going on; I have felt touched when a daughter gently, sensitively and *sotto voce* explained carefully the point of a joke or tried to suggest a "little better way of saying it". I have also felt grateful that my children have not used Chinese as a "secret language" to exclude me.

Lawrence Elliott (1977) gives a deliberately exaggerated, yet amusing account of the difficulties which can be encountered in a family if one parent is not very proficient in one of the languages being acquired by the child. Elliott's family lived in America, and his French wife Gisèle spoke only French to their son, Nicholas, while he himself addressed him in English, as well as occasionally in broken French. He reports that he had considerable difficulty in following his son's French utterances and "In self-defence, I kept a French dictionary by my side ..." However, even this did not work all the time. On one occasion, Nicholas told his father: "Papa, le potage est en train de bouillir." *(Dad, the soup's boiling.)* By the time Elliott had puzzled this out with the aid of his trusty dictionary, the stove, walls and floor were covered with soup!

In Ernesto Zierer's family, however, both parents were proficient in both languages, and it is unlikely that any conflict due to lack of comprehension would have eventuated. It appears that restricting the child to German until he was 2 years 10 months old may not have been entirely conducive to "the integration of the family", since his monolingual Spanish-speaking maternal grandmother, who visited the home daily, was requested not to speak to him in Spanish until that time.

There is probably no single method which can guarantee success in achieving bilingualism in the family, since there are simply so many variables involved. A method which works well in one family may encounter difficulties in another. The studies mentioned above have endeavoured to separate the child's two languages according to interlocutor or according to certain fixed times. All the parents, including those in the present study, have avoided indiscriminate switching from one language to the other, believing this would confuse the child.

Jules Ronjat (1913:109) mentions, for example, a Swiss friend whose mother tongue was French and whose wife was a native speaker of (Swiss) German. In the home, situated in the German-speaking part of Switzerland, the parents used Swiss German and French to each other and to the children, but without any system. Once the children started school, they no longer wanted to speak French. Ronjat believed that this would not have happened if the one-person–one-language method had been applied:

The children, who are affectionate and intelligent, would undoubtedly have remained attached to a language which they would have, above all, felt to be the language of their father.
(Translated from the French)

But again we may well be underestimating the child. Ana Huerta (1977) reports on a Mexican-American boy's simultaneous acquisition of Spanish and English in a home environment where frequent switching between the two languages is the dominant style of speaking, e.g. his mother speaks to him in both Spanish and English. Although she describes only the period from age 2;1–2;10, Huerta concludes that this method has no detrimental effect on the child's developing bilingualism and believes it may even enhance it. A special feature of this situation, though, is that this system of communication in the home receives support from the linguistic behaviour of the community. According to Huerta, such code-switching is common among Spanish-English bilinguals in the South-West of the USA where the family lives.

Another study in which most of the persons in the community with whom the child comes in contact use two languages alternately is that by Padilla & Liebmann (1975). They studied the speech development of three young Californian Spanish-English bilingual children whose language input was not dichotomized by person, and found no evidence that the bilinguals had a reduced rate of linguistic development in comparison with that of monolingual children.

In a two-year investigation of 13 Canadian French-English infant bilinguals with a commencing average age of 34 months, Doyle *et al.* (1978) also came to the conclusion that there is no evidence that the bilingual child's languages must be separate by person or location, at least as far as optimal vocabulary growth is concerned.

Experiments by Bruce Bain (1974) did, however, indicate some advantage for dichotomizing the child's two languages. Bain tested and compared three groups of children on their ability to relay messages from one parent to the other. Two of the groups were two types of Alsatian-French bilinguals, one in which the children were being raised according to the one-person–one-language principle, and one in which both parents used both languages indiscriminately with their children. The third group consisted of monolingual children who spoke either only Alsatian (a German dialect) or only French. The bilinguals from the one-person–one-language group scored 69.7% correct responses, whilst the other bilinguals and the monolinguals scored almost the same, namely 55.0% and 55.7% respectively. These results suggest that separating a child's two languages by person results in accelerated cognitive development compared to using them indiscriminately or even compared to using only one language. The results also suggest that bilinguals exposed indiscriminately to two languages fare just as well as monolinguals.

A possible danger of *not* separating a child's two languages by person can be seen in an account by Robbins Burling (1959). Burling, an American anthropologist, and his wife worked for two years in the Garo Hills of Assam, India, among the Garo people. Their son, Stephen, aged 1;4, was spoken to in English by his mother and in English and Garo (a Tibeto–Burman language) by his father, and he also had constant contact with monolingual Garo speakers. When the family left the Garo Hills when Stephen was aged 3;4, Burling writes that: "...there was ... no doubt that Garo was his first language ..., but English had become a flexible means of expression as well." Back in the USA, his father, who then became his only source of Garo, tried to speak the language with him *"from time to time"*. However, this was not sufficient to maintain Stephen's Garo:

> For a couple of months he would respond to Garo when I spoke to him, but he refused to use more than an occasional word. After this, he began failing even to understand my speech ... and within six months of our departure, he was even having trouble with the simplest Garo words ...

This severely reduced contact with Garo and the fact that even in India the father had not established himself as a Garo-only interlocutor for Stephen ("...when he was two and one half years old ... he developed a taste for speaking English with native English speakers and to my chagrin he came to prefer to speak English with me"), meant the loss of Stephen's Garo. Had the father consistently spoken Garo to his son, it seems probable that Stephen would have (eventually) recognized him as someone to whom he was to speak Garo and would have considered using it to him (compare the temporary reluctance of two of the children in this study to use German to their father, described in chapter 6).

In families where two languages are spoken, there is, therefore, a considerable advantage in having one parent speak to the children consistently in one language, the other parent consistently in the other language, as this ensures that the children have regular exposure to, and have to make use of, each language. This is particularly important for the language which has little outside support, and parents who do not wish to follow the one-person–one-language system, but prefer each to use both languages with their children, should take care that this more weakly placed language is used in the home at least as much, preferably more, than the other language.

3 Communication in the family: how it works

General remarks

Each individual bilingual family will, of course, have its own particular circumstances which will determine who speaks which language to whom, and when. What may evolve as a satisfactory linguistic arrangement in one family may, therefore, need to be modified in some way in another family. And not only do circumstances vary between families, but even within the one family. Children will have differing personalities, and their position in the family may also exert considerable influence. What works with one child may not necessarily succeed with another.

The description of communication in my family is therefore offered merely as a guide to what can be achieved, and indeed in a situation which is in some ways less than ideal for creating bilingualism. I am virtually the children's sole contact with German, and consequently their exposure to English is at least four to six times greater. Such a situation would not appear conducive to achieving a good standard of bilingualism. If it were their mother passing on German, for example, the hours of contact the children would have with the language, particularly in the years before the commencement of school, would be significantly increased. Nevertheless, such drawbacks can be countered to a certain extent, and it is hoped that the results obtained in this case and detailed in the following pages will prove encouraging to any family which is contemplating, or is in the process of raising its children bilingually.

This study gives a more accessible insight into the effect of fathers' speech to children than would be the case in a monolingual family, since most of the children's German comes from me. Rondal (1980) calls fathers "the forgotten contributors to child language development", and Friedlander (1971, 1972) offers some encouragement to fathers who are solely responsible for passing on a language to their children but who have limited time to do so, by suggesting that the emotional intensity which seems to characterize many father-child interactions compensates at least partially for the limited time spent in interaction.

Stages of linguistic development

What can parents expect to occur in the linguistic development of an infant bilingual? Firstly, there is no evidence that an infant who is exposed to two languages in the home will, in comparison with children living in a monolingual environment, be delayed in any way with regard to the production of his or her first word. In one study, for example, Doyle *et al.* (1978) compared thirteen young French-English bilingual children with thirteen monolingual children and found that the age at which the first word occurred was 11.2 months for the bilinguals and 12.0 months for the monolinguals.

Subsequent bilingual development will, again, vary with individual children and their particular circumstances, but generally, as found by Nygren-Junken (1977), Volterra & Taeschner (1978), and Taeschner (1982), they will pass through a three-stage developmental sequence:

Stage 1

This stage lasts roughly from the beginning of speech until age 2;0. The majority of a child's sentences will be single-element ones (e.g. "Ball") until about 18 months, and then two-element ones (e.g. "Ball gone") until about two years. During this stage children really possess only one lexical system containing words from both languages. Their active vocabulary is very limited, and when they can give a name for something in one language, they will most probably not be able to do so in the other. This applies very much more to the production of words than to their comprehension. By age 1;4, for instance, Frank understood and responded to both *horse* and its German equivalent *Pferd,* these being very important words for him, since his bedroom overlooked a paddock where horses regularly grazed. But in his speech he used only *Pferd* (pronounced initially as [d ∂t]), regardless of whom he was speaking to, until he reached the age of 2;0. At age 1;4 *heiß* was the other German word in Frank's active vocabulary (but not its English equivalent, *hot*). At the same age he could say another eight words, all English. He could, of course, understand much more than he could say in both languages. But even in his receptive vocabulary there were some items he knew, or at least reacted to, in only one language. When asked in English at age 1;9 what noise a bird made, Frank would reply with a hearty "Ahk! Ahk!", this particular sound being a result of his being especially impressed by crows which frequently landed on a tree in his backyard. However, if I asked him the same thing in German, he looked puzzled and made no response; the word *Vogel* (= bird) was obviously not yet part of his vocabulary. When asked the same sort of question about an ambulance, he would respond with siren noises only if the question were put in German.

Unfortunately, even at this early stage of what is called by Imedadze (1967) "mixed speech" and referred to perhaps more appropriately by Oksaar (1976) an "overall code", where children seemingly unsystematically name things in one of their languages, rarely in both, some parents begin to worry that their children are acquiring neither language properly. (This is a fear which, as will be seen, will probably recur at later stages.) It is thus important to realize that what occurs in this stage is neither unusual nor cause for concern. It seems that for the moment the child regards the two languages as one system containing many synonyms, and in his or her small active vocabulary uses only one of the "synonyms". Thus Frank used *Pferd* from the possible choice of *horse* and *Pferd*. The same process also takes place in a monolingual environment, although in a less noticeable way: a child who hears and understands *horse, horsie,* and *gee-gee* will initially most likely produce only one of them, say *gee-gee*. Since the child in a bilingual environment is at this stage not yet aware that he or she is dealing with two separate linguistic systems, he or she obviously cannot yet be expected to address adults only in the language heard from those adults. Towards the end of the first stage, the child will gradually start to use a word from each language to refer to the same concept, but at first this will be done indiscriminately. At age 1;10 Frank had three words to express to his parents that his nappy was wet and needed changing: English *wet,* German *naß* (= wet), and also a form which could belong to either language, namely *piss*. He was not at all consistent as to which form he would use to which parent or even to other people. Only later, in Stage II, would he become fully aware that *naß* was to be used to his father, *wet* to most other people, and that the socially not quite acceptable *piss* was best used only within the family.

Stage II

This stage begins sometimes around a child's second birthday. The child will have soon acquired an active vocabulary comprising words which designate the same item, action or function in both languages, and he or she will increasingly use the appropriate language when addressing different people. However, he or she may still produce utterances containing elements from both languages, since the same concept will not always be acquired simultaneously in the two languages and may continue to be bound to the context in which it was acquired. For example, Katrina, aged 2;4, holding a stick and pretending to fish, said to her mother, "I caughting fish with my *Angelrute* (= fishing rod)". Similarly, Thomas, aged 2;2, watching a flock of seagulls with his paternal grandfather, remarked, "Lots of *Möwen* (= seagulls), Granddad!" In both cases the children knew the corresponding English words and could produce them on request, but for a time they showed a definite preference for the German terms in their speech, irrespective of interlocutor. This preference is perhaps attributable to the fact that these particular words had featured much more

prominently as topics of conversation in German with me than in English conversations.

Some children go through an initial phase at this stage where they often refer to an object or activity in *both* languages. Frank, for example, at age 1;11, would frequently communicate to anyone willing to listen that he understood the dangers of touching the gas fire in the lounge room. Pointing at the fire, he would earnestly exclaim, "Hot heiß!" The child is here apparently becoming increasingly aware that there are two languages, that there are two words for everything, and that it is appropriate to address certain people in a certain language, but as yet he or she is unsure when or to whom to use which, so, to be on the safe side, resorts to both. As the child's awareness of the distinction between the two systems increases, the number of these double-barrelled terms will decrease. A similar use of synonyms to ensure understanding can also be observed in the speech of monolinguals: a small girl, aged 2;1, was heard urging her father to throw her up in the air yet again with the request, "More! Again!"

Even when a child begins actively to employ a term from each language appropriately, confidence that it is in fact the right term in the right language may take some time to develop. By age 2;0, for example, Frank would usually request a drink from me with the word "Flasche!" (=bottle!) and from his mother with "Drink!" However, as can be seen in the following exchange, if no immediate acknowledgement of his request was made, he would repeat it in his other language:

Frank (to mother): Drink! Drink!
Mother (failing to hear because of background noise): What?
Frank: Flasche! Flasche!

Els Oksaar (1977:300) observed a similar strategy employed by her Estonian-Swedish bilingual son, Sven, between the ages of 2;4 and 2;10. When he asked his parents for something in one language and they did not react instantly, the request was repeated in the other language.

In fact, parents may well find the existence of two languages to be quite an asset at this age when the child's pronunciation of words is not always readily intelligible. The child's spontaneous or elicited repetition of an unclear word in his or her other language gives the parents a double chance to comprehend (not unimportant if a child is prone to tantrums if not understood!) This is well illustrated in the following example:

Katrina (2;2,15) (to her mother): Did Katrina and Kathryn go in the *ceek?*
Mother (who, without any contextual clues, cannot deduce what is meant): What does Daddy say?
Katrina (after a moment's reflection): In der Wasser. *(In the water.)*
Mother: Oh, in the creek!
Katrina: Hm.

At this stage, parents can also help to speed up the development of a child's awareness of which words belong to which language by pretending not to understand (although this should not be overdone and only when it is known that the child knows the word for a particular concept in both languages), or by making the child aware of which parent says what, by

(a) supplying the word, e.g.:

Father: Was hast du da? *(What have you got there?)*
Katrina (1;8,14): Money.
Father: Geld, ja. *(Money, yes.)*

This could also be expressed more directly: "Ja, Mutti sagt *money* , Bert sagt *Geld." (Yes, Mummy says* money, *Daddy says* Geld.)

(b) by asking the child to supply the word, if it is thought that he or she knows it, e.g. "Was sagt Bert für *money*?" *(What does Daddy say for* money?)

Carl Dodson (1984) even recommends that this be made into a game to help young bilingual children to separate their two languages. He has observed that many young bilinguals often play with language by saying to themselves a word, phrase or sentence in one language, followed immediately by an equivalent utterance in the other language. He believes that parents should encourage such bilingual language play at other times as well, as it serves as an important mechanism which helps developing bilinguals to separate their languages, reduce cross-language interference, and to switch easily and effectively from one language to the other whenever required. Provided parents do this only when it is within their children's capabilities and make sure that it is fun, not a chore, for the children, this sort of bilingual game can be very useful.

During this second stage, children's rapidly developing ability to keep their two vocabularies reasonably separate may not be matched by a corresponding flexibility in differentiating the syntactic rules of the two languages, i.e. the rules which govern the order of words in sentences.one of the children in Virginia Volterra & Traute Taeschner's (1978:322) investigation, Lisa, for example, appeared for a long period of time, until the age of 2;9, to have acquired only one syntactic system for her Italian and German (although the evidence given is not completely convincing). However, this was not observable in the case of Thomas, Frank and Katrina except with regard to particular types of syntactic structures or on infrequent occasions. For instance, in English compound tenses, the past participle is placed straight after the auxiliary verb (e.g. The dog *has eaten* the bone.), whereas in German the past participle is in the *final* position in the clause, e.g. Katrina (2;2,20): Hast du das Brot und der Zeitung *gekauft?* (Literally: Have you the bread and the newspaper *bought?*) All three children made this differentiation between the two languages with the appearance of their first past tenses, and it was only on very rare occasions that an utterance was heard in German which followed the English pattern, e.g.Katrina (2;10,24): Ich habe *gepflückt* Löwenzahn. (= I've *picked* some dandelions.); *gepflückt* (= picked) should be last in the German sentence. But, as already stated, there was practically no evidence of a fused syntactic system. Where syntactic structures differed in the two languages, these differences were, on the whole, observed. To take just one other example: sentences with modal verbs (can, must, want, etc.) require the following verb to be placed at the end of the clause in German, but immediately after the modal verb in English. The three children's speech always showed this differentiation, as can be seen in the following dual language utterance made by Frank to both his parents when he was aged 2;7,0:

Frank: I wanna wash my hands. (And then continuing after a barely perceptible pause:) Ich will meine Hände *waschen.* (Literally: *I want my hands to-wash.*)

Jürgen Meisel (1986, 1987), after analyzing the relevant literature and the results of his own research with young German-French bilingual children in Hamburg, also believes that bilingual children do not have to pass through a stage where they use only one syntactic system for both languages; his research shows, for example, that bilingual children consistently use different word order in both languages no later than they start to make utterances of two or more words.

Stage III

In this final stage children now speak the two languages differentiated in both vocabulary and syntax, their speech revealing minimal interaction between the two languages. If being brought up in an environment where each language is bound to particular persons, children will now consistently address interlocutors in the appropriate language. The transition from Stage II to Stage III is gradual, usually far from smooth, and may take considerable time. The time taken for this transition, as well as the degree to which the two languages are finally differentiated, will depend on many factors, such as the child's personality and natural ability, the parents' attitude, and the proportions of time of exposure to each of the languages. Children will relatively quickly acquire an almost uncanny ability to speak to people only in the appropriate language. However, as many researchers into bilingualism (e.g. Leopold (1939–49), Haugen (1956), Clyne (1967)) have clearly shown, it is very rare to find a bilingual person, child or adult, who can completely avoid one of his or her languages influencing the other in some way or other.

With regard to the separation of the two languages by conversation partner, it will be seen in the present study that it was not really until the age of 3;9 that Thomas was addressing me predominantly in German (98%), whilst Frank and Katrina reached this point much sooner, Frank already speaking 95% German to me at age 3;0, and Katrina 99% German to me at age 2;6 (see chapter 6 for more details).

The children's communication strategies

In the present study, a fairly stable communication routine has developed in the family: the three children and I communicate with each other in German, the three children and their mother use English to one another, my wife and I speak English to each other, and between themselves the children speak mostly English.

Since all family members understand both languages, no-one is left out of a conversation. The children switch with apparent ease from one language to the other depending on who it is they are speaking to. The following examples show how harmoniously the two languages co-exist in the family and how communication in a variety of situations is in no way impaired by the parents using different languages; if the family were monolingual, communication would most probably take place in much the same way:

Father: I'd better take a photo of you two (i.e. his wife and Katrina) — you two haven't had your photo taken together.

Katrina (5;1,19) (To her mother): Only once I think. (Looking at me): **Weil ich kann mich erinnern.** *(Because I can remember.)*

Frank (11,1,22) (to Thomas): Four days before I said to Dad that Boris Becker would win, (to me) **nicht wahr, Bert?** *(didn't I, Dad?)*
Father: Ja. *(Yes.)*

(Thomas is telling his parents about arrangements to meet a friend.)
Thomas (10;11,21): ... I see him in politics tomorrow, and in maths, Mum. I can tell him where I'll be waiting, Mum.
Mother: Hm-hm.
Thomas: I have to wait forty minutes.
Father: Oh, das ist nicht sehr lange. *(Oh, that's not very long.)*
Mother: I know. That's a shame, though, isn't it?
Father: Yeah.

Children addressing both parents simultaneously

There are occasions when the children may wish to speak to both parents at the same time. But which language are they to use? In this investigation, Thomas adopted, around his third birthday, a certain strategy to overcome this problem, a strategy later also adopted by his younger brother, Frank, at about age 3;6, and by his sister, Katrina, shortly before her third birthday. Faced with such a predicament, the children's solution is to address one of the parents by name, establish eye contact with him or her, and then proceed in the language appropriate to that parent, knowing that the other parent will understand anyway. In the initial stages of establishing this routine, Thomas obviously felt somewhat uncomfortable in such situations and would avoid eye contact with the parent whose language he was not using. If he did happen to glance at the other parent, this would often cause him to falter in his delivery and switch to the other language, e.g.:

Thomas (4;3,17) (holding one of his favourite storybooks about a cat called Charlie and telling the story to his mother. While he is doing this, I come in and sit down beside them to listen. Thomas continues with the story, looking at first steadfastly at his mother, but at one point he catches my eye, falters in his delivery, and switches to and completes the account in German): ... And Charlie looks at him up on the big rubbish-tin, and, and the tomcat went away. Charlie went in there and further and further. And then a fire eng— (looking at me) **— und dann hat ein Feuerwehrwagen gekommen. Und Charlie hat auf der Straße gegangen ...** *(— and then a fire-engine came. And Charlie went on the road ...)*

This uncomfortableness had practically disappeared by Thomas's fifth birthday. In fact, by that time he was beginning to use this strategy to his advantage. When having difficulty expressing himself or finding a word in one language, he would establish eye contact with the other parent and switch to his other language, often in mid-sentence. In the following example, Thomas (5;6,24) is talking about mountain climbing and has chosen to address his remarks, which are obviously intended for both parents, to his mother in English. However, the word *summit* is not yet known to him in English and the simpler and more usual children's word *top* seems not to have occurred to him. To extricate himself from this difficulty, he switches to German and addresses me:

> **Thomas:** Mum, I want to climb a mountain ... and then put a flag up when I've climbed it. It shows that I've, I've, that I've, ah, **Bert, das zeigt, daß ich der Gipfel erreicht habe.** *(Dad, that shows that I've reached the summit.)*

This switch to German would not have occurred if I had not been present. Thomas would then have either used the German word *Gipfel* (= summit) in his English, most likely in a hesitant manner, showing that he realized the word was not English and suggesting a desire for assistance, or he would have paused briefly and made a direct request such as "How do you say *Gipfel* in English?"

The above procedure for addressing both parents at the same time is basically still employed by Thomas, and also by Frank and Katrina. But there still sometimes seems to be a little bit of conflict in the children's minds about which language they should choose in such situations, which may lead them to state expressly that *both* parents are being addressed, e.g.:

> **Thomas** (12;11,29) (To mother): I'm trying to tell you something, but Dad keeps making these sick jokes. (Smiles at me:) **Ah, ich sage es auf deutsch** *— (Ah, I'll say it in German —)* (looking at his mother) but I'm telling both of you, right? **Heute** ... *(Today ...)*

The same sort of problem can, of course, also arise in written communications which are intended for both parents. An interesting solution to this problem was found by Thomas when he was aged 9;7,22. He had written and stuck on his bedroom door a notice with the words "KEEP OUT! The only people allowed are Kevin, Shane, Frank, Ross and Tim." Then, underneath he had added a postscript: "NOTE. Mum, you and Dad are allowed. I only made the chart to include my friends." By apparently writing directly only to his mother he found a way out of the difficulty he was no doubt in. It would have seemed strange to him to begin "Mum and Dad, you ...", since he never addressed me in English. It would also have seemed peculiar to him to address his mother in German by beginning " Bert und Mutti ..." *(Dad and Mum ...)* The only other solution which he would have found acceptable would have been to write two separate messages, one in German to me, one in English to his mother!

When one of the children is addressing both parents simultaneously in one language, each parent answers freely in the same language we would normally use to the child, e.g.:

Frank (4;1,10) (specifically to his mother, but glancing in mid-sentence at me to indicate that I am included): Can we go for a walk?
Father: Aber das Abendessen ist doch beinahe fertig. *(But tea's just about ready.)*
Frank: Oh, blöder Mist! *(Oh, damn!)*
Mother: Perhaps we can go after tea.

Even when one of the children addresses a remark to one parent only and the parent does not hear, or for some reason does not reply, the other parent may answer in the other language, e.g.:

Thomas (4;1,23) (to me): Hat dein Hemd ein Loch da drin? *(Has your shirt got a hole in it?)*
Father: Ein kleines, ja. *(A little one, yes.)*
Thomas (to me): Flickt Mami das für dich? *(Is Mummy going to fix it for you?)*
Mother: Yes, Thomas, I've got a few things to do.

Or one parent may add information or some comment in the other language, e.g.:

Thomas (11;0,18): Matthias hat seinen Füller vergessen, Bert. *(Matthias has left his pen here, Dad.)*
Father: Oh—
Mother: How will you remember it tomorrow, then, Thomas?
Thomas: Oh, I'll just have to bring it.
Mother: Will I clip it on to your parka? That might be a good idea.
Thomas: Yeah...

When I wish to address my wife and at the same time one or more of the children, I may use German, e.g.:

Father (to Katrina and her mother): Möchtet ihr ein Eis?
Katrina (5;10,8): Oh, ja bitte! *(Oh, yes please!)*
Mother: Yes, that'd be nice.

Or I may instead use English and ostensibly address only my wife, this second alternative often being followed by some comment in German to the children to let them know that they are included, e.g.:

Father (to wife): I think we might go to the beach a bit later on. (Then to the boys who are also present): Möchtet ihr das tun? *(Would you like to do that?)*
Frank (5;0,5): Ja, Bert... (Yes, Bert...)

Children addressing father plus monolingual(s)

Even more problematical for the children are situations where the children wish to address me and a monolingual English-speaker simultaneously. The children then usually opt for English and address the monolingual, knowing I will understand, e.g.:

> **Father** (asking Frank about a fishing trip with a great-uncle): Hattest du eine Schwimmweste? *(Did you have a life jacket?)*
> **Frank** (11,2,30): Ja. *(Yes.)* (Then, to include his grandfather and grandmother, who are also present:) Jack didn't have one — a life jacket. He said, "You only drown once."
> **Grandmother:** That'd be enough, too, wouldn't it?

However, whilst this is the children's usual solution in such cases, it is apparent that, being conditioned to using only German with me, it can at times cause conflict in their minds. As if to allay this conflict and to indicate to me that they do not wish to break their arrangement of German only, they may occasionally:

(a) make short asides to me in German to indicate that I am included in the remarks, e.g.:

> **Frank** (11,9,26) (taking part in a conversation with me and two monolingual relatives): The day that we came back one year, um, it was 42 (degrees), **nicht wahr, Bert?** *(= wasn't it, Dad?)*
> **Father:** Hm.
> **Frank:** That was really hot...

(b) use English to the monolingual English speaker and then repeat basically the same information for me in German, e.g.:

> **Katrina** (5;10,8) (seeing dog drinking quickly from a bowl, to grandmother): Jock must be thirsty!
> **Grandmother:** I'll say.
> **Katrina** (to me, sitting next to the grandmother): Jock hat Durst, Bert. *(Jock's thirsty, Dad.)*

Alternatively, I may be addressed first in German and the information then be repeated in English for any monolinguals present, e.g.:

> **Frank** (6;3,17) (returning from an unsuccessful hunt with me and a great-uncle, hears the loud, human-like laughter of a kookaburra *(Dacelo gigas)* coming from a nearby gumtree): Bert, der Lachende Hans lacht, weil du hast nichts geschossen! *(Dad, the kookaburra's laughing because you didn't shoot anything!)* (Then immediately to his monolingual great-

uncle): Jack, I think the kookaburra's laughing because you didn't shoot anything.

Another possible strategy, but one not used all that often, is for the children to address the remark to me in German and leave it to me to make any explanation necessary to monolinguals included in the utterance, e.g.:

> **Frank** (7;1,22) (watching his uncle skin a rabbit): Ich mag die Eingeweide nicht, Bert. *(I don't like the innards, Dad.)*
> (I laugh at Frank's screwed up face.)
> **Uncle:** Eh?
> **Father:** Frank said he doesn't like the guts.

Child to child communication

That English is the language predominantly used, even in private, between Thomas, Frank and Katrina, is a situation which has developed naturally, that is, practically without parental intervention.

During the time until Frank's second birthday, that is, while his active vocabulary was still very small and he had not yet begun to differentiate between the two languages, Thomas tended to respond in the language Frank used to address him in. This was normally English, since most of Frank's utterances were in that language, a predictable result of his being exposed to it very much more than to German. In fact, many of the utterances Thomas directed at Frank at this stage were a mixture of English and German, particularly when they referred to me or to activities engaged in with me, e.g.:

Frank (1;4,4) (looking for me): Dad dad dad.
Thomas (3;2,27): Dad dad's in the front room **schreiben Bücher** *(writing books)*, Frankie.

Frank was thus not clearly classified as someone to whom only English was to be used. Thomas obviously realized that he understood German and also occasionally spoke it. However, when Frank, at age 2;0, began speaking in more than one-word sentences, his utterances were at first largely in English, even to me, from whom he continued to receive only German. Consequently, Thomas (3;10) spoke to him almost exclusively in English.

When Thomas was aged 4;0, I tried to make one afternoon a week, when the mother was absent, a time when only German would be spoken by me and the children. This was more an attempt to encourage Frank (2;2) to speak more German than an attempt to induce the children to speak German to one another. This experiment worked reasonably well, Thomas accepting it cheerfully, but initially becoming frustrated with Frank's failure to speak only German. He made disapproving remarks if he heard Frank speaking English to me and, on occasions, even disapproved when Frank addressed *him* in English. He would then either voice his disapproval or refuse to answer , e.g.:

Frank (2;6,22) (pointing at a car): What's that, Tom? (Thomas [4;5,4] ignores him. Frank repeats the question three times, but still no response is forthcoming. Finally he resorts to German.) Was ist das? *(What's that?)*
Thomas (visibly pleased, answers immediately): Das ist ein Auto, Frankie. *(That's a car, Frankie.)*

Despite Thomas's initial despair, Frank did respond well to the setting aside of a regular time for German only, and his use of German on these occasions increased quite dramatically. Eventually a situation developed where Thomas would, if he initiated the exchange and I was in close proximity, address Frank in German. If Frank was the initiator of an exchange to Thomas, he was not as consistent about using German in my presence; if he did this in English the reply from Thomas would usually also be in English. When I was absent or not close by, the children would, with a few exceptions, to be discussed later, use English to each other. Thomas himself (4;10,15) summed up the situation succinctly when I walked in on an animated conversation between the two brothers and jokingly commented:

He, ihr zwei, heute ist doch unser deutscher Tag! *(Hey, you two, today's our German day!)*

Thomas's surprised, spontaneous reply was:

Aber, Bert, nur wenn du da bist! Dann sprechen wir Deutsch! *(But, Dad, only when you're here! Then we speak German!)*

No attempt was made to interfere with this reasonable assessment of the situation.

Smolicz & Harris (1977) show that this type of situation is by no means uncommon in Australian bilingual families. After questioning 838 children of various ethnic backgrounds (Polish, Italian, Greek, Dutch and Latvian), they came to the following conclusion:

> In regard to active linguistic experience in speaking ... the basic finding, which held for all ethnic groups in these surveys, was that even in those families where the ethnic language was spoken by the second or 1b generation (= children who immigrated before their speech habits had become fixed, i.e. before about age 12) with ethnic elders, the language used with peers was almost invariably English.

Similar findings are reported by Michael Clyne (1970:35) and Camilla Bettoni (1981:50). Clyne questioned 74 children of German-speaking immigrants in and around Melbourne. The children, all of whom attended a German-language Saturday school, "generally spoke English among themselves". In her book *Italian in North Queensland,* Bettoni says of the Australian-born children of Italian parents:

> Among themselves they always speak English. They started doing that as soon as they went to school and saw no reason to change their habits later on. Only with their parents, their parents' friends and generally with first generation migrants who know little English do they speak their native Italian ...

After a period of approximately 13 months (Thomas 4;0 to 5;1, Frank 2;1 to 3;2), opportunities for me to be alone with the children decreased owing to the presence of playmates and also their mother's no longer being absent for an eight-hour period each week as previously. Consequently, their use of German to each other in my presence gradually declined. By the time Thomas was 5;11 and Frank 4;1 the children were using English to each other even if I was alone with them, although German has never completely disappeared from such communication.

German is still used when one of the children (including Katrina, who is discussed in more detail in the next section) addresses the other but wishes at the same time to include me in the remark. This is particularly the case when an attempt is being made to convince not only a brother or sister of an argument but also at the same time to make an appeal to me to recognize the validity of the argument, since in many cases I am the one who has the final decision in the matter in question. In the following typical example, the children have been told that they must eat all their main course if they wish to have dessert. Thomas has not quite finished his main course when he reaches for his dessert:

> **Frank** (4;1,23) (protesting to me): Ernie hat sein Gemüse nicht gegessen! *(Thomas hasn't eaten his vegetables!)* (Implying that he therefore does not deserve dessert.)
> **Thomas** (6;9,15) (turning to Frank): Das macht nichts! *(That doesn't matter!)*

German may be used by one of the children to another not just when seeking support from me, but also simply to convey information to me. This usually happens in the excitement of a game with me, particularly when the majority of exchanges are between me and one of the children, that is, in German. In the following incident, the two boys and I are engaged in a rather hectic pirate game. Playing the arch villain, I am being assailed by two sword-wielding pirates:

> **Father** (succumbing to a vicious sword thrust and slumping to the floor): Aua! Ooh!
> **Frank** (4;10,1) (to me): Du blödes — *(You stupid —)*
> **Thomas** (6;8,24) (to brother): Er ist tot! *(He's dead!)*

This remark by Thomas seems to be conveying both to Frank, to whom it is ostensibly directed, and to me, a stage in the game, that is, that the villain is dead (and should therefore pretend to be such). In this and the examples above it is likely that English would have been the language employed if there had not been a definite need to include me directly in the remarks.

In games in which I am a participant, the children do use quite a bit of German to each other even when I cannot be considered a direct addressee. Usually in such games the children are playing a certain role, assuming temporarily a different identity, often disguising their voice to fit the part they are playing. Since they have become, as it were, temporarily different people, they can speak German to each other without any feeling of strangeness or sense that they are breaking the established pattern of communicating with one another in English.

If I participate in a game and have to leave before it is finished, my influence may linger for some time after my departure. For example, on one occasion I had been playing cops and robbers with Thomas (6;11,9) and Frank (5;0,17), but had been called away. A tape-recorder left running revealed that the boys continued playing the game completely in German for about a minute.

When I am not present at all, the children do still use German to each other under certain circumstances. In role play, for instance, if the character in question is perceived as being a German-speaker, then that language will be used. At one time one of the boys' favourite stories in German was a dramatic recording of

Aladin und die Wunderlampe (Aladdin and the Magic Lamp). So German was the language chosen when the two of them played a game modelled on that story:

> **Thomas** (7;3,2): Ich bin der Geist der Lampe. Meister, dein Wunsch ist mir Befehl. *(I'm the Genie of the lamp. Master, your wish is my command.)*
> **Frank** (5;4,10): Hol mir eine interessantes Buch. *(Get me an interesting book.)*
> **Thomas** (fetching a book and handing it ceremoniously to Frank): Hier ist dein Buch, Meister. *(Here is your book, master.)*

Frank browses briefly through the book. After this interaction they move on to play something else, and their dialogue reverts to English. (Alvino Fantini (1978a:290) made a similar observation with his own Spanish-English bilingual children, Mario and Carla: "Roleplays were usually performed in the language of the person being portrayed, whether a playmate, a teacher, or Bionic Woman".)

Interactions in German between the children may be associated with activities they frequently engage in with me, although at times it is difficult to determine what motivates the choice of German when they are by themselves. German may be used for brief, high-spirited utterances of a teasing nature, e.g.:

> **Frank** (4;8,0) (seizing Thomas in a bear-hug): Ich schmeiße dich in diese Mülltonne! *(I'm going to throw you in this garbage can!)*

The incident culminated in a good-natured tussle, following which the conversation returned to English. An explanation for this sort of temporary switch to German may be that the children enjoy teasing and wrestling with me in this way, but not with their mother, and thus associate this amusement with German, at least within the family.

On a few occasions the children have been observed using German to each other to reinforce a request which has already been made in English and which has been rebuffed, e.g.:

> **Thomas** (6;8,8): Put the arrow back!
> **Frank** (4;9,16): No!
> **Thomas:** Steck der Pfeil zurück! *(Put the arrow back!)*

Evidently the use of German is seen as giving the request more authority; perhaps it makes the request sound more like one from their father.

Whilst, apart from the exceptions discussed, English is the language predominantly used by the children to each other when by themselves, it is an English which may contain quite a number of lexical transfers from German. This was particularly so when the two boys were younger, e.g.:

> **Frank** (4;0,7): There's a *Kaninchen* (= rabbit), Thomas! Let's get him!

Since in most cases like this the brothers knew the corresponding vocabulary items in English, there was no linguistic necessity for their using German words. They seem rather to be deliberately indulging in a kind of linguistic game for their own amusement. Sometimes the use of German words in their English occurs because the conversation is about an activity associated with me and with speaking German, e.g.:

> **Frank** (11;0,27): Tom, how much did you lift in *Stoßen?* (= clean and jerk)
> **Thomas** (12;11;19): Forty-five kilos...
> (Practically all the boys' experience with, and discussions about, weight-training are with me and therefore in German.)

This use of German words in English does not occur if monolingual English speakers are present, unless as a means of teasing a monolingual, but this occurs only rarely.

During the family's six month stay in Hamburg in 1984, English still remained the language the children normally used to communicate with each other, although the number of German words used in their English increased. Sometimes there was a clear reason for the use of the German word, e.g.:

> **Frank** (8;9,26) (talking about German ice-cream): I like strawberry and ***Heidelbeer.***

Heidelbeere (= bilberry or blueberry) was a flavour not available in Australia and therefore the English term was not yet known. In other cases, the use of a German word was prompted by there being no exact equivalent in English, e.g.:

> **Frank** (9;0,7): Tom, guess what we're doing in ***Werken*** now.

Werken was a school subject which did not really correspond to any subject at Frank's school in Australia — it included woodwork and various kinds of craft work. In tapes sent from Germany to their monolingual relatives in Australia such lexical transfers were usually not used, but replaced by an explanation or a near-translation, e.g. *Werken* was referred to as "craft".

When speaking English to each other, the children also almost invariably used German to give direct quotations of conversations they had had or heard in German, e.g.:

> **Frank** (9;0,13) (telling his brother about a film he has seen at school): ...And, well, I saw a bus in India, and they had the windows open and they were all — and he said (i.e. the German commentator of the film), **"Auf diesem Bus gibt es dreißig Leute."** *(On this bus there are thirty people.)*, and it was only a little bus, Tom ...

In Hamburg, even when German friends were present who could not under-stand English, Frank and Thomas normally still spoke to each other in English; only rarely did they use German when just addressing one another. They preferred to speak English to each other and then if necessary explain in German to their friends what they were discussing. Their friends did not seem to mind, but rather showed considerable interest and curiosity. This tolerance was probably helped by the fact that proficiency in English does have quite a bit of prestige in Germany. If their brother *and* a German friend were to be included in a remark, then German was used.

Once back in Australia, the pattern of communication between the children did not change very much. English remains, and will probably remain, the primary means of communication between them, but by no means to the total exclusion of German.

Communication between brothers and sister

When Katrina was born on 13 February 1981, her mother and I began straightaway to address her just as they had her two brothers, in English and German respectively. Whilst Thomas showed no surprise that I addressed Katrina in German, Frank initially expressed scepticism that a baby could understand Ger-man, she being the only baby he had ever heard spoken to in German. However, he readily accepted the explanation that his sister would be like the other children in the family and understand both languages. Before Katrina could talk, her brothers usually addressed her in English when I was absent and the mother or other English speakers were present. If they were playing with her and I was the only other person in close proximity, they tended to address her predominantly, but not exclusively, in German. When alone with her they spoke mainly English, although an occasional sentence in German was to be heard.

When Katrina was aged 10 months, I taught her to touch her nose in response to the question "Wo ist Katrinas Nase? *(Where's Katrina's nose?)*, an achievement which impressed her brothers greatly and really established her credibility as someone German could be spoken to. It was made even more impressive by the fact that at first she did not respond at all to the same question in English. Consequently German became the language which Thomas and Frank used to get her to show off her "tricks" to their friends and relatives. Her first word to accompany her pointing was also German, namely "Da!" *(There!)* (established by age 1;0), which rein-forced this practice. Monolingual English speakers found it amazing that such a little girl could understand German. Friends of the boys were fascinated by this and some of them also learned to ask Katrina in German to perform for them, e.g. to run through her repertoire of animal sounds (beginning at age 1;1,25 with a woof in response to "Was sagt ein Hund?" *(What's a dog say?)*)

In the subsequent five years there has always been some German used between Katrina and her brothers, not only when I am present (which increases the likelihood that at least some of their exchanges will be in German), but also when I am absent. This has particularly been the case when Katrina and Frank play together, which occurs quite frequently. Tapes made of them playing together reveal that whilst on such occasions their main means of communication is English, they do switch every now and then into German, sometimes for a few sentences only, sometimes for longer stretches of conversation. On average, German comprises about 10–20% of what they say to each other. Most of the German switches are instigated by Frank, perhaps continuing a practice he established with Katrina when she was just beginning to speak. The switches from one language to the other appear not to follow any logical system, although reasons for some of them can be surmised, e.g. on one occasion, Frank (8;4,17), who was speaking English to Katrina, suddenly changed the topic of conversation and switched to German:

> **Frank** (8;4,17): Here's your cornflakes. (Short pause.) Wir gehen heute zu Timo. *(We're going to Timo's today.)*
> **Katrina** (3;0,5): Ja. *(Yes.)*
> **Frank:** Wirst du mit ihm spielen? *(Are you going to play with him?)*
> **Katrina:** Ja. Und du auch? *(Yes. And you, too?)*
> **Frank:** Ja. (Slight pause.) Look at this, Katrina … (Conversation continues for a while in English.)

Here, the switch to German most probably occurred because the new topic, Timo, is a friend with whom the children always speak German. However, as mentioned above, the reasons for other switches into German and back to English defy easy interpretation. When asked about this, Frank simply said that sometimes he just felt like saying things in German to Katrina. Whilst he found it somewhat unnatural to speak German to his brother in normal conversation, he had no such feeling of strangeness when speaking German to his sister, it felt the same as when he was speaking English with her. Thus, when German-speaking friends are present, for example as during the family's stay in Hamburg in 1984, the proportion of German Katrina and Frank speak to each other rises to about 80%. In such circumstances, Thomas, too, who normally does not speak nearly as much German to Katrina as Frank, increases the amount of German he uses when talking to her.

Sometimes I capitalize on Frank's natural inclination to speak partly in German to his sister by asking him to increase the amount of German he speaks to her, explaining to him that this will increase her exposure to and practice in speaking the language; he usually does this willingly, although sometimes Katrina obviously finds it a little strange if Frank continues to speak *only* German to her for long periods of time, and she begins to answer him in English.

In some bilingual families, parents insist that the children also speak the home language among themselves. This may indeed be quite possible when there is only one home language, but even then it seems that most children do this only when their parents are actually present or within earshot; otherwise they speak the dominant language of the community with each other. In a family such as mine, where the children speak one language with their mother and another with their father, it is more difficult to encourage the children to use their "weaker" language to each other, especially as the children get older. However, it may be possible, as above with Frank, to enlist the older children's aid in maintaining the "weaker" language by speaking it to their younger siblings, or perhaps by setting aside certain times when, unlike normal family practice, the "weaker" language is used by the whole family.

Private speech

The three children nowadays use mostly English in their monologues, although until around their fourth birthdays quite a bit of German was also used for this purpose. In that early period, there sometimes seemed to be no particular reason for the choice of language, while sometimes the choice appeared to be governed by topic, e.g. if talking to themselves about a game usually played with me or about a conversation with me, the children would be inclined to speak predominantly German, e.g.:

> (Frank is playing with a toy plane and talking to himself. He is re-enacting an incident just seen in an English-language television program in which a light plane has crashed. Although the program itself was in English, he has discussed it thoroughly afterwards with me in German.)
> **Frank** (3;5,24): Oh, oh, es hat abgestürzt! *(Oh, oh, it's crashed!)* Broke to pieces Total Kaputt! Verflixt noch mal! *(Completely wrecked! Damn it all!)*

Els Oksaar (1973) reports on similar experiences with her Estonian-Swedish bilingual son, Sven. In an incident when he was aged 2;8, for instance, Sven was recalling aloud to himself the day's activities. He switched from Estonian to Swedish whenever he mentioned experiences which he had had during the day in a Swedish-speaking family. Werner Leopold (1949b:127) also noticed much the same in Hildegard's monologues, her private speech in play being considered as an extension of games played with her monolingual peers. He made the following observation when she was aged 5;7,26: "When she plays alone she speaks English because her solitary games continue her games with other children." Theodor Elwert (1959:330) refers to this type of phenomenon as *Nachhallsprache* (= echo language), and describes how, having read a book in a particular language, he continues for a while to think about the book and discuss it with himself in the language in which it was written.

As found also by Ronjat (1913:10), Leopold (1949b:62), Rū̄ke-Draviņa (1967:37) and Oksaar (1973), during monologues the children make appropriate language switches when pretending to address people, real or imaginary, who are associated with a particular language, e.g.:

> **Katrina** (2;3,13) (playing with her doll Anna): Anna's sick. Where's my telephone? (Finds her toy telephone.) I ringing up Daddy. (Speaks on phone.) Guten Tag, Bert. (In a sad voice) Anna ist krank — und weinen. *(Hullo, Dad. Anna's sick — and cry.)*

In solitary games where the children act out the parts of actual or made-up people, they assume the language of the person whose role they are playing (see also chapter 4 for additional details on role playing). The process involved is practically the same as in games played by monolingual children where each imaginary character is given an appropriate tone of voice, accent, etc. A bilingual child simply extends this to have characters speaking more than one language. A typical example of this occurred when Thomas was aged 7;5,24 and was playing with a set of toy soldiers, consisting of American, Australian, German and Japanese troops. In the course of the game he gave each group of soldiers the language and/or accent appropriate to their nationality, including even a short stretch of invented Japanese.

Another factor which could affect a child's choice of language in private speech is the presence in the same room of one parent, even though the parent is otherwise occupied and does not speak to the child. Jules Ronjat (1913:10) writes that his son, Louis, behaved in much the same way. His monologues were in either French or German, depending on the subject which inspired them or the persons who were within earshot. It was Ronjat's impression, therefore, that his son's monologues were more often in German than in French, since they generally took place in the presence of the mother and/or the maid, with both of whom Louis spoke German.

In the case of Thomas, Frank and Katrina, my presence, particularly if only one of the children and I are present, may still cause them to use some German in their monologues, although this was much more noticeable in the period before each child started school. In that period, Thomas and Katrina were more influenced by my presence than Frank who, until about age 4;6, mostly became so engrossed in his play and in his monologues that he seemed oblivious of anyone's presence. It was apparent, for example, that even at age 4, Thomas preferred English for his private comments to himself, even when alone with me, e.g.:

> (Thomas, age 4;3,25, is playing mechanics with me and speaking German. But in an aside to himself he switches to English.)

Thomas (to me): Ich habe diese Räder abgenommen. *(I've taken these wheels off.)*

Father: Warum? *(Why?)*

Thomas (engrossed in his game, does not seem to hear my question, and talks to himself): I try — they sort of push in and out.

Father: Was? *(What?)*

Thomas (suddenly realizing I am there): Sie kommen raus ... *(They come out ...)*

It seems that in an examination of the children's private speech, a difference needs to be made between situations where they are pretending to address or assume the roles of other people and those situations where they are *conversing with themselves*. In the first type of situation, the language chosen is determined by the language perceived as appropriate for the imaginary people in question. However, which language does one use to address *oneself* when one speaks and understands two? From quite an early age, all three children seem to have preferred English for this purpose. This preference reflects the fact that English is the dominant language of their environment and that, with the exception of communication with me, the children are practically always addressed in English. I have made no attempt to interfere in this essentially private sphere, except for a few occasions when, on overhearing the children speaking to themselves in English, I have teasingly asked, "Was?" *(What?)*. This has typically provoked responses such as:

Thomas (5;0,9): Ich spreche mit mir selbst Englisch, Bert. *(I speak English to myself, Dad.)*

Frank (5;7,11): Ich spreche nicht mit dich! *(I'm not talking to you!)*

Katrina (5;3,1): Bert! Ich spreche mit mir! *(Dad! I'm talking to myself!)*

Dreams

A particular type of private speech occurs in sleep. Which language do bilinguals use in their dreams? Theodor Elwert (1959:331) scoffs at what he calls a widespread naive belief that a person dreams only in his "mother tongue": "Als ob man nur in einer Sprache träume!" *(As if you dream in only one language!)*. Because the children in this study have talked only rarely while asleep and because of the difficulties of observing them when they do, examples of this type of speech are not plentiful. However, it seems that in general the language used by the children in their dreams is determined in much the same way as when awake, i.e. English is used unless I (or someone else classified as a German speaker) appears in the dream, in which event German is used to address them. Similarly, Elwert (1959:331), reporting on his own experiences with dreams, writes that if people appear in a dream, they are addressed in the language in which they would be spoken to in a real life situation. Velta Rūķe-Draviņa (1967:37) also comes to the conclusion that the choice of language in a dream depends on the persons and circumstances occurring in the dream.

In fact, a dream can become more a nightmare if the linguistic arrangements of real life are upset, as illustrated in the following excerpts from a taped conversation between Thomas (10;11,26) and his mother. After having lived for four months in Hamburg, the family had spent a week's holiday in England, and it was there, placed suddenly once again into an English-speaking environment, that Thomas's dreams took a strange turn:

> **Thomas:** In my dreams that I had in England, Mum, I was confused... because I didn't know which language to speak... My dreams were just all mixed up — like, I'd speak German with my friends in Australia, and they wouldn't answer or anything, Mum, and I was just so confused... Like, Leslie asked me something and I said **"Was?"** *(What?)*, Mum...

However, this was an isolated incident, and is really not unlike the type of nightmare monolinguals may have, in which their actions in the dream are at variance with their normal behaviour and seemingly beyond their control. There is no evidence for what Edith Harding & Philip Riley (1986:125) call "the old legend" that bilingual children have more nightmares than monolinguals.

Communication with animals

Until the children went to Germany in 1984 they, as a general rule, assumed that animals understood only English, a reasonably logical assumption in a predominantly English-speaking society where they almost always heard animals addressed in English. This assumption applied to both live and imaginary animals. In the following example, Thomas (4;9,11), during a game with me, switches to English to address an imaginary horse:

> **Thomas:** Ich gehe, um Milch zu holen. *(I'm going to get some milk.)*
> **Father:** Okay. Wo holst du die Milch her? *(All right. Where will you get the milk from?)*
> **Thomas:** Ah, von Kühe. *(Ah, from cows.)* (Pretends to mount a horse.) Giddy up, horsie, giddy up. Da sind meine Kühe. Da ist eine. *(There're my cows. There's one.)*

On one occasion, Frank (3;9,21) even attributed a cat with the power of speech and quoted it (but not himself) in English:

> **Frank:** Eine weiße Katze war auf das Baum, und ich habe gesagt: "Komm runter, Katze!", und das Katze hat gesagt: *(A white cat was on the tree and I said, "Come down, cat!", and the cat said:))* "I'm coming down." Und dann hat sie runtergekommen. *(And then she came down.)*

This tacit assumption that animals could understand only English persisted unless the children were confronted with an experience which suggested that the assumption needed to be revised as far as a particular animal was concerned. (This was practically the same procedure as adopted when meeting people for the first time.) An amusing example of this occurred when Thomas (5;6,20) and Frank (3;7,28), on a walk with me, passed a house with a white cockatoo in a cage on the verandah, and attempted to coax it to talk to them. When their efforts (in English) met with no success, I jokingly suggested that the cockatoo might respond in German. Much to the children's surprise (not to mention my own!) there was an almost immediate response from the cockatoo:

Thomas: Hullo, how're you?

Frank: Good day, cocky. Hullo, cocky. (To me): Er kann nicht sprechen. *(He can't talk.)*

Father: Vielleicht versteht er kein Englisch. Versuch's mal auf deutsch. *(He might not understand English. Have a go in German.)*

Frank (visibly amused by this suggestion, but doing it anyway): He, Kakadu! Guten Tag! Sag etwas! *(Hey, cockatoo! Good day! Say something!)*

Cockatoo: Hallo, hallo.

Thomas (amazed): Du hattest recht, Bert! Er versteht Deutsch. *(You were right, Dad! He understands German.)*

Frank (also astonished and delighted): Er hat "Hallo!" gesagt. *(He said "Hullo!")*

From that time on, this particular cockatoo was, to my amusement, identified as understanding German and was addressed accordingly. I did not have the heart to spoil their obvious delight and excitement at discovering a German-speaking cockatoo by pointing out that its responding to their overtures in German was purely coincidental.

The assumption that animals were addressed in English even carried over into games where I assumed the role of an animal. The fact that I was assuming a role (see section entitled "Role play" in chapter 4) meant that I had temporarily changed identity and was to be addressed according to this new identity. However, since I persistently insisted on being able to understand nothing but German in any animal role the children persuaded me to adopt, they quickly learned that they needed to use German to achieve the results they wanted, e.g.:

Thomas (4;9,0) : Du bist mein Pferd, Bert. Ein sehr schnelles Pferd. *(You're my horse, Dad. A very fast horse.)* (Climbs on my back) Giddy up! Giddy up! (The "horse" does not budge.) Ah, ah, hüh, hüh! *(Ah, ah, giddy up, giddy up!)* (The "horse" neighs and sets off at a reckless gallop, Thomas clinging on for dear life.) Whoa! Whoa! Ah! Stop! Ich meine Brrr! Brrr! *(I mean Whoa! Whoa!)* (The "horse" obeys, to Thomas's amusement — and relief.)

Before their 1984 stay in Germany a few animals well-known to the children seemed to be classified by them as belonging to the same category as themselves, that is, able to understand both German and English but spoken to in German by me and in English by most other people. One such animal, their paternal grandparents' dog, Jock, had, for instance, usually been addressed in German by me in their presence, although they themselves addressed him in English. When, on one occasion, I spoke English to the dog, Thomas (5;1,17) was clearly puzzled, indicating by his reaction and comments that he thought that Jock, like himself, should be spoken to in German by me.

In Germany in 1984 the children quickly realized that practically all animals there were addressed in German, and they accepted this as logical and normal in a German-speaking environment. And in Wales, also in 1984, they met a family who spoke to their cat in Welsh. Questioned in 1986 on which language was to be used to animals, Katrina (5;10,10), for instance, replied that animals understood and therefore should be addressed in the language which their owners spoke to them; thus, in general, animals in Germany were to be addressed in German and animals in Australia in English. She thought that only a few animals were bilingual and they were animals which for some reason or other were in contact with more than one language, e.g. the dog, Jock, mentioned above.

Communication with toys

Toys such as dolls, teddy bears, etc. are also normally considered by the children to speak the same language as their owners. Their own toys have thus usually been seen as being, like themselves, bilingual in German and English. For instance, when Thomas was very young, he frequently played with a green cloth doll who was, appropriately, called Greenie in English and Grüni in German. She was clearly bilingual, as can be seen in the following examples:

Mother: Did Greenie like her biscuit?
Thomas (3;10,13): Yes. Her said, "A nice biscuit".
Thomas (3;10,16) (arriving at beach): Wir sind jetzt hier, Grüni. *(We're here now, Greenie.)* We're here now, Mum.

Interestingly, Greenie had special status in that she could be addressed in either German or English by Thomas (at that time, and still today, the children normally address German-English bilinguals in only one of the two languages). In fact, he also used phrases to her which he knew from other languages.

The choice of language used by the children to their toys and which they make the toys produce seems to depend very much on the situation created for a particular game and the toys' role in that game, and also on what other persons are present. My direct participation in a game can cause a switch to German as the language used to and "by" the toys, unless it is important for the purpose of the game that the toys be identified as English speakers.

4 Departures from normal language choice in the family

Introduction

As in communication with each other (see chapter 3), and in contrast to communication with monolingual English-speakers, the children have always been inclined to employ a number of German words (i.e. lexical transfers) in their English when addressing their mother. The frequency with which this occurs and the apparent motives for it have varied both with the individual child and with time.

Until he was aged about 3;8, Thomas had a small number of German words which he consistently used when speaking English to his mother, words such as *Ersatzrad* (= spare wheel), *Müllwagen* (= garbage truck), *Maschendraht* (= wire netting) and *Krankenwagen* (= ambulance). Wendy not only accepted the use of these words but at times employed them herself when speaking to him. Despite this, he still obviously considered English to be the appropriate language for her to speak to him, as can be seen in the following example, where, prompted by Thomas's use of German *wo* instead of English *where*, she attempts to address him in German, and he steadfastly sticks to English:

Thomas (3;8,18): *Wo*'s the cows?
Mother: Was? *(What?)*
Thomas: Where's the cows?
Mother: Was? *(What?)*
Thomas: Where's the cows? Where's the cows?

His tone of voice indicated that he was not simply repeating his question but also making a very conscious choice of language.

In communication with English-speaking monolinguals Thomas did not always remember to use English equivalents for the German words he normally used to his mother. It was apparent that he was beginning to regard them as belonging to both languages. As a result, Wendy began pointing out that these words were in fact German and that most people outside the family could not understand

75

them. He quickly and quite consciously modified his English speech, reducing significantly the number of German lexical transfers. Within a month he was criticizing Wendy if she happened to forget the "new arrangement", e.g.:

Thomas (3;9,22) (looking in boot of car): What's that?
Mother: That's the *Ersatzrad.*
Thomas (very emphatically): No, you say spare wheel, not *Ersatzrad.*

However, Thomas's period of linguistic vigilance lasted only for about a month. He then again began using German words occasionally when speaking to his mother, though rarely to English-speaking monolinguals when he would use the corresponding English terms. It seems that he did this more or less unconsciously, sometimes realizing in mid-sentence what was happening, e.g.:

Thomas (3;11,18): Mum, at the hardware shop you can buy nails, screws, *Maschendraht* (= wire netting), lawnmowers, saws, *Wellblech* (= corrugated iron), *Dachziegel* (= roof tiles) - (pauses momentarily and chuckles) I talkin' a bit of German!

Werner Leopold (1949b:70) reports a similar reaction by Hildegard (4;7,14): "When she says a sentence with too much admixture of English she often comments: That is funny German."

Even so, Thomas's preference that his mother use only English to him continued, e.g.:

(Thomas and his parents are looking at a picture book together.)
Thomas (4;3,17) (to father): Was ist das? *(What's this?)*
Father: Ein Käfer. *(A beetle.)*
Thomas: Ein Käfer.
Mother: A *Marienkäfer,* is it? *Marienkäfer,* literally "Mary beetle", is German for "ladybird".)
Thomas (reproachfully): Ah, ah, ladybird.

This situation has more or less continued through to the present time, with Thomas (13 years old) from time to time deliberately inserting a German word in his English to his mother, as if simply to take advantage of another means of expression which they both have. The lexical transfers from German are generally clearly marked off by a change in tone of voice, which shows that he is aware that he is using them. She may accept them without comment, respond in kind (which surprises and/or amuses him), or ask him if he knows the English equivalent, e.g.:

Thomas (5;11,27) (swinging round and round a tent pole): Mum, when I do this I get *schwindlig.*
Mother (laughing): What's that in English?

Thomas (ponders for a few seconds): I don't know.
Father: *Dizzy* oder *giddy* heißt das auf englisch. *(It's called* dizzy *or* giddy *in English.)*

In the case of Frank, he began, around his third birthday, to object to his mother's occasional use of German lexical transfers, even though he himself was prone to such words, e.g.:

Frank (3;2,0) (to his mother): I want to play with *Spielteig.* (*Spielteig* itself is a word coined by Thomas and used by the family, it being a literal translation of English *playdough,* a home-made substance similar to plasticine.)
Mother: What?
Frank: *Spielteig* — playdough.
Mother: Oh, playdough. You want to play with *Spielteig.*
Frank: You don't say that. You say "playdough".
Mother: Oh. Who says *Spielteig* ?
Frank: Daddy does. He says it in German.

However, this period of vigilance with regard to his mother's speech lasted only a few months; by age 4;0, for example, he was apparently unconcerned if she occasionally used a German word or phrase when speaking to him. Between the ages of 3;6 and 5;2 Frank frequently deliberately inserted German words into his English when talking to his mother, usually as an amusing way of teasing her, e.g.:

Frank (3;11,8) (to mother): This is my bottle of *Milch.* (= milk) (He laughs with obvious amusement. His mother smiles, indicating that she knows that he is using a German word, but makes no comment.) This is my *Milch.*
Mother: Is that an English word?
Frank (grinning): *Deutsch.* (=German.)

After age 5;2, Frank's use of German words when speaking to his mother declined noticeably, most probably due to the influence of the long summer holidays occurring then, during which time he rarely had occasion to speak to his mother without monolingual English-speakers being present, a definite inhibiting factor; and secondly, because of his commencing school at age 5;4, which substantially reduced his contact with his mother.

Katrina has been much less inclined to use any German words when speaking English to her mother than her brothers. Her desire to keep the two languages separate developed earlier than with her brothers. By age 2;0 she was already very aware that she was dealing with two separate languages, one of which she was to use to her father and one to her mother. Accompanying this awareness was a sense of what she considered acceptable linguistic behaviour, so that even at this age she began to reprimand her mother for using the "wrong" language, e.g.:

Father (seeing a dog cock its leg): Was macht dieser Hund?
Katrina (2;0,20): /ə/ Hund pinkelt. *(The dog's doing a pee.)*
Mother: Der Hund pinkelt?
Katrina: No! The dog's doing a pee!

Interestingly, such objections came at a time when Katrina was seemingly unaware that she herself did not always keep the two languages separate, e.g.:

Mother (who is about to go for a run): What's Mummy going to do?
Katrina (2;0,14): Ah, a *Lauf* (= run).
Mother: A *Lauf*?
Katrina: Bert sagt *Lauf*. *(Daddy says* Lauf.*)*
Mother: What does Mummy say?
Katrina: Ah, nun (= run).

In the almost four years which have passed since then, Katrina's attitude to the use of German words in English to her mother and by her mother has relaxed considerably, although such words are now mainly used to create a special, mainly humorous, effect, as in the following example where she is teasing her mother:

Mother: Katrina, come here for a minute.
Katrina (5;6,5) (with a cheeky grin): I'm just *frag*ing Dad something. (Giggles.)
(Katrina is using the German verb *fragen* (= ask) as if it were an English verb.)

The type of deliberate lexical transference described above is not used nearly as often by the children when speaking to their father (the main exception being when they forget or do not know a German word). This is most probably because I have as a rule discouraged this practice, mainly because of the weaker and particular position of German in the children's lives. If I accepted the use of English words in their German, I felt and still feel that, without the counterbalancing effect of any monolingual German speakers who would not understand such words, the children could come to regard them as *German* as well as English. My aim, however, is for the children to acquire and maintain a variety of German which would be easily intelligible to someone who knows only German. Wendy, on the other hand, can afford to be much more tolerant of the children's occasionally using German words to her in their English, and, in fact, as she does, at times to employ certain German words and phrases herself when addressing them. Because of the influence of a predominantly English-speaking environment there is, at least after commencement of schooling, little danger that German words will become fixed as part of their English used with people outside the immediate family. The children are, as a rule, fully aware that they are employing German words and that such a speech style would be inappropriate when addressing a monolingual speaker of

English. As a result, there exists a mutual tolerance of occasional lexical transference from, or even brief switches to, German between the children and their mother.

The consequences of parents using too many words from the majority language when speaking the minority language to their children are demonstrated by Traute Taeschner's (1983:223) experiences with her daughters Giulia and Lisa, with whom she speaks German in Italy. When the girls were 7 and 8 and speaking both German and Italian (their father's and the national language) well and keeping them separate, their mother decided that it was perhaps no longer necessary to be so careful about keeping the two languages completely distinct. So she began using Italian words often in her German. As a result of this, less than a month later all the utterances made by her daughters contained lexical transfers from Italian. The message for the parent in such a situation, where he or she is responsible for providing most of the children's input in the minority language, is therefore quite clear: if you want your children to speak your language without inserting a large number of words from the majority language, remember that *your own speech* serves as their model.

The fact that Wendy has always used an occasional German word or phrase to our children in ordinary conversation, whilst I have endeavoured to speak to them exclusively in German, is reflected to a certain extent in the children's own attitudes. When Thomas was aged 5;4 and 7;7, for instance, Wendy and I, out of interest, occasionally reversed language roles to gauge his reactions. He was apparently unaware of Wendy's switches to German or, if he was aware, completely unconcerned, simply answering her in English, the language he normally used with her. However, he reacted with annoyance whenever I attempted to address him in English, e.g.:

Father: Why is it dangerous to go outside during a thunderstorm?
Thomas (5;4,8): Ah, sag das auf deutsch! *(Ah, say it in German!)*

He had obviously come to consider any use of English with me as taboo (except for quotational switching and role play (both discussed later in this chapter), and for seeking linguistic assistance (see the first part of chapter 6)), and obviously felt uncomfortable or upset if this arrangement was broken. At age 13 his attitude is still basically the same. At that age, for instance, one of his friends and he were overheard discussing how they could persuade me to allow them to go to see a certain film at the cinema together. The friend wanted Thomas to do the negotiating in English so that he could offer supporting arguments. However, Thomas said he just could not do this, it "just wouldn't feel right". (They went to the film!)

An interesting aspect of the type of "experiment" in using the "wrong" language described above was that it had a similar effect on me. So accustomed was I to speaking only German to Thomas, that I felt quite strange when addressing him in English, a definite sense of incongruity being created. Werner Leopold (1949b:143) voices similar sentiments: "I sometimes say something in English to (Hildegard) when other children are present; but I have a feeling of constraint and unnaturalness when I do."

Frank's attitude has been slightly different from that of Thomas. At age 4;0 he also paid no apparent attention to unexpected switches to German by his mother in the course of a conversation, simply replying unconcernedly in English, whilst an unexpected switch to English by me resulted in his looking somewhat ill at ease. At age 4;4,5, when I addressed him in English, Frank was half annoyed, half amused, responding with:

Frank: Du bist nicht Mutti! *(You're not Mummy!)*

At age 5;7–5;8, however, Frank (unlike his brother at the same age) did not object, nor show any surprise or unease, when I addressed him in English, although this was a very unusual experience. Frank simply replied in English. Similarly, when Wendy unexpectedly spoke German to him, he showed no surprise, but just replied in German or English. The explanation for these differences may, at least in part, be due to the children's different experiences in the family due to their position in the family. Being first in the family, Thomas at age 5;4 was relatively unaccustomed to having me address him in English. So when I did so, it came as a shock. However, by the time the experiment was conducted with Frank at age 5;7–5;8, two years had passed, and he was quite used to hearing me help Thomas with homework projects, which were of course in English, as well as with quizzes and the like in English-language magazines. In such cases, the question itself might be discussed in German but since the answer was required in English, it would often be necessary to state the question in its original English form in order to formulate an appropriate answer. Frank was also used to hearing Thomas sometimes ask Wendy, on occasions when I was absent, for assistance with short German writing exercises which I set (for more details on these, see chapter 8), e.g.:

Thomas (7;3,18): Mum, this one's a bit hard: Was ist ein Synonym für *schroff? (What's a synonym for* precipitous?)
Mother: That is hard. I don't think I know that word.
Thomas: It's when a mountain's like that (indicating a perpendicular wall with his hand.)
Mother: Oh, real steep?
Thomas: Yeah.Oh— I could put *steil* (=steep).That's nearly the same:Ein Synonym für *schroff* ist *steil. (A synonym for* precipitous *is* steep.*)*

By Frank's seventh birthday he also, like Thomas, objected to my addressing him in English in normal conversation, and this attitude has continued ever since.

As already mentioned above, Katrina showed at a very early age (about 2;0) a desire to keep her two languages separate. She not only reprimanded her mother but also me for using the wrong language. She even "corrected" me for using in my German words such as *Shorts*, which she identified as English, but which are now also part of the German language, e.g.:

> **Father:** Deine **Shorts** sind schön. *(Your shorts are nice.)*
> **Katrina** (2;7,12): Ich habe keine — ah, ah, nein, du sagst **Hosen.** *(I haven't got — ah, ah, no, you say pants.)*

Although by about age 3;0 Katrina had come to accept that there were certain English loanwords like *Shorts* which were commonly used in German and perfectly acceptable, she nevertheless still objected from that time on to any attempt by me to address her in English in normal conversation. Like her brothers, she has obviously to a large extent adopted the attitudes of her parents: since I have always expected the children to speak only German to me (except when they cannot remember or do not know a particular German word or phrase, and except for the purpose of role play, or in quoting English speakers), they in turn expect the same behaviour from me; they obviously consider this basically to be a set arrangement which should not be broken. However, since Wendy has always been tolerant of the children's insertion of occasional German words or phrases into their English, their stronger language, they accept the same sort of linguistic behaviour from her. Adding to this acceptance of German with their mother is the fact that on certain occasions the children and she do converse *in German.* Once a month, for example, the children attend a playgroup in Sydney for German-speaking families with me. If Wendy comes too, she and the children have agreed that at the playgroup they will speak German to each other, so as not to upset the German-speaking atmosphere of the playgroup; if they used English, other children present could also be tempted to speak English, and that would rather defeat the main purpose of the playgroup.

Role-play

The only circumstances in which the children have been happy to accept my speaking English to them and to address me also in English has been in role-play. If, for the purpose of a particular game, I assume the identity of an English-speaker, I can then speak English to the children without any protests from them and without their feeling ill at ease. However, for such a situation to be accepted by the children, I must usually disguise my voice and my "new" identity must be established before the game proceeds, i.e. the illusion has to be created that it is not really their father who is speaking English to them. This type of role-play began shortly after Thomas's fifth birthday and has occurred with him and the other children up until the present time, although only infrequently. Between the ages of 3;2 and 4;2 Frank found it difficult in such games to divorce role-play from reality and replied to my English only in German. After age 4;2, however, he addressed me in English if I was playing the part of an English-speaker. At age 5;10 Katrina developed a variation of this sort of role-play which to the outsider would sound not like role-play, but as if she were actually being herself and speaking to her father in English. In the company of her English-speaking cousins of similar age, she occasionally addressed me in English, just as her cousins did. It seems, however, that she was here in fact playing a type of role, being as it were a niece rather than a daughter. She addressed me as "George" just as her cousins did and spoke with a slightly different tone of voice from usual, indicating that her identity was now slightly different. Significantly, Katrina made no attempt to continuing addressing me in English once her cousins were no longer directly involved in the conversation, but immediately reverted to being my daughter and switched to German.

Despite the children's acceptance of me as an English-speaking interlocutor for the purpose of role-play, it is apparent that there is still some sense of strangeness about it, for none of them is keen for such a game to persist for very long.

The mother's knowledge of German

We have seen how the children and their mother sometimes use German words when conversing with one another. Despite this, in the years before they began school, the children occasionally seemed to forget that she knew German, perhaps because in their minds she was so closely associated with English, e.g.:

Mother: Good night! Schlaf gut! *(Sleep well!)*
Frank: (4;4,20) (surprised): How can you speak that?
Mother: Speak what?
Frank: Speak that? Speak Deutsch *(German)*?
Mother: What did I say?
Frank: You said, ah, "Gute Nacht". *(Good night)*
Mother: I learned it from you and Daddy. Did it sound good?
Frank: It sounded funny.
Mother: Why did it sound funny?
Frank: Mummies don't speak Deutsch. *(German)*
Mother: What do they speak?
Frank: English.

This type of generalization recalls that made by Werner Leopold's (1949b:58) daughter at almost the same age:

Hildegard: (4;9,30): Mother, do all fathers speak German?

Otherwise, as can be seen in other sections of this study, the children are obviously aware that their mother has a good knowledge of German. At times, for instance, they ask her for assistance in remembering an English equivalent of a German word or phrase (or vice versa), e.g.:

Frank: (9;0,30): Mum, I like, um, — what would you call *Basteln* ?
Mother: Um, building things out of paper and —
Frank: (continuing with his original sentence): I like building things
Mother: (suggesting another translation): Craft —
Frank: Yeah, craft, but it's a bit different to craft...

If I happen to be absent when they are doing short German writing exercises I have prepared for them and they encounter difficulties, the children have no qualms about seeking their mother's assistance. This was also the case when the children attended school for five months in Hamburg in 1984 (see chapter 10) and they occasionally called on their mother for help with their homework. However, they do not always accept her advice on German usage uncritically; they recognize that she, like them, does at times have difficulties with certain aspects of German grammar and vocabulary. This probably came about originally when the children were quite young, because they sometimes heard Wendy asking me about points of German usage. By the time we spent the six months in Germany the boys at least were old enough (8 and 10) to realize that they had much in common with their mother - in some respects their German was better than hers and she sometimes sought their help (e.g. with children's colloquial expressions), while in other respects they could see that she had more linguistic knowledge and could assist them (e.g. with spelling, with the meanings of "adult" technical words). Mother and children also offered each other assistance with German when they could see that the other was in some sort of linguistic difficulty.

The children usually accept unquestioningly my advice on German usage, as indeed they do both parents' advice on English usage. However, the children are aware, from their experiences with their parents, that no-one is linguistically infallible and that sometimes the answers to questions of language usage may have to be sought in books or in discussions with other speakers of the language.

Privacy

Sometimes a language can be used advantageously for reasons of privacy. In Australia Wendy does at times use German for this purpose in somewhat delicate situations, e.g. to remind them of their manners, without turning her comments into a public announcement, as would virtually be the effect if she said these things in English, and thus saving the children from unnecessary embarrassment. In Australia she also uses German in notes which she leaves for them and which she does not wish other people to be able to understand. For example, the following note was once left on the back door for Thomas (12;9,12):

> Dear Thomas
> Der Schlüssel ist unter der Apfelsinenkiste. Wir sind im Supermarkt.
> Love
> Mum
> *(German section: The key is under the oranges box. We're at the supermarket.)*

Fortunately, German-speaking burglars are not common in the neighbourhood where the family lives!

While in Germany, Thomas once used English to me, a very unusual occurrence, in order to keep a remark private which could have offended if heard and understood:

> **Thomas** (10;9,6) (seeing a woman load about twenty packets of cigarettes into her supermarket trolley): Kuck mal, Bert! *(Look at that, Dad!)* She's got heaps of cigarettes. Siehst du? *(See?)*

Edith Harding & Philip Riley (1986:59) also mention similar examples of language switches by children to avoid embarrassment to themselves and/or others, e.g. Emily (17;5), a trilingual who lives in France and speaks English with her father and Swedish with her mother, switches briefly to Swedish during a conversation at dinner, which because of the presence of a friend is being held in French, to let her mother know that she doesn't think the friend really likes the dish her mother is offering her more of.

Storytelling by the parents

At bed-time on most days the children are read a short story or a chapter of a book by each of their parents (see chapter 8). As a general rule, this means that I read to them in German and Wendy in English. Exceptions to this are infrequent, but do occur nonetheless.

I have rarely read to them in English. Before they could read themselves and they asked me to read them something printed in English, I almost always translated it into German, something which the children not only accepted but came to expect. This applied, and still does apply, to magazines, books, etc. present in the household in other languages such as French, Dutch, Afrikaans — they expect a German rendition. Although at times it would have been easier for me to read particularly more technical types of literature to the children in the original English, I have been reluctant to do so, mainly because this would take away precious contact time with German.

However, under certain circumstances, I may read to the children in English, but practically only on infrequent occasions when Wendy is prevented by illness etc. from reading their story to them. The children accept this as a special occasion brought about by the particular circumstances. Whilst I read the story in English, aspects of the story are discussed in German and explanations of vocabulary etc. are given in German, e.g.:

> **Father** (reading from *The Bobbsey Twins at Snow Lodge* by Laura Lee Hope): "I do hope Papa will be home for Christmas," sighed Nan, for Mr Bobbsey's business trip, in relation to lumber matters had kept him away —"
> **Frank** (5;3,5): Was ist "lumber"? *(What's lumber?)*
> **Father:** Bauholz. Das ist amerikanisches Englisch. In Australien sagt man meistens "timber". *(Timber. That's American English. In Australia we usually say "timber".*

When the children began to read material by themselves, they would, regardless of the language involved, ask whichever parent was available for help with words they could not decode. Such assistance could be given in both languages. For example, I could help them with reading difficult English words and then perhaps give a translation of them in German, following this up if necessary with an explanation, also in German:

> **Katrina** (5;10,8) (reading an English comic): Bert, was ist dieses Wort? *(Dad, what's this word?)*
> **Father:** *Conceited* — eingebildet *(conceited).*
> **Katrina:** Was bedeutet das? *(What does that mean?)*
> **Father:** Das bedeutet, daß man glaubt, daß man besser ist als andere Leute — *(That means that you think you're better than other people —)*
> **Katrina:** O ja, ich weiß — wie *vain. (Oh yes, I know — like "vain".)*
> **Father:** Ja, sehr ähnlich. *(Yes, very similar.)*

Code switching and triggering

In this study, most switches which are made from one language to the other are (as seen in the section entitled "The children's communication strategies" in chapter 3) attributable to the fairly clear-cut patterns of communication which have developed within the family. That is, they are predominantly dependent on who the person being addressed is and which language has been established as being appropriate to speak to that person in. Some exceptions to the normal pattern have been discussed in the sections on child–child communication and on parents and children in chapter 3, and the particular use made of switching from one language to the other for the purpose of directly quoting utterances in the original language is to be described in the next section.

Other reasons for switching from one language to the other in discourse may be linguistic ones. In an analysis of language switching in Martin Luther's *Tischreden* (Table Talks), Birgit Stolt (1964) identified certain "linguistically neutral" words, that is, words which could belong to either language, which caused the speaker to lose his "linguistic orientation" and to continue his discourse in a different language from that in which he started. Michael Clyne (1967) gave the name *trigger word* to this kind of word since it triggers a switch from one language to the other, a switch which the speakers themselves often, initially at least, are unaware of. Clyne (1972:24; 1975:29) lists five types of words which may act as trigger words: *lexical transfers* (i.e. words from one language used in the other but which are not normally considered part of the other, e.g. Frank's (5;5) continued use of *Panzerwagen* (= armoured car) in his English), *proper nouns* (e.g. Sydney, Adidas), *homophonous diamorphs* (i.e. words having the same meaning and sounding the same or similar in both languages, e.g. German *Glas* and English *glass),* *loanwords* (i.e. words originally belonging to only one of the languages but now also considered part of the other, e.g. *kindergarten*), and *compromise forms* between the two languages (i.e. forms which may arise in a bilingual's speech which strictly speaking belong to neither language but are close to the equivalent word in both, e.g. [ɪs] for German *ist* [ɪst] and English *is* [ɪz]. Clyne found that trigger words caused about 30% of his German-Australian informants to switch from one language to the other when they were being interviewed.

To this list of trigger words we can add a quoted word (or phrase) from the other language which triggers a language switch either in the speaker or in a listener, e.g.:

> **Frank** (5;6,26) (showing his mother some German writing he has just done for his father): Look what I wrote, Mum.
> **Mother**: Gee. Can you write *Hund*? (= dog)
> **Frank**: Ja. *(Yes.)*

Here the quoting of the German *Hund* causes Frank to reply in German, rather than, as usual to his mother, in English.

Examples of switching languages due to triggering are quite rare in the speech of Katrina, Frank and Thomas. One possible reason is that their phonological systems are, unlike those of many of the bilinguals studied by Clyne, quite distinct for English and German. This decreases the number of potential trigger words, since in their speech most loanwords, proper nouns and homophonous diamorphs are, as far as pronunciation is concerned, clearly assigned to one language or the other, e.g. their pronunciation of *Poster* (now also a common German word) is quite distinct for German and English; they are felt to be different words. Another reduction on the number of potential trigger words is caused by the relatively low number of lexical transfers in the children's speech, in turn a result of my encouraging them to avoid them unless absolutely necessary.

Michael Clyne (1967:84ff.) isolates four types of triggering: *consequential triggering* (i.e. following a trigger word), *anticipational triggering* (i.e. in anticipation of, before a trigger word), *sandwich words* (i.e. words "sandwiched" between two potential trigger words), and *contextual triggering* (i.e. triggering not because of a trigger word but because of the context of the situation). The trigger word setting off a language switch need not occur in the speaker's own speech but may be used by somebody else who is present (including voices on radio and television). A closer look will now be taken at these types of triggering, using examples from the children's speech.

(a) Consequential triggering

The speaker reaches a trigger word and then, becoming momentarily disoriented and forgetting which language s/he is speaking, continues in the other language. It is almost a reflex reaction, which in the case of Katrina, Frank and Thomas is usually detected by them immediately and laughingly corrected, but which in the speech of some bilinguals can go unnoticed and result in a switch to quite lengthy stretches in the other language. In the following example, the German word *Mami* , which means the same as and is also pronounced practically the same as the Australian English *mummy*, acts as a trigger, causing Thomas to be momentarily confused about which language he is speaking. However, as is often the case, he realizes his mistake and quickly re-orients himself to German:

Thomas (4;3,17) (praising his mother's home-made bread, to his father): Der Ladenbrot ist nicht so gut wie Mamis *bread*, ah, Brot. *(The shop bread isn't as good as Mummy's bread, ah, bread.)*

(b) Anticipational triggering

This type of triggering takes place when a speaker is thinking ahead to what he or she is about to say and, anticipating the imminent occurrence of a trigger word, switches from one language to the other just before reaching the word in question, e.g.:

Frank (3;6,7) (talking to his father about a gift he has received from a family friend): Das war nett *of* Jim. *(That was nice ...)*

Here, the name Jim, belonging as it does to both English and German, functions as a trigger and induces Frank to switch to English just before it.

Sometimes a trigger word can be anticipated prior to commencing a whole sentence or clause, causing this to be uttered entirely in the other language. For example, on one occasion Thomas (7;6,2) had searched high and low for one of his German books, which he eventually located. Just as he found it, his mother walked in, and he excitedly showed it to her:

Thomas (to mother): Kuck mal! Ich habe das Buch gefunden — "Onkel Pauls Laster." *(Look! I've found the book — "Uncle Paul's Truck.")*

Here, the German title of the book seems to have triggered off a switch into German for the whole utterance directed at his mother whom he would normally address in English.

(c) Sandwich words

This type of triggering is in effect a combination of consequential and anticipational triggering. When a word or phrase is sandwiched in between two potential trigger words, particularly if they are loanwords, proper nouns or a short quotation, this word or phrase may be said in the language with which the trigger words are identified by the speaker at that moment rather than in the language s/he began in and/or continues in. In the following example Thomas (7;6,23) is telling me about two television programs he will watch that evening:

Thomas: Ich werde mir "Grange Hill" *and* "The Changes" ankucken. *(I'll watch "Grange Hill" and "The Changes".)*

The word "and" is said in English because of the powerful effect of the two trigger words surrounding it, namely the titles of two English film series. Thomas is, to use Michael Clyne's (1967:87) words, "unable to switch in and out of German quickly enough to avoid adapting the sandwich word to the two trigger words."

However, generally Katrina, Frank and Thomas do manage to cope with keeping such sandwich words in the appropriate language, albeit often with some noticeable effort, indicated, for example, by hesitation in the flow of speech.

As already mentioned, triggering occurs only rarely in the children's speech, and is not regarded as a problem when it does, but rather as a source of amusement. In their speech to monolingual English speakers triggering is practically non-existent, since in such communication there are many fewer potential trigger words than in communication within the family; lexical transfers scarcely occur and proper nouns and loanwords are usually distinctly anglicized, thus reducing the chance that they could be associated with German and trigger a switch to that language.

(d) Contextual triggering

This type of triggering is not brought about by a particular word or expression as shown in the first three types, but rather by the context of the situation. A certain activity or situation is closely associated with a particular language and this may trigger a switch to that language, a switch which appears to be more or less unconscious, although sometimes detected and corrected by the speaker, e.g.:

Frank: (4;4,5): Mum, can you speak lots of German?
Mother: A fair bit. I speak a lot to Ilda's mother.
Frank: Why a lot?
Mother: She doesn't understand English. You've heard me speaking German to Ilda's mother, haven't you?
Frank: Hm. And we play with Ilda.
Mother: Hm. Do I speak good German then?
Frank: Ja. *(Yes.)*

The context of the German language together with the frequent mention of the word German triggers a switch from English to German.

(e) Blocked switching

The same kind of words which can trigger a switch from one language to another can at times also cause a speaker to bypass a normally expected language switch. This mostly occurs in conversations with fellow bilinguals. Even so, the children quickly become aware of what is happening and then make the appropriate switch. Blocked switching virtually never occurs in communication outside the immediate family, and when it does, it is nipped so quickly in the bud that the person being spoken to remains unaware of it, e.g.:

Frank: (5;2,26) (to father): Hat Graeme Fische gefangen? *(Did Graeme catch any fish?)*
Father: Ich glaube ja. Frag ihn. *(I think so. Ask him.)*
Frank (to his uncle): *Ha—,* did you catch any fish, Graeme?

Here, there is a slight carry-over effect from the German remarks immediately preceding the question to the uncle which temporarily checks the switch to

English. *Ha*— is the first syllable of the same question in German: *Ha*st du Fische gefangen?

The reason the children detect so quickly such failures to switch when talking to monolinguals seems to be that they are very much aware that these people cannot understand German. Inside the family it is not so crucial if this happens, as everyone will still understand.

(f) Triggered switches in style in the one language

Triggering is not confined to switching between languages but may also occur between varieties of the one language. The trigger involved may be the use of a certain lexical item (e.g. "Bloody oath!" used as an affirmative answer to a question such as "Do you like it?" rather than "I certainly do" or the like), a certain pronunciation (e.g. *'ouse* instead of *house*), a grammatical construction (e.g. "That *ain't* fair" instead of "That *isn't* fair"), or the context of the situation and the person being spoken to. The following is a typical example of such style switching. Thomas (6;9,25) is talking to a great-uncle, a former tin miner and skilled raconteur, who embellishes his anecdotes with many colourful expressions and expletives, particularly the so-called Great Australian Adjective *bloody*, and to whom Thomas listens with obvious pleasure. Normally Thomas uses *bloody* sparingly in his speech, probably because it meets with disapproval at school. However, as can be seen in the conversation, his great-uncle's use of *bloody* quickly triggers off a switch by Thomas to this style of speech. But it is not only the word acting as a trigger but the whole situation. Just as it appears appropriate to switch to German to address his father so it also seems appropriate when addressing his great-uncle to switch to the style of speech he associates with him. In the last line of the excerpt it can be seen that Thomas corrects his speech, changing Standard English *those* (which he normally says) to *them*, the form appropriate to this variety of English, a switch set off no doubt by a similar use of *them* by his great-uncle a few seconds before:

> **Thomas** (seeing his great-uncle for the first time for several months): Good day, Georgie!
> **Great-uncle:** Good day. How are you, mate?
> **Thomas** Good.
> **Great-uncle:** By bloody oath you're growin'!
> **Thomas** (smiling, excited): Georgie, in Sydney we went to this beach and saw these hang-gliders fly off these bloody cliffs.
> **Great-uncle:** Yeah?
> **Thomas** Yeah. Remember you said we could go up to Scamander and practise flying on the sandhills? (A standing joke between the two is that

the great-uncle can fly, a joke supported by a trick photo showing him doing exactly that.)
Great-uncle: On them beaches, yeah, when we get up on them sandhills.
Thomas: Yeah, those beaches.
Great-uncle: We'll have bloody fun then.
Thomas (chuckling): Yeah. It's bloody good at those beaches — them beaches.

Quotational switching

When monolingual speakers wish to quote directly what someone has said, they may reproduce the person's tone of voice, accent, dialect, choice of vocabulary and the like. Something of the original is injected into the quotation, and it is thus made to sound more credible. If this is not done, at least partially, then the quotation can sound out of place or even unauthentic, as, for example, if the Queen of England were quoted verbatim in a broad Australian accent.

In communication between *bilinguals*, the decision as to how to quote someone is a little more complex, since often a choice has to be made between translating an utterance for the purpose of quotation or leaving it in its original language. According to Haugen (1953:65), reporting on Norwegian-English bilinguals in the USA, Timm (1975:475), writing about American Spanish-English bilinguals, and Kouzmin (1976:108), discussing Russian-English bilingualism in Australia, the desire of bilingual speakers to quote in the original language is perhaps the main factor promoting language switching. Fantini (1978a:297) also reports that his children, when speaking Spanish to him and his wife, switch to English to quote English speakers.

In this study, all three children, when quoting a person or a section of a story, etc., *verbatim*, usually do so in the language in which the original was made when speaking to each other, to their parents, or to other English-German bilinguals, e.g.:

> **Frank** (8;11,7) (telling his mother about what his Hamburg friend Hendric's dog once did): And Schieta — once he took one of Hendric's Smurfs and he bit his nose off. And Hendric said,"Das war mein ganz neuer Schlumpf!" *(That was my brand-new Smurf!)*

However, when the children report in *direct* speech what somebody has said (e.g. She said *that* ...), the language used is the one normally used to the particular parent, e.g.:

> **Frank** (8;11,7) (telling his mother about a conversation with his monolingual German friend): And Hendric told me that once this robber wanted to break in their house and Kanto (a watchdog) sprang on him and nearly ripped his arm out.

The children's wanting to quote someone in the original language seems to be motivated by one of three factors (or, in certain cases, by a combination of these factors):

- A feeling of incongruity at quoting someone in a language he or she does not speak.
- A desire to capture the flavour of the original utterance(s).
- To extricate oneself from a vocabulary difficulty.

The most important motivating factor is that the children have a definite feeling that it is incongruous to quote someone in a language they know he or she cannot speak; it would be inappropriate to portray the person as being a speaker of that language. The sense of incongruity seems to be especially strong if the person is quoted in the first person. It is as if the children then temporarily assume the role of that person, a role for which only one language is seen as appropriate.

When quoting what they themselves have said in a particular situation, there is nowhere near as much reluctance to present the quotation in a translated form and not in its original form. Since they speak *both* languages, there is not the same feeling of strangeness and incongruity about doing this; they are not depicting themselves as being capable of something which they are not, even though it does not give a true picture of a conversation.

If the children do present a quotation in translated form, the feeling of incongruity is difficult to escape, and this often leads to their making an explanatory remark indicating that the actual words used in the original were in the other language, e.g.:

> **Thomas** (6;0,13) (talking to me about Helen, his best friend at school at this stage): Bert, weißt du, Helene wird sehr streng, wenn Leute ihre Dinge kaputt machen. *(Dad, you know, Helen gets very stern if people break her things.)*
> **Father:** Kein Wunder. Was sagt sie? *(No wonder. What does she say?)*
> **Thomas:** Sie sagt: "Du mußt das flicken!" **Aber auf englisch.** Sie sagt das sehr laut. *(She says, "You'll have to fix that!" But in English. She says that really loudly.)*

This strategy of switching languages to quote people in the original was not something the children acquired from their parents, since at least until both the boys had started school both Wendy and I nearly always translated quotations into the language we speak to them. At times, particularly before the children started school, this seemed to puzzle them and they would ask questions such as "Hat sie Deutsch gesprochen?" *(Did she speak German?)* or even indicate that they found this inappropriate. Gradually, Wendy and I have come more and more to use the same strategy as the children, i.e. giving direct quotations in the original language. However, I do try to avoid quoting too much of English conversations directly in English, simply so that the children can hear as much German as possible from me.

Besides the desire to avoid a feeling of incongruity, another reason for the children's wanting to quote in the original language is the wish to capture accurately the flavour of the original utterance which they feel may be lost in translation.For example, at age 4;10,15, Thomas was speaking to me about the American children's television program *Sesame Street* and wished to quote one of the characters, Cookie Monster. In order to capture the effect of this character's deviant English phonology and syntax, he switched to English:

> **Thomas:** Und dann hat Krümel gesagt: Ich — ah, auf englisch hat er gesagt: *(And then Cookie said, I — ah, in English he said:)* Ah, me not real understan. (Uttered in a gruff voice.)

As in the above example, the quotation is sometimes preceded by a switching marker in the form of an expression such as "Ich sage es auf englisch." *(I'll say it in English.)*, which warns the listener that the other language is going to be used briefly and that the speaker is not really violating the usual language arrangement. Nils Hasselmo (1970:198), in a study of the speech of Swedish-English bilinguals in the USA, identifies a similar desire on the part of his informants to explain a language switch. One informant, in a stretch of discourse in Swedish, switches to English to quote an English-speaker, explaining in Swedish: "För hann talte ängelska, vet du." *(For he spoke English, you know.)*

The flavour of the original which the children wish to preserve when quoting does not necessarily consist of deviant pronunciation or sentence structure as in the last example. The speaker may have used a particular accent or particular words, the exact effect of which could be lost in an attempt at translation, e.g.:

> **Frank** (8;11,7) (telling his mother about problems with a boy at school in Hamburg): He says, "Du blöder Arsch." *("You stupid bastard.")* and that Mum, but I just thump him ...

Here the insult is given in its original form probably both to preserve its precise nuance and to avoid the problem of trying to find an English equivalent with the same connotations.

This brings us to the third reason for the children's quoting someone in the original language: to extricate themselves from a vocabulary difficulty. That is, they are uncertain about how the original utterance should be rendered in the other language. Einar Haugen (1953:53) mentions a similar strategy by second generation Norwegian-English bilinguals in the USA who did not hesitate to switch to English when their Norwegian vocabulary was inadequate. In the following example, Frank (4;0,9) is called upon to relay two messages from his mother to his father. With the first, telling his father what time it is, he encounters difficulties because the task is beyond his conceptual development at this stage, being more than a matter of simple translation; he cannot tell the time in either language. To circumvent this problem, he therefore quotes this message in the actual words of the original. The second message is much more straightforward and is easily and confidently reproduced in translation:

> **Father** (to Frank): Frag mal Mutti, wieviel Uhr es ist. *(Ask Mum what the time is.)*
> **Frank** (runs to his mother): What's the time, Mum?
> **Mother:** A quarter to three.
> **Frank** (returning to his father): Mutti hat, "It's a quarter to three." gesagt. *(Mum said...)*
> **Father:** Oh gut, danke. *(Oh good, thanks.)*
> **Frank** (going back to his mother): Does Daddy have to get Thomas?
> **Mother:** Yes. Tell him it's just about time for him to get him.
> **Frank** (again to father): Mutti hat gesagt, du mußt Thomas jetzt abholen. Ich komme mit. *(Mum said you have to get Thomas now. I'm coming with you.)*

Normally Wendy and I give assistance when we foresee any linguistic difficulties in relaying a message (see chapter 6), but in this case Wendy was not aware that the time information was to be passed on to me. Walburga von Raffler-Engel (1970) also observed that a satisfactory translation depends on whether a child has a clear conceptualization of the message. Jules Ronjat (1913:94) similarly reports that his son Louis (aged about 4;0) could normally translate messages very well, but: "It can be seen that his skill as a translator sometimes fails in the face of an expression which is a little abstract." (Translated from the French.) Sometimes the children themselves will foresee such a difficulty and, rather than having to quote in the other language, seek assistance before conveying a message, e.g.:

> **Mother** (camping, seeing ominous black clouds approaching): Frank, go and ask Daddy if he's put the flaps down on the tents.
> **Frank** (5;3,17) (starts to leave, then pauses, obviously a little puzzled): How do you say "flap" in German?
> **Mother:** Oh, I don't know either, Frank. I know — go out and say to him: **"Mutti hat gesagt: Sind die Zelte in Ordnung?** *(Mummy said, "Are the tents all right?")*
> (Frank runs off happily to deliver this message.)

Another means of extricating oneself from a vocabulary predicament in one language is to quote what someone else (or even oneself) says (or would say) if speaking the other language, e.g.:

Thomas (5;10,0) (telling me about a boy at school): Und, Bert, er will alles zuerst machen. Er is, ah, ah — auf englisch würde ich sagen *(And, Dad, he wants to do everything first. He's, ah, ah — in English I'd say): "He's a real greedy-guts."*

The problem encountered here is that Thomas cannot think of an adequate way of expressing the colloquial term *greedy-guts* in German.

A rare method of circumventing a problem with vocabulary which is related to the above type of quotational switching is to actually request to be permitted to say something in the other language, that is, to quote what one would ask or tell the other parent if he or she were present. At times this is absolutely necessary, for example in the case of untranslatable jokes, puns, and the like:

Thomas (9;5,26) (to father): Ich will dir ein' Witz auf englisch erzählen. *(I want to tell you a joke in English.)*
Father: Auf englisch? *(In English?)*
Thomas: Ich muß das auf englisch sagen, das wirkt nicht auf deutsch. *(I have to say it in English, it doesn't work in German.)*
Father: Okay. *(All right.)*
Thomas: Where did Napolean keep his armies?
Father: Ooh — ich weiß nicht. *(Ooh — I don't know.)*
Thomas: In his sleevies.

Einar Haugen (1953:63) observed similarly that many of his Norwegian-English bilingual informants switched to Norwegian in anecdotes they had begun in English to give what he calls the "untranslatable and inimitable punch line". Nils Hasselmo 1970:204) found much the same in the speech of Swedish-English bilinguals in America.

When the children switch from one language to the other for the purpose of quotation, the original utterance is sometimes not given in its entirety, only significant elements of the original version being cited (something also observed by Clyne, 1972:139). There does not always appear to be a special effect which has to be recreated nor a phrase which is difficult to translate which could explain retention of part of the original utterance. It seems rather that, in recalling the original utterance, part of it, usually that containing the main idea or piece of information, is still strongly felt and persists in the language of the original:

Frank (4;10,15) (to his mother): Daddy said he made the bath **sehr tief.** *(very deep)*

Another aspect of quotational switching occasionally observed in the speech of the children is that a section of discourse which is not part of the quotation unit itself may also occur in the language of the quotation, a phenomenon which Nils

Hasselmo (1970:201) refers to as "morphological raggedness". The quotation unit itself has a triggering effect (cf. Clyne, 1972:140), i.e. it triggers off a language switch either before the quotation unit (called by Clyne (1967) "anticipational triggering"), or after the quotation unit (Clyne's "consequential triggering"); the following example, with two quotations, could fit either category — the words sandwiched between the two quotations should really be in German, but are in English:

> **Frank** (10;8,14) (telling me about the Australian film *Crocodile Dundee*): Und im Wald hat er eine Eidechse für sie geholt, und sie hat gesagt *(And in the bush he got a lizard for her and she said):* "Do you expect me to eat this?" **And he says:** "Yeah, you can live off it, but it tastes like shit," Bert. Und ... *(... Dad. And ...)*

An amusing kind of quotational switching, which is really a double switch, occurred on occasions when the children were under six years of age; the utterance quoted is not the actual original utterance but a translated version of it which has been heard from one of the parents. In the following example, Thomas (3;8,17) quotes a monolingual English-speaking cousin to his mother, but quotes not his original English utterance but a German rendition of it which he has heard from his father:

> **Mother**: What are you laughing at?
> **Thomas:** What Mikie said.
> **Mother:** What did he say?
> **Thomas** (laughing): Mikie said, "Kommt nicht ins Haus, ihr doofe Hühner!" *(Don't come into the house, you silly chooks!)*`

The cousin's actual words had been: Don't come inside, you bloody chooks!" (*Chooks* is the Australian English equivalent of British English *hens* or US English *chickens.*) Normally, in an English conversation, the children would quote an English speaker in English. Here Thomas seems to be recalling not the original amusing incident but a later gleeful discussion of it with me.

Quotational switching in storytelling

The three children have had somewhat different attitudes with regard to quoting sections of stories (including films) to their parents or other bilinguals in the original language, showing again that even when growing up in the same family under basically the same conditions, children do not necessarily acquire bilingualism in exactly the same way.

Thomas has always been quite prepared to retell in one of his languages a story he has heard only in the other, although doing so perhaps with a slower and less fluent delivery than would be the case in the original language, indicating that a definite, conscious effort may be required to divorce a story from its familiar form in one particular language and reproduce it in another. If, while doing so, he does switch languages, it is usually only for some direct quotations of characters' utterances. It seems that he attempts to tell the whole story in one language but, particularly when reporting characters' utterances, the pull of the actual wording and language of the original at times proves too strong. The following excerpt from his telling in German at age 5;7,1 of *Jack and the Beanstalk,* a story until then known to him only in English, illustrates this struggle against the force of the original language of characters' utterances:

Thomas: ... Und dann hat der Koch gesagt: *(And then the cook said:)* "Ah, ah, **will you — do you want some cook—**, ah, willst du Kekse?" *(Do you want some cookies?)* Und Johann hat gesagt: "Ja." Und er hat ihm Kekse gegeben ... *(And Jack said, "Yes." And he gave him some cookies.)*

Nowadays, the situation with Frank (age 11) is virtually the same as that just described for Thomas — he has no qualms about retelling an English story in German or vice versa. However, it has not always been like that. Until about age 7, Frank was very reluctant to retell a story, in part or in whole, in anything but the original language. That is, he associated a story he had usually or only heard in a particular language closely with that language. It is not that he memorized the actual wording of a story and was simply reproducing it, since each story was recounted using his own particular style of expression. Nevertheless, he obviously did have a strong feeling that a particular story was a German story or an English one. Stories were for Frank similar to what Nils Hasselmo (1970:201) calls a "preformulated sequence", in which a speaker finds it very difficult to depart from the language in which the particular sequence was formulated (Saunders, 1982c:108). One of Hasselmo's informants, even when asked in English to retell a certain story, switches to Swedish to do so, although an aside to the interviewer during the narration is in English.

Just how strong the influence of the language associated with a particular story can be, became evident when Frank was asked at age 5;5,14 to retell several of his favourite stories in English and German. He found no difficulty in doing this if he was familiar with the story in both languages, e.g. *The Three Pigs*, even though his two versions still reflected the slight differences between the English and German versions he had heard. However, faced with the task of retelling a popular story about an Eskimo boy heard only in German, *Ootahs Glückstag* (= Ootah's Lucky Day), Frank was very insistent that German was the only language in which it should be told:

Frank (rather pathetically): Ich will das in Deutsch ... Ich kann das nicht in Englisch. *(I want to do it in German ... I can't do it in in English.)*

He reacted in the same way when asked to retell in German a story he had heard only in English. This meant that Frank at that age usually refused to tell a German story to someone he knew understood only English. However, he was prepared to make comments *about* the story, which could, in fact, amount to a summary of the story. It was only when he felt he was *retelling* the story that he could not depart from the language of the original.

Similar findings are reported by Nils Hasselmo (1970:204). He shows what happens when a speaker is forced to render a Swedish preformulated sequence in English:

> Very strong prompting of English, viz., a direct request that English be used, was required in order to get the informant to retell the story in English. The poor performance, as far as story telling is concerned, is in flagrant contrast to the informant's normal performance. ... (He) ... is involved in something that is quite difficult, viz., breaking the rules of his private speech economy by rendering in English a sequence which is preformulated in Swedish only, and that is ... a reason for the poor performance.

When Katrina was aged 2–3 she willingly produced for me German versions of stories which she had heard in English only, and for her mother English versions of stories she had heard in German. But since then she has become less willing to retell English stories in German, and now, at age 5;10, does so rather reluctantly and hesistantly. There is no such reluctance to retell German stories in English, which she does easily and fluently. The reason for her reluctance in German does not, however, seem to be any desire on her part not to depart from the wording of the original English text, but rather due to the fact that at this stage her oral English, which is excellent compared with that of monolingual children of the same age, is substantially superior to her oral German. The task of telling a story in German, especially if it has been heard or read only in English, simply requires much more effort from her, as her active vocabulary is not at the same level in German as it is in English.

5 Influences from outside the immediate family

Attitudes of monolingual English speakers

Unfortunately, bilingual children in probably any bilingual situation may be exposed at times to hostility from people who (usually monolingual themselves) are so intolerant that they cannot bear a language other than the majority language being spoken in their presence, even if the people speaking the other language are engaged in a completely private conversation. This antipathy is typified in a letter by a Mrs R. C. Miller to the editor of the *Sydney Morning Herald* (13.2.1981):

> Nothing annoys me more than two or more 'ethnics' jabbering away in their native language in the company of English speaking people, particularly in a work environment. Is it really too much to ask them to observe simple politeness by refraining from resorting to their native language in the company of English speaking persons.

Accompanying this view is undoubtedly a fear that things are perhaps being said about one in a language one cannot understand. People who hold this view fail to realize that even in a completely monolingual environment we do not expect to hear and understand everything said by people who are not speaking specifically to us. Nor do we in such circumstances by any means always speak loudly and distinctly so that all present will understand us. Why should the use of a foreign language be any different? It is surely only impolite if a person is linguistically excluded from a conversation in which he or she is a definite participant. However, there seems little justification in objecting to people who share a common language using that language for their private communication simply because it is not understood by other people who are within earshot.

Silke Hesse (1980:55), in an article reflecting on her own experiences as a German-English bilingual in Australia, makes a pertinent observation on this aspect of bilingualism:

Socially I found that it was not always rude to use a foreign language in the presence of monolinguals; it could be courteous to mark out areas of privacy and turn a private conversation into a mere background noise. Most people are grateful if they cannot understand what does not concern them.

Thomas, Frank and Katrina have usually seemed quite at ease speaking German to me in the presence of monolingual English-speakers. However, they have been fortunate in that they have never actually encountered any overt antagonism towards their speaking of German from anyone present while they are using the language; such antagonism could obviously adversely affect children's willingness to use their home language outside the immediate family circle.

There is also a covert type of antagonism that can be encountered: although certain persons do not object directly, one clearly gets the impression that they have a negative attitude towards, or are uncomfortable or embarrassed about another language being used in their presence. Thomas is the only one of the three children to have been affected by this. His awareness that someone was not favourably disposed towards the use of German appeared at about age 4;3. His reaction was to avoid speaking German as much as possible while such people were within earshot. By age 6;6, whilst he may still have sensed such antagonism, he seemed to have ceased to be intimidated by it, perhaps influenced by his younger brother Frank's complete lack of concern. Frank has always remained blissfully ignorant of any disapproval of his use of German and has happily spoken German to me wherever we may be or whoever may be present. In this respect Katrina has followed closely in Frank's footsteps.

Often the attitudes of people in positions of comparative prestige and authority, such as teaching and medical personnel, can have a decisive influence on how children and also their parents view their bilingualism. A negative attitude can obviously have an adverse effect on a family's resolve to raise its children bilingually, particularly if this attitude is expressed in the guise of helpful advice with the children's welfare in mind. Parents, who naturally wish to do the best for their children, may be inclined to accept such advice from people they regard as experts. Unfortunately, such adverse opinions may be based on personal conjectures or prejudices rather than on any objective evidence.

In my own family's case, we were warned by a child health doctor just after Thomas's third birthday that speaking two languages was too great a burden on him and was impairing his acquisition of English, and it would be in his best interests for him to be addressed in English only. This pronouncement was made after a fifteen minute examination. Thomas's failure to perform adequately on several verbal tests, due in part to his being shy of performing in front of a stranger, was attributed immediately to his being bilingual. The unfortunate part about this particular case was that the doctor in question worked in a clinic which was located in an area where a considerable proportion of the population which she would be required to advise came from non-English speaking countries. One wonders whether this sort of advice was also given to such families in which the parents' ability in English would usually be far less than in their mother tongue. Abandoning the mother tongue, particularly for another in which the parents lack proficiency, could have far-reaching consequences for parent-child communication and rapport.

In her book *The Sun is Feminine*, Traute Taeschner (1983:22) relates an incident in which a pediatrician advised the German-speaking mother in a bilingual German-Italian marriage in Italy to give up speaking to her daughter in German because the child had not begun to speak by the age of 18 months and the use of two languages was obviously the cause of this delayed linguistic development. The mother followed the advice and "two months after the 'treatment' had begun, the 'miracle' occurred, and the child began to speak." Traute Taeschner then makes the caustic, but so true, remark:

> Many monolingual parents whose children have not begun speaking until shortly before their second birthday have also been perplexed, worried, and somewhat disappointed. But they were luckier, because no pediatrician told them to keep quiet in order to resolve the problem.

Medical personnel may also attribute other problems which children can have with speech development, such as unclear speech or stuttering, to their bilingualism, and advise the parents to expose their children to only one language, or at least to delay the exposure to two languages (such advice being mentioned, for example, in articles by Métraux (1964:650) and by Berthoz-Prouz (1976:121)). There is, however, no evidence that bilingualism *per se* causes stuttering. According to Edith Harding and Philip Riley (1986:139), countries with a high proportion of bilinguals do not have significantly higher statistics on stutterers than monolingual countries. Wendell Johnson (1967), Professor of Speech Pathology and Psychology at the University of Iowa, for example, in a 100-page discussion of research into stuttering and its causes, does not even mention bilingualism. What does become clear, however, from his work on disfluency in speech, is that *all* children speak disfluently to some degree, but it usually only becomes a problem for the child when it is seen as such by adults. Johnson writes that "...in case after case, stuttering as a serious problem developed after it had been diagnosed. The diagnosis of stuttering — that is, the decision made by someone that a child is beginning to stutter — is one of the causes of the stuttering problem, and apparently one of its most potent causes."

Johnson stresses the importance of the attitude of parents and others towards children whose speech is not always fluent. To label them "stutterers" will only aggravate the problem, whereas to accept them as "normal" or "good" or "acceptable" speakers will most likely lead to quite a different kind of behaviour.

When bilingual children have difficulty in expressing themselves in one of their languages and have to grope for words or struggle with various grammatical constructions, resulting in a certain amount of repetition and hesitation, it is quite possible that this will attract the attention or even arouse the impatience of listeners and perhaps be considered stuttering. The children's self-consciousness and anxiety about their speech, or more exactly, about listeners' possible negative reactions to it, are the most likely causes of such disfluency, or at least the causes of its becoming a problem. Indeed, the disfluency may be conspicuous in only one of a child's languages, in the one which has to be used in circumstances causing uneasiness.

Attributing the problem to children's bilingualism and trying to solve it by removing one of the languages would seem to be not at all satisfactory. In fact, such an action could have the opposite effect, merely increasing children's anxiety, especially since, in most cases, it would be the language of the home which would be the one to go. If children are suddenly told that they cannot use the familiar home language, the language associated with the warmth and security of the family, perhaps even the language in which they feel most confident and at ease, they cannot fail to become aware that people consider that they have a speech problem, undoubtedly a serious one at that for such drastic action to be taken. It is very doubtful that such an experience and realization would lead to improvement in fluency in the language remaining.

The solution lies rather in the attitude of the listener, and much of the advice given by Johnson (1960:299,543ff) to parents, teachers, etc., who have contact with children with disfluent speech applies equally well to people coming into contact with bilingual children:

(i) Make talking enjoyable. See to it that the children have as much a feeling of success as possible in speaking. (One) should do all (one) can to make the children's speaking enjoyable and rewarding. Certainly (one should) not make a point of criticizing them for mistakes in grammar and pronunciation ... or for other things about their speech that are not important in relation to the fun and satisfaction they get from speaking as well as they can.

(ii) Try to be the kind of listener (the) children like to talk to ... when they are "talking over their heads" be patient, and now and then supply them with a new word which they have not yet learned but which they need at the moment. To a reasonable extent and in meaningful ways help them to add to their vocabulary — preferably at those times when they need words they haven't learned in order to tell you things they have never tried to say before.

(iii) Read to (the children) whenever you can. In reading or speaking to them, enunciate clearly, be interested in what you are reading and avoid a tense, impatient, or loud voice. Enjoy this reading and make it fun and companionable. Do some of it every day, (if a parent) preferably just before bedtime, if possible.

As can be seen, this advice, if followed, reduces children's anxiety about speaking and makes it an enjoyable experience for them. Whilst Johnston mentions these steps specifically as effective means of building confidence in the disfluent speaker, they would seem to be a sound procedure for assisting also bilingual children who are having difficulty in expressing themselves.

During bilingual children's education they and their parents may have the misfortune to encounter members of the teaching profession who are intolerant of bilingualism. Most of this intolerance is, fortunately, not as vehement as an example mentioned by Eve Isaacs (1977:90) in her book *Greek Children in Sydney*: "I heard one teacher advise a soap-and-water mouth rinse for those using other languages (i.e. not English) within the school grounds." Nor is the intolerance usually rigidly institutionalized as set out in the rules of a French high school in Truchtersheim in East Lorraine, a school attended by many pupils whose home language is German (and mentioned in Hoffmeister's (1977:34) report on the language situation in that region):

Article 5 — General Discipline
French must be the usual language of all pupils, in their games and their conversations, in the playground and in the buildings, as well as on the school buses.
(Translated from the French)

Generally, this sort of antagonism seems to be based on the mistaken belief that the children's acquisition of, and competence in the majority language, and hence their overall level of participation in school affairs will be improved by outlawing the language of the home. Besides not being supported by research evidence, this view again entirely ignores the harmonious functioning of the family unit. In such cases, firm action should be taken by parents to protect the interests of their children. Even antagonistic teachers will usually tone down their views in the face of strong protests from determined parents.

Even if teachers are not directly antagonistic towards the children themselves they may still be quick to blame any school problems on children's bilingualism and advise as a remedy that parents cease speaking to their children in their own language, again in the unfounded belief that this will be to the children's benefit. In such cases, more assertive parents may wish to inform the teacher of the overwhelming evidence against this point of view, others may prefer, initially at least, to avoid direct confrontation and simply ignore the teachers' advice. In Eveline de Jong's (1986:90) book, *The Bilingual Experience*, one mother describes how this problem was dealt with in her family:

> Maxime appeared to have problems with reading at school and just before the Christmas holidays the teacher told us to stop speaking French to him at home. Of course, we didn't, but we did sit down with him to read in English. When he went back after the holidays, it soon became clear that he had caught up with the rest of the class. The teacher triumphantly told us that apparently her remedy had worked.

From all this it would appear to be *essential* that health workers and teachers who have to deal with children from bilingual homes should have basic, factual information about bilingualism incorporated into their training programmes. Unfortunately, this is not often the case. In most countries, for example, most doctors, nurses, health visitors, social workers, speech therapists, etc., receive little, *if any*, training in dealing with bilingualism (Saunders,1986b:5). Edith Harding and Philip Riley (1986:123) are very blunt — and to the point — when they write in their book *The Bilingual Family*: "It makes as much sense to ask your doctor for advice about bilingualism as it would to ask him about your car."

There are, of course, doctors, nurses, etc., who do have the necessary knowledge and experience working with bilingual families, or perhaps who come from a bilingual family themselves, to be able to offer sensible advice. The difficulty is knowing where to find them. Parents of bilingual children should therefore be wary of advice they receive from medical workers, etc., concerning their children's bilingualism, particularly if that advice is to drop one of the languages. They should ask about the reasoning behind the advice and, if sceptical, seek other opinions (preferably from other *bilinguals* who themselves have *bilingual* children).

Unfortunately, misleading advice on bilingualism is also sometimes issued by government departments. In 1986, for example, the *Jugendamt* (= Youth Welfare Department) of the city of Cologne in the Federal Republic of Germany *issued Elternbrief 18,* a pamphlet of advice for parents of two-year-old children. One section deals with the language situation in families with a German and a non-German parent. Parents are told that:

> The advantage of growing up bilingually is often bought at the cost of insecurity in both languages, and this development should be avoided if at all possible. ... Often a foreign father will wish his child to speak

his, the father's, language, even when he has left his homeland for ever. In such a case the father should try to put aside his understandable feelings in favour of his child's interests. (Translated from the German)

This is very dubious advice indeed. How can a parent know for sure that he (or *she* — presumably foreign women also marry German men) will remain in Germany for ever? Even if this is the case, the parent may not feel comfortable using German to his/her children, the family may visit the homeland during holidays, people from the homeland may visit them in Germany, etc., etc. It is most regrettable that such advice should be given an official stamp of approval by appearing in a government publication. On this subject, Edith Harding & Philip Riley (1986:145) make the following valid point:

... talking to children in a language in which you are not fully competent may not be the favour you think it is. ... it is rather sad and illogical to see a parent ... having problems communicating with his/her child in order to avoid the 'dangers' of bilingualism.

In his study of his own bilingualism, Theodor Elwert (1959:293) also mentions another factor worth considering with regard to the use of a minority language in the home: although his mother spoke German fluently, she did so with not quite accurate grammar and with a distinct English accent, and the children did not like to hear her talking German because "it was positively embarrassing for us to hear her speaking 'incorrectly', to see her in a position of inferiority" (translated from the German). Thus, for Elwert the use of English with his mother in Germany put her on a superior or equal footing with her children. This is a sentiment I have also heard voiced by the children of immigrants in Australia: communicating with their parents in their own language allows them to see their parents as people who, in that language, are as linguistically competent as members of the dominant English-speaking community.

In this study, Thomas, Frank and Katrina have so far had the good fortune to encounter in Australia only teachers who have simply accepted, usually even without comment, the fact that they also speak German. (Katrina was especially fortunate in that her first teacher, whom she liked very much, was also bilingual, having grown up in Australia speaking Estonian to her parents; she was very much in favour of bilingualism and wished eventually to have bilingual children herself.) Perhaps the attitude of the teachers may have been different had the children not been able to function linguistically as well as their monolingual English-speaking classmates. (Further details of the children's schooling in both Australia and Germany are given in the last few pages of this chapter and in chapter 10.)

Relatives and friends

There have been very few problems with monolingual English-speaking relatives and friends accepting the children's bilingualism, perhaps for the simple reason that the children are able to function linguistically in a way which is practically indistinguishable from that of their monolingual Australian-English-speaking peers. These relatives and friends accept good-naturedly the children's use of German to me in their presence, and occasionally ask, often teasingly, for an English translation, which is usually given readily and with good humour, e.g.:

> (I am giving Thomas (5;6,10) a long explanation on how to carve wood safely with a sharp pocket-knife. My mother is sitting nearby, reading.)
> **Grandmother** (teasingly): Whatever's your dad saying to you, Thomas?
> **Thomas** (smiling): Just how to carve.

Sometimes a translation is forthcoming unsolicited when the children re-member that someone present will not have understood something in German and it is wished to include him or her in the conversation, e.g.:

> (Frank (3;7,22) informs me of the fate of a biscuit he had just dropped and then repeats his statement in English for the benefit of a great-aunt.)
> **Frank** (to me): Das hat kaputtgegehen. (*That breaked.*) (Then immediately to his great-aunt): Dot, that did broke to pieces.

Usually Wendy and I make an effort to prevent a monolingual speaker of English, who is participating in a conversation with the family, from being excluded from those sections of the conversation conducted in German. Being used to the linguistic situation in their own family, the children may forget that the German segments of their conversation are not intelligible to others present. If this happens, either parent may briefly inform the English-speaker about what has been said, e.g.:

> (Thomas (6;1,20) is watching an aunt breastfeeding her baby daughter.)
> **Aunt** : Madeline's having her tea.
> **Thomas**: Oh. (Looks on with interest, then turns to me): Ich will etwas zu trinken, Bert. (*I want something to drink, Dad.*)
> **Father:** (amused, to aunt): He wants something to drink, too, Maree.
> **Aunt:** (laughing): Does he?
> **Thomas:** (to me): Ich will schwarzen Johannisbeersaft. *(I want blackcurrant juice.)*
> **Father**: Okay. *(All right.)* (To aunt): He doesn't want milk, though, he wants blackcurrant juice.

Or the children may be reminded by a parent that someone present cannot understand German and be asked to repeat or explain something in English, e.g.:

(Thomas (5;1,12) is questioning me about a childhood incident involving a tiger snake. Two relatives with no knowledge of German are present):
Father: ... und ich bin durch die Brombeeren gegangen, und plötzlich habe ich etwas gehört. Ich habe mich umgekuckt, und da war eine große Tigerschlange ... *(... and I was walking through the blackberries and suddenly I heard something. I looked around and there was a big tiger snake ...)*
Thomas: Bist du sehr gesaust? *(Did you really zoom along?)*
Father: Ja, und ob! Erzähl jetzt mal Maree und Graeme, was passiert ist. Sie können nichts verstehen. *(Yes, I'll say! Now tell Maree and Graeme what happened. They can't understand anything.)*
Thomas: (to relatives): Ah, ah, do you know, when Daddy was a little boy, he was going in the blackberries, when he heared something and he looked around and there was a big snake ...

The various procedures just described appear to be an effective way of keeping monolingual listeners informed and preventing possible disharmony in such interactions. The only other solution would be for the children and I to speak English to each other on such occasions, as Leopold (1949b:58) did with his daughter Hildegard when monolingual visitors were present. However this would mean a fairly drastic reduction in the children's contact with German, especially during school holidays and as the children acquire playmates who visit regularly. It could also perhaps have the unfortunate effect of giving the children the impression that the speaking of German was something to be ashamed of or concealed. Sometimes a compromise between these two possibilities is made. When I am addressing the children as part of a group, I sometimes do use English, or a bilingual version, e.g.: "Who'd like to go to the beach?", with or without the addition of the German equivalent "Wer möchte an den Strand gehen?" An interesting development from doing this bilingually is that some of the children's young cousins (aged 4–7 in 1986) actually asked that the German version be said first, preferably with a pause before the English version, so that they could first have a chance to try to work out what had been said; over an extended period of contact (e.g. the summer holidays) they become quite proficient at decoding common German expressions and even begin to sprinkle their English with German words and phrases, excellently pronounced, not only when speaking to their uncle (me), or Thomas, Frank or Katrina, but also to each other. This obviously gives these young cousins a lot of pleasure, and their very positive attitude towards German is clearly appreciated by Katrina, Frank and Thomas.

Of course, the children have been fortunate in that practically all relatives and friends, most of whom are monolingual English-speakers, have been sympathetic to their acquisition and use of German. Such favourable, or at least non-antagonistic, attitudes certainly make it easier for both parents and children to establish and maintain a minority language in the immediate family. Opposition and negative reactions from relatives and friends with whom a family has regular contact could have a very damaging effect on the parents' resolve to continue raising their children bilingually and also, of course, on the children's confidence and desire to use the minority language.

A rather sad example of this is given in an article by Bent Søndergaard (1981). A native speaker of Danish, he and his wife, whose native language is Finnish, failed in their attempt to raise their son bilingually in Denmark. There are several reasons why this attempt failed, with Søndergaard himself considering relatives' negative attitude one of the most decisive:

> ...during the whole experiment the parents were under severe pressure from (monolingual Danish) members of the family who maintained that the boy would suffer, perhaps permanently, from this double acquisition of language.

Unfortunately, Søndergaard did not feel confident about countering this opposition:

> It was difficult to resist this (pressure), because we could not consult any expert on bilingualism, and because at that time we did not know any families where bilingual children were being brought up.

In this regard, I heartily endorse one of the 'golden rules' put forward by Edith Harding & Philip Riley (1986:79) for parents bringing up their children bilingually:

> When all is said and done, the decision is yours. Or at least it should be; don't let outsiders, whether family or 'authorities', push you around. Remember, you know best. Remember, too, that there is no evidence that bilingualism does any intellectual harm (if anything, the reverse is true) and that bilingualism can be of great social benefit.

I have found in the few cases where relatives and friends have expressed doubts about the advisability of the children's bilingualism, that a discussion of what is involved, including some reference to the research evidence on infant bilingualism, allays most of the doubts. Their doubts are really a fear of the unknown, but once they receive some sort of comprehensible explanation, much of the mystery, and consequently also the concern, disappears.

Playmates

By about age 2;0 the children were aware that few people of their acquaintance could understand or speak German. Even at that young age they obviously classified German as a language to be spoken only to me, except in exceptional circumstances. In Thomas's case, however, this assessment was temporarily upset when he was aged 3;8. At that time we enrolled him in a German kindergarten in Melbourne which ran for two and a half hours on Saturday mornings. He was surprised to find that there were other children who, unlike the few playmates he already had, could understand German. But now he seemingly began to equate children he did not know with his new acquaintances at the German kindergarten, that is, children capable of understanding German. Thus, when an acquaintance of his mother's visited with her two monolingual English-speaking children, Thomas immediately began talking to them in German, much to their bewilderment. Wendy had to explain to him that the children could not understand German. From then on he distinguished carefully between children at the German kindergarten and other children.

Of course, the presence of children's monolingual playmates may call for certain modifications to be made to a family's normal way of communicating with each other. Although bilingual children, as mentioned above, realize very early who can and cannot be *addressed* in their home language, it will usually take them longer to realize, and then always to remember that their monolingual friends do not understand interactions in that language between themselves and a parent. This is particularly so in the case of longtime friends who visit the home regularly, e.g.:

> **Father:** Hast du meine Schlüssel gesehen, Frankie? *(Have you seen my keys, Frankie?)*
> **Frank** (5;5,7): Nein. *(No.)* (To friend): Did you, Shane?
> **Shane:** No.
> (Both children return to their game. It is very doubtful that Shane understood my question to Frank in this case.)

Normally, in such a case I would, if the playmate looked puzzled or bewildered, either remind the child that the friend could not understand German or would myself repeat the question in English for the friend's benefit.

Some people see the presence of children's friends as an almost insurmountable obstacle to the use of the home language, e.g. an anonymous contributor to the *Journal of Multilingual and Multicultural Development* (1981, 2(1):83) commenting on earlier reports on family bilingualism, particularly one by me (Saunders: 1980a), writes:

These other fathers appear to have contact with their children; but not with their children's friends. It is impossible to insist on speaking the 'foreign' language when that excludes other people and everyone *knows* that the language of the environment is available.

He is supported by Mike Byram (1981:213):

> I have every sympathy with the reader who points to the importance of the influence of children's friends.

However, the situation is not as difficult as suggested. Parents *can* have contact with their children's friends without on those occasions refraining from using the language they normally use with their own children. The important thing is not to allow the use of the other language to *exclude* the monolingual friends, since this, understandably, could well cause embarrassment or even resentment. In my family this is done in a number of ways. Thomas, Frank and Katrina may independently explain to their friends in English what has been said between them and me, or when they forget (through absentmindedness, excitement, etc.), they may be prompted to do so by me or Wendy, or one of us may explain; if none of these happen, the friends themselves may ask for an explanation. It has been found that once the friends know that they will be kept informed of what transpires in German, they readily accept the situation, even listening with interest to the German and trying to deduce the gist of what is being said before being told. A few examples can best illustrate how German continues to be used in our family in the presence of the children's monolingual playmates:

> (I see Thomas (6;11) and Frank (5;0) with a friend looking at the web of a dangerous redback spider.)
> **Father** (to Thomas and Frank): Faßt die Spinne doch nicht an! *(Don't touch the spider, will you?)* (To friend): Don't touch the spider, will you, Shane?

If I do not do this and the children consider that something I say is also relevant in some way to monolingual playmates, they will supply them with an explanation in English. For example, I catch sight of Thomas (7;0,1), Frank and a friend Shane, playing on the roadway in front of our house:

> **Father**: Das ist zu gefährlich. Spielt doch hier auf dem Rasen, sonst müßt ihr reinkommen. *(That's too dangerous. Play here on the lawn or else you'll have to come inside.)*
> **Thomas** (to Shane): If we go on the road again we have to go in.

Admittedly, to outsiders the above procedures may seem rather tedious or artificial when the children and I *could* speak English to each other in such situations. However, this would mean breaking a firmly established communication routine between father and children in which German is used exclusively. It would also mean a drastic reduction in the amount of German the children would hear and speak and perhaps jeopardize the language's viability in the family.

Werner Leopold (1949b:143,149) adopted a different solution to the problem of how to communicate with his daughter in the presence of her friends. He then addressed her in English, "being conscious of the group which is to participate in my communication". He reports that at ages 6;7,11 and 7;1,21 and also still at age 11;0,16, Hildegard would usually answer him in *German,* "disregarding the fact that the other children are thereby excluded from the conversation". Significantly, this was not regarded unfavourably by her monolingual friends:

> Her playmates always admire her for her knowledge of German. That helps much. During her (eleventh) birthday party, after the obligatory singing of 'Happy birthday to you', the twenty sprightly eleven-year-old girls demanded a 'speech' of her, and they wanted it in German.

Clearly, the use of the majority language of the community between parents and children in the presence of monolingual friends is one solution to the problem for those who feel ill at ease with the approach which incorporates the use of the minority language plus translation/explanation. In some families such a system is established early, with a particular language being used only if all present can understand it. Harrison & Piette (1980:220), for instance, tell of a Welsh-English bilingual boy, Eiran, who by the age of four had adopted the same strategy as his elder brother and mother, namely using Welsh in the family except when the monolingual father was present, in which case they all spoke only English.

I have only once used English with one of the children (i.e. when not teasing or assuming an English-speaking role in a game, as mentioned elsewhere). This occurred when Thomas was aged 12;5, not in the presence of a friend, but during discussions with one of Thomas's teachers about a difficult matter. The teacher was not aware that either Thomas or I spoke German, and we both instinctively felt that the matter would be more quickly resolved if the teacher were not distracted or annoyed by the use of German. Afterwards, Thomas and I discussed the matter and agreed that this might be the best solution in such official encounters in the future.

The reactions of children's friends when confronted with their using another language are obviously important. When new friends of Thomas, Frank and Katrina first encounter them speaking to or being spoken to by me in German, their initial reaction is usually one of surprise and/or puzzlement, e.g.:

> **Thomas** (8;1,25)(To friend): I'll ask my dad. (Turning to me): **Bert, kann man diese Garnelen essen?** *(Dad, can you eat these shrimps?)*
> **Father:** Ich glaube ja. *(I think so.)*

Thomas (to the friend who is looking a bit bewildered): He thinks you can. I asked him in German because he talks German to me and Frank, and we talk it to him.
Friend: Oh yeah.

Some children accept such an explanation and the situation without much comment. Others become very curious and show considerable interest, wanting to learn German words and phrases. This pleases Katrina, Frank and Thomas, as well as the other children when they are able to say a few things in German.

Occasionally the children have been observed teasing monolingual playmates by exploiting their non-knowledge of German, but such instances are rare and fortunately are quite without malice, e.g.:

> (Thomas (7;3,13) is listening to a German story, *Ali Baba und die vierzig Räuber* (Ali Baba and the Forty Thieves) when his friend Shane arrives.)
> **Thomas:** Hi! My dad and me are listening to a story on cassette. Do you want to hear it, too?
> **Shane:** Yeah.
> **Thomas:** Bert, Shane will die Geschichte auch hören. *(Dad, Shane wants to hear the story, too.)*
> **Father:** Aber sie ist auf deutsch. *(But it's in German.)*
> **Thomas** (a little sheepishly): Ich wollte ihn nur ein bißchen necken, Bert. *(I just wanted to tease him a bit, Dad.)*

This type of teasing is carried out only with some close friends or relatives, in other words only with people the children know intimately and who they know can take and appreciate a joke. Alvino Fantini (1978a:290) mentions that his children, Mario and Carla, also amused themselves in a similar way: "To tease their grandparents, they rattled off words in Spanish."

Mike Byram (1981) considers that the influence of children's friends becomes stronger as they grow older and says that most studies do not "document the 'loss' of a language as children become older, say from age nine or thereabouts". This "loss" does occur in come cases, but it is by no means inevitable. There are many documented cases of children who have friends in the majority language group but who continue to speak a minority language within the family until adulthood and beyond (e.g. Elwert, 1959; Haugen, 1972; Lowie, 1945; Schmidt-Mackey, 1977).

We ourselves have been warned by various bilingual people, whose own children are monolingual, that their children would stop speaking German at various stages in their development: firstly when they started kindergarten, then when they begin primary school, then when they went to high school. So far this has not eventuated, and it is doubtful if it ever will, since the speaking of German is so firmly entrenched and does not interfere with the children's functioning perfectly adequately in a predominantly English-speaking environment. Einar Haugen's (1972:11) comments are very relevant here. Recalling his own childhood experiences as a Norwegian-English bilingual in the USA, where he spoke Norwegian with his parents and their friends and English with his playmates and teachers, he writes:

> In each of these contexts I found satisfaction in playing a role which gave me acceptance and praise. This seems to me to be the answer to the worries many people have about making their children bilingual. If the contexts are satisfying and the problems of integration not too overwhelming for the child, no harm can result.

Peer group pressure

In certain situations it does sometimes happen that bilingual children come in for teasing or aggression from monolingual children because they speak another language with their mother and/or father. This could cause sensitive children some anguish or even make them resentful of their home language. Mike and Marjukka Grover (1982), the parents of two Finnish-English bilingual children living in England, make the following valid points on this subject:

> All children will be teased by their peers and especially when they stand out from the group — 'four-eyes', 'carrot top', or after an accident, 'smelly pants' are all common. But if in the case of bilingualism children can be brought to understand that they have something that other children do not and that teasing is very often the manifestation of jealousy, then that is a large step in the right direction.

The realization that being bilingual *is* something special and an achievement to be proud of is a significant weapon against any antagonism from peers. If necessary, suggestions could also be given to the children of more practical ways to counter such teasing: a comment such as "Can you only speak *one* language?!", uttered in a suitable tone of disbelief, is usually quite an effective counter attack.

In a discussion of outside influences on the maintenance of bilingualism it is important for parents not to underestimate the counter-influence of the family itself. Whilst it is difficult for parents to intervene directly against children's friends or acquaintances who may react negatively to bilingualism, their attitudes and prejudices can be discussed and countered in the home. Elwert (1959:293) and his sister always spoke only English to their English-born mother, first as young children in Italy and then as teenagers and adults in Germany, including in not altogether favourable times for the use of English in Germany, namely during two world wars. Elwert says that the family did not allow outside events to interfere with their family language.

Thomas's, Frank's and Katrina's experiences would suggest that most monolingual English-speaking children are not hostile to their knowing and using another language, but simply very curious because it is something outside their immediate experience. If parents, and particularly teachers, took time to satisfy this curiosity by giving even a brief, simple explanation, this would help monolingual children to realize that speaking more than one language is nothing unnatural and nothing to be ridiculed.

Use of the "wrong" language

It is very rare that the children have addressed monolingual speakers in the wrong language, except occasionally for the purpose of teasing as mentioned above. Most other examples occurred before the children were five years old and the person they were addressing was not visible, did not respond, and I was present, e.g. when I got the children to speak on tape to relatives. In such circumstances I often had to remind them that they should use English, e.g.:

> **Father:** Komm mal her, Tom. Wir machen eine Kassette für Oma. *(Come here, Tom. We'll make a cassette for Grandma.)*
> **Thomas** (4;4,3) (holding microphone): Guten Tag. *(Hullo.)*
> **Father:** Ah, ich glaube, es wäre besser, wenn du Englisch sprechen würdest. Okay? *(Ah, I think it would be better if you spoke English. All right?)*
> **Thomas:** Hullo. How're you?
> **Father:** Grüß auch die anderen. *(Say hullo to the others, too.)*
> **Thomas:** Guten Tag, Marie — (2.5 second pause) — hullo, Maree, hullo, Granddad ...

It is the lack of response which seems to be the deciding factor in this type of failure to use the right language. In similar circumstances, but talking instead on the telephone, the children did not depart from the language appropriate to the person they were talking to, even when I was present and suggesting things they could say.

The children and German-English bilinguals

Although the children's contact with native speakers of German in Australia is sporadic, they have never had any difficulty in communicating with them in

German, once they have overcome initial shyness. The nature of the first encounter with a person is crucial as far as determining which language will be used with that person on that first occasion and in the future. The children's initial shyness and reticence, for instance, are usually interpreted by German native speakers as an inability to understand or speak German (despite assurances from us, the parents, to the contrary), and they immediately switch to English. However, once a person speaks to one of the children in English, particularly in an initial encounter, that person is likely to be classified as an English-speaker and, from that moment on, will most probably be addressed in English. This was particularly so until the the the children's first few years of school, although with increasing age they have become more adaptable and not as bound to the language used in an initial meeting with someone. Elwert (1959:291) reports similar experiences. For instance, a German nurse-maid, engaged expressly to impart German to him and his sister in Italy, made the mistake of addressing them first in Italian:

By doing this she was classified by us as one of those persons one spoke Italian to. And, having got used to this, it would have seemed to us unnatural and affected to speak another language with her.
(Translated from the German)

Even as an adult Elwert always preferred to speak to a person in the language in which they had their first conversation.

The language used by interlocutors to Wendy or me in the presence of the children need not be the language used between the interlocutors and the children. For example, even if a person addresses me in English and receives English back, but speaks to the children in German, they seemingly do not regard this as anything out of the ordinary and are quite happy to communicate with that person in German (provided the person does this in a consistent way). Actually, such a situation would, in any case, be little different from that already existing within the family.

Until their six month stay in Hamburg in 1984 (see chapter 10), the children had no contact at all with monolingual speakers of German. All the native speakers of German they met (and still meet) in Australia, have some proficiency in English. Many of these speakers incorporate numerous lexical transfers from English in their German, and/or they make frequent switches from one language to the other, a situation not unusual where there is contact between languages. Michael Clyne (1973:100), for example, found that switching to English in the middle of a stretch of German discourse — and often in mid-sentence — occurred in the speech of 36 out of 50 pre-war immigrants in Australia. Ironically, the children used to classify such speakers as not proper speakers of German and, consequently, English was the language chosen for conversing with them. Alvino Fantini (1978a:288) similarly notes that his bilingual son, Mario, showed intolerance of language mixing by

Mexican-American peers in a Texas kindergarten: because, in his judgement, they did not speak Spanish convincingly, he spoke to them solely in English. (However, in a subsequent article Fantini (1978b:186) reports that by age 7;0 Mario had undergone a change in attitude: "If his interlocutors switched or mixed codes, he did likewise even though he normally maintained a rigid separation of his languages." Thomas, Frank and Katrina still (at ages 13, 11 and 5 respectively) feel somewhat uncomfortable speaking German to such speakers (although they now do so), but later in private often express a strong preference for the two languages to be kept fairly separate.

Interestingly, in both the above cases it was the dominant language of the community which was chosen by the children when they considered a speaker's fluency inadequate. In the present study, this occurred even when an interlocutor's English showed great phonological, lexical and syntactic deviations from the norm. There are several probable reasons for this. Firstly, my German, which until 1984 was virtually their only model for this language, contains practically no lexical transfers from English. Secondly, both children were accustomed to encountering people from a variety of language backgrounds (e.g. in many local shops) whose English deviated often considerably from Australian English. Thirdly, TV pro-grammes, particularly the American series *Sesame Street*, had influenced the children's acceptance of deviant English. Some of the characters in this show, particularly Cookie Monster, speak a type of English which deviates from that of native speakers of (American) English. The result of this continual exposure to deviant varieties of English was that they were tolerated by the children, whereas deviant forms of German were not.

Jules Ronjat's (1913:83–4) son, Louis, showed a more adverse reaction than any of the children already mentioned. He was upset by anyone who addressed him in an imperfect form of either of his languages when he knew that the person spoke the other language. At age 2;3, for instance, Louis showed great distrust of a German visitor who addressed him in heavily accented French and also in German. Almost a whole day of urging was needed before he would talk nicely to the man. If, however, people were reasonably competent in one or both of his languages, he was quite willing to speak it with them. At age 3;7, for example, when addressed alternatively in French and German by a friend of the family, he answered her in the same way without showing any surprise or embarrassment. The crucial difference in this case was that this particular person spoke both languages approximately equally well.

Until my children spent six months in Hamburg in 1984 there was only one exception to their non-acceptance of a deviant form of German, namely when they met Mrs K who spoke German as a second language, fluently but with a distinct accent, and whose English was restricted to only a few words. A native speaker of

Turkish, she worked in Germany for ten years before coming to Australia. Her daughter, Ilda, was in first grade with Thomas at school. Wendy and Mrs K communicated in German, with Wendy occasionally acting as an interpreter for Mrs K in dealings with school personnel. Although the children were somewhat puzzled by Mrs K's German (e.g. Thomas (5;11,11) remarked, "Sie spricht es komisch." (*She speaks it funny.*), they soon realized that English was of no use when addressing her. They both obviously found the situation strange and were shy about speaking German to her although they would eventually do so if urged by their mother. This strangeness was perhaps compounded by the fact that such occasions were the only times when they heard their mother conversing at length in German.

In Hamburg in 1984, the children also encountered other people like Mrs K who spoke German as their second language but knew no English, and they quickly accepted this as a normal state of affairs. They also encountered a few people whose native language was German but who spoke English well and with whom they sometimes spoke German, sometimes English, depending on which language these people wished to speak on a particular occasion; this was a novel situation for them, but one which they accepted. However, they were reluctant to speak much English to Germans whose English they did not consider to be of a high standard.

When an English-speaker who knows some German tries out his or her German on the children, they are amused and pleased. Even a few words are viewed positively. But, unless the person can continue convincingly with the conversation, the children just treat it as a kind of game and fairly quickly revert to English. On such occasions the children tend to slow their rate of German speech and speak very distinctly, e.g.:

> **Grandfather** (coming out of bedroom): Guten Morgen, Tom. (*Good morning, Tom.*)
> **Thomas** (6;2,0) (smiling, always being impressed if his grandfather uses one of about a dozen German phrases he knows, and answering slowly and clearly): Guten Morgen. Es ist schlechtes Wetter heute. (*Good morning. The weather's bad today.*)
> **Grandfather:** I didn't understand that last bit.
> **Thomas:** That means "The weather's bad today."
> **Grandfather:** Yeah, it's not too good, is it?

Leopold (1949b:132) reports on a similar attitude of his daughter Hildegard (5;9,3):

> My brother-in-law George, who knows very little German, insists on saying brief German sentences to her ... She criticizes his defective German but always replies in German, as she does with the few other people who speak to her in German.

Ronjat's (1913:83–4) son, Louis, was obviously distressed when confronted with such a situation. At age 3;4, for example, when a family friend, who had always spoken French to him, started to address him in rather primitive German, he refused to reply and turned his back on her. No amount of scolding by his maid could get him to answer the lady or shake hands with her as he normally would.

Fantini (1978a:288) shows that his son Mario's attitude changed with age:

... between his fourth and fifth years Mario met several individuals who had achieved varying degrees of fluency (in Spanish) through study. Yet because they did not speak Spanish convincingly, Mario went into English, despite their attempts to maintain conversation in Spanish.

But Fantini (1978b and 1985:116) reports that "by 7;0 Mario had learned to accept the attempts of others to speak to him in Spanish even if they lacked sufficient fluency and native pronunciation."

Kindergarten and school

Thomas began kindergarten, in Australia, at age 4;3, Frank at 3;4, both spending two hours three days a week in completely monolingual English-speaking groups. Thomas became somewhat hesitant about speaking to me, i.e. speaking German, in the kindergarten environment, but otherwise his year at kindergarten did not affect his willingness to speak German. Frank readily spoke German to me at all times in the kindergarten. I originally thought (Saunders 1980a:141) that the age difference might explain the difference in the children's attitude towards speaking German at the kindergarten, since by age 4;3 Thomas was already developing an awareness that some people react unfavourably to the use of a language other than English in their presence. However, Frank's attitude has remained unchanged over the years; even at age 11, after six years at school, he is still completely uninhibited about speaking German to me whoever happens to be present. At age 5;2,29 Thomas began primary school in the preparatory class. This had an unexpected favourable effect on his bilingualism, since in his class there were a number of other bilingual children whom he heard speaking to their parents in the schoolyard in Greek, Turkish, Italian and Serbo-Croatian. He showed considerable interest in this and obviously took some pride in the fact that he, too, could speak a language other than English. Wendy and I capitalized on the situation to portray bilingualism as something natural, but special. He showed no inhibitions about speaking German with me in front of his classmates or teachers.

When Thomas was aged 6;5,12 we moved interstate and he was enrolled at a school where he had some difficulty settling in and where he heard no other language but English. The trauma of the move and readjustment did temporarily affect the quality of his German (as discussed halfway through chapter 6), although he still freely spoke German to me in the school precincts.

In some bilingual families, parents and children speak the language of the school when meeting in the school grounds and then switch to the other language once away from the school. This may be done for a variety of reasons, e.g. the school may be seen as a domain in which only the school language is appropriate; the children and/or parents may not wish to appear different from the other children and their parents; they may be apprehensive about the reactions of the other children or parents. The Dutch scholar Meijers (1969), in his book *De taal van het kind* (= The language of the child), reports on a typical such situation involving some of his grandchildren:

> One daughter, married to an Englishman, lives in England. In the home English is always spoken, to and of course also by the two children. The mother attaches importance to the children's also learning Dutch and they speak it pretty well, albeit with an English accent. In the home the children have no objections to Dutch when their mother speaks it to them. But the children have given her the emphatic instruction: 'Don't speak Dutch to us when you come to pick us up from school. The other kids think that's dumb.'
> (Translated from the Dutch)

However, if teachers and other children are tolerant of the use of other languages, it is unlikely that the children will feel uneasy or embarrassed about speaking to their parents in another language within the school precincts. If the parents use the language naturally and confidently in such situations, their children will be given confidence to do likewise. From observation it would seem that the usual initial reaction of most other children and teachers is one of interest and curiosity, which should be interpreted as such, that is, a natural inquisitiveness about something different, rather than a sign of hostility. (See also the section "Peer group pressure" earlier in this chapter for further discussion of this point.)

The fact that I speak only German to them has caused several minor dilemmas for both Thomas and Frank at school. When Thomas was aged 7;9 his teacher issued the class with a stencilled card which on its front cover had the message "Happy Father's Day" and a picture to be coloured in. The children were asked to write appropriate greetings to their fathers on the inside of the card. At first Thomas wanted, and attempted, to leave the card blank so that he could fill it in later at home in German. (He did not think it would be acceptable to write in German in what was part of an English lesson.) But, being embarrassed about having to explain why he was not writing anything, he then wrote in pencil:

To dear Dad
Happy Father's Day
Thomas

However, when he arrived home, and before giving the card to his father, he carefully rubbed out this message and replaced it with the following:

Lieber Bert
Alles Gute zum Vatertag
Ernie XXX
(Dear Bert,
All the best for Father's Day
Ernie XXX)

It is probable that Thomas would still have been faced with a difficulty if he and I spoke English to each other but still had our respective nicknames, Ernie and Bert, since this, too, would clash with the expected "normal" forms of address between a son and his father. As it turned out, Thomas's teacher proved to be very understanding when the incident was mentioned to her, making the comment, "He could have written it in German, it wouldn't have mattered."

Thomas did have some problems in grades 6 and 7 with a very small minority of his fellow pupils because they found out that he spoke German to his father; they ridiculed him for this and even called him a "Nazi". When this first happened in grade 6, Thomas became rather depressed and then reacted quite violently against his tormentors; at this stage I intervened by going to the school principal who quickly put a stop to the victimisation. In grade 7, when he began high school in Australia, the teasing was less intense and less persistent, although still irritating, and Thomas was able to ignore/put up with the few *Ignoranten* (= ignoramuses), as he aptly called them, who thought anyone who spoke anything but English was stupid. However, these unfortunate experiences did not cause any decline in his willingness to speak German to me; if anything, the opposite was probably the case, as he seemed to find speaking German at home after a trying day at school a welcome escape from the difficulties he had encountered with this small group of English speakers.

It is important that parents try to help their children through such periods of mindless attack and help them to see that abandoning the home language would not really solve the problem, since such people would simply find something else to ridicule. In fact, Bent Søndergaard (1981) describes just such a case. Although he (a Dane) and his wife (a Finn) discontinued the attempt to raise their son JH bilingually in Denmark when he was nearly three years old, JH was still teased ten years later by his classmates at school, because he had a Finnish mother and was therefore half-Finnish, an attitude which Søndergaard aptly calls "grotesque" in an area where bilingualism of another sort, namely Danish/German is accepted. The tragedy here is that JH's *not* using Finnish regularly in the home with his mother did *not* save him from the illogical taunts of his classmates: he was penalized in any case just because his *mother* was not a native Dane!

Frank has not yet met any such problems, although his more aggressive temperament may well have deterred intending tormentors. He seems proud of his German; at age 11, for instance, he was happily taking German comics and magazines along to school to read in a time of the day set aside for the children's free reading. (This also had an ulterior motive, since he could then read in peace without any of the other children wanting to read his reading material!)

Katrina's situation was somewhat different from that of her brothers, since from age 3;6 to 3;10 she attended an all-German kindergarten in Hamburg, but only for two hours on Wednesday afternoons. As she was at that age extremely shy and unwilling to speak to adults other than her parents, I always took her to kindergarten and collected her afterwards so that her teachers would at least hear her speaking German to me and not interpret her silence as not knowing German. On her return to Australia, Katrina attended kindergarten from age 4;0 to 4;10 for four and a half hours every Thursday, and the following year, at age 5;0, began school in the preparatory class. She has never shown any reluctance to speak to me in German in the presence of teachers or other children. Although no other children in her class spoke anything but English, she was fortunate to have as her very first teacher a woman who was brought up in a similar way to her: her teacher had always spoken Estonian to her parents in Australia and was most enthusiastic about the benefits her two languages had brought her. She had also studied other languages and knew some German. This enthusiastic acknowledgement of, and support for, their mutual bilingualism obviously impressed Katrina very much, coming as it did from someone she already admired very much.

Even so, the Australian school is clearly seen as an English-language domain (in contrast to her "German school", as she calls the reading and writing lessons she does at home with me). At age 5;6,16, for example, she was telling Thomas (12;9,20) that she had at school made a Father's Day card for her father:

Thomas: What language did you write the card in?
Katrina: In English.
Thomas: Why didn't you write it in German?
Katrina (quite indignantly and definitely): I made it *at school*!

During the children's stay in Germany in 1984 (see chapter 10), when the situation regarding their two languages was, as it were, reversed, they never displayed any reluctance to speak English to their mother in the presence of others. Occasionally, in the presence of people who understood no English, Wendy would

— to save continual translating — address them in German, and sometimes they replied in German. This more flexible attitude on Wendy's part was because the family was going to be in Germany for only a brief time and their English was not going to be under any threat of being swamped by German.

6 Further possible problems in establishing bilingualism

Children's reluctance to speak the home language

In trying to establish or maintain bilingualism in a family, the parents may at certain times become discouraged and be tempted to abandon the attempt. Such discouragement may come from outside the family (e.g. from teachers or medical personnel who may attribute any speech difficulties or learning problems to a child's bilingualism) (for a discussion of this, see chapter 5) or from within the family itself (e.g. through conflict caused by the parents unrealistically expecting the child to be not only bilingual but *equilingual*, i.e. equally proficient in both languages, or from the child's reluctance to speak one of the languages, usually the language which is not the dominant language of the community). Discussions with Australian families, in which attempts to bring up the children bilingually have failed, indicate that it is mainly these periods when a child avoids using the language other than English, or speaks it with large numbers of lexical transfers from English, which persuade the parents that the attempt is futile. In addition, the child's English may contain a considerable number of transferences from the other language, e.g.:

Frank (3;6,16) (to his mother): I need a SABBERLÄTZCHEN *(bib)*.

In the face of such language mixing, the parents may fear that the child is acquiring neither language properly. This anxiety is understandable, but provided the parents persist with raising the child bilingually, such periods of language mixing should, if not disappear, be reduced to a minimum

In some cases it may not be the mixing of the two languages which causes concern and doubts, but the failure of one of the languages to be used at all for some time. For example, Walburga von Raffler-Engel (1965, 1970) reports that she addressed her son in Italian whilst her American husband spoke to him English, but that the boy at first spoke only Italian. He initially had only a passive knowledge of English and did not utter his first English words until age 2;8, but from then on used both languages, rewarding parental persistence. This demonstrates the advisability of parents not giving up, if, at the onset of speech, or for some time thereafter, a child uses predominantly only one language. Continuing to talk to a child in the language he or she is reluctant to speak, will ensure that he or she is acquiring a passive knowledge of that language which will, in most cases, eventually be activated.

In my own family, both boys have gone through short periods where they have shown reluctance to speak German to me, preferring to address me in English. An analysis of the taped corpus reveals that at the age of 3;5,3 the percentage of all-English utterances used by Thomas to me was a quite high 58%. Only 25% of utterances were completely German, while 17% were a mixture of English and German. The percentage of German words (tokens) directed at me on this 45-minute tape was a mere 28%. The same problem did not arise with his speaking of English, most probably because virtually all linguistic contact at that stage, apart from with me, was with English-speakers. At virtually the same age (3;5,0), for example, 95.1% of the utterances Thomas directed at his mother were completely English, 2.4% completely German, and 2.4% a mixture of English and German. 97.8% of words (tokens) spoken to his mother were English. When communicating with English-speaking monolinguals the percentage of English words used was even higher.

Frank's resistance to German occurred at around age 2;7, when his utterances to me contained only 40.3% German words. But by age 3;0, this percentage had increased to 95.1%, and by age 4;0 to 98.5%, below which it has never since dropped. Like Thomas, Frank has shown no resistance to speaking English; from age 2;6 to age 5;7, for instance, the *lowest* percentage of English words recorded when addressing his mother was 98.5%.

The figures just mentioned for Thomas's German at age 3;5,0 and for Frank's German at age 2;7,6 do not really give a true picture of their active ability in the language at those times, i.e. they show what they *did* produce, not what they *could* produce. The figures are more an indication of their willingness to speak German. This could be seen when I pretended not to understand something they said to me in English. They then demonstrated that they were capable of producing predomi-nantly German utterances:

Frank (2;7,0): I'm driving a little truck, George.
Father: Was? *(What?)*
Frank: Ich fahr 'n Lastkraftwagen, Dad. *(I'm driving a truck…)*

Father: Und wo hat der Zimmermann das Holz herbekommen? *(And where did the carpenter get the wood from?)*
Thomas (3;5,3): He got it off sawmill.
Father: Woher? *(Where from?)*
Thomas: Aus 'n Sägewerk. *(From a sawmill.)*

This "pretending not to understand" strategy can be very effective in encouraging a child to use the "right" language to the right people. Traute Taeschner (1983:200-205), married to an Italian and living in Italy, used this technique to good effect to increase the amount of German her daughters Lisa and Giulia spoke to her. Some people (e.g. Anne Bödiger, 1985) regard such a procedure as cruel. But it need not be, provided it is not done excessively (i.e. certainly not every single time a child uses the "wrong" language), is carried out with some sensitivity (i.e. ceasing when the child shows distress), and is not carried out before children are old enough to be conscious that they are dealing with two separate language systems and that there are two ways of saying almost everything; most children will have reached this stage by or shortly after their second birthday (see chapter 3). Moreover, the language behaviour of most children, be they bilingual or monolingual, is regulated in some way by their parents. For example, a parent may well pretend not to understand a child who says "Give me a drink!", responding with "I beg your pardon?", indicating that a request such as "Could I have a drink, please?" would be preferred. In my own case I found it more difficult, in fact, to get Thomas to remember to put a "please" on the end of requests than to speak only German to me!

Another possibility, which proved effective in our family, is to prompt a response in the 'right' language, e.g.:

Father (talking to Thomas about a girl who had cut her arm): Wer hat ihren Arm verbunden? *(Who bandaged her arm?)*
Thomas (3;5): Her mother, Dad. Her mummy and daddy.
Father: Oh, ihre — *(her)* (Expecting Thomas to complete.)
Thomas: Mutter und ihr Vater. *(Mother and her father.)*

However, this period did mark the lowest point in the boys' use of German. It is my impression that if I had relented at these points in time and spoken English to them, they would have been quite happy to have abandoned German. However, only a few months after these periods of resistance to German, judging from their adverse reactions when I addressed them in English, they would have accepted a change to all-English communication with me only with some difficulty. It is also my impression that even if I had continued to speak German to Frank and Thomas but had not persisted in eliciting German responses from them they would have become receiving bilinguals only, with their knowledge of German confined to comprehension and their ability to speak the language limited. Such situations are not uncommon in immigrant families, where parents continue to address their children in the language of their country of origin, but the children reply in the language of the new country. For example, Michael Clyne's (1968) investigation of seventy-four families with German-speaking parents and children either born in Australia or arriving in the country before the age of 5, showed that in fifty-six (75.7%) of the families the parents spoke only German to the children. Yet in only sixteen (28.6%) of these fifty-six families did the children speak only German to the parents. In twenty-seven (48.2%) the children spoke a mixture of English and German, and in thirteen (23.2%) the children always answered their parents in English. A similar tendency is revealed by the research of Smolicz & Harris (1976) into the linguistic behaviour of other immigrant groups in Australia: the percentage of Polish, Dutch, Italian and Greek-speaking parents using only their language to their children is considerably higher than the percentage of children responding in that language only.

When children for some reason show reluctance to speak the language of their parent(s) or begin to interlard their speech with numerous lexical items from the dominant language of the community, it would seem that the problem can be successfully overcome provided the parents are persistent, yet show understanding and good humour. In this, the children's individual personalities obviously have to be taken carefully into account. It is important that the language does not assume any negative connotations for the children. With some children, for instance, to insist that they never resort to the dominant language of the community could cause frustration and resentment and have an adverse effect on their willingness to speak the other language. Instead, children should be given every encouragement to speak the language and should be helped when their linguistic knowledge is not adequate to express their thoughts. When they either consciously or unconsciously use elements from the other language or, to avoid doing this, struggle to find an appropriate way of expressing themselves, the parent(s) can casually supply the missing vocabulary item, help with an idiom, etc. If this is done in moderation it should not inhibit the children's desire to communicate. After a few gentle reminders of this kind the children will in most cases adopt the word or expression appropriate to the language in question. Of course, this will not always work immediately, and a particular word or expression may persist for some considerable time. For instance, at age 3;5 Thomas predominantly used English *her* instead of German *sie* and *ihr*. Five months later *her* was being used side by side with *sie* and *ihr*, e.g.:

Thomas (3;10,0): Warum HER gern singt? Hat SIE Musik für mich gemacht? *(Why her likes singing? Did she make music for me?)*

Isolated examples of *her* were still to be found in Thomas's German as late as age 3;11,7 but by 4;0,7 the word had finally disappeared. However, apart from such stubborn cases, most lexical transfers survived for only a very brief period.

As mentioned above, *excessive* correction of children's speech may have a negative rather than the desired positive effect. In her book, sadly titled *Young people's Dyirbal. An example of language death from Australia*, Annette Schmidt (1985:18,38–40) describes how in an Australian Aboriginal community the traditional language, Dyirbal, is dying and being replaced by English. One of the reasons is that not only do most young people in the community speak English much better than Dyirbal, but they are also inhibited from speaking Dyirbal to older fluent speakers because of the *constant correction* they receive from these older speakers who attempt to uphold traditional linguistic norms. "The main objection by traditional speakers appears to be a contamination of young people's Dyirbal with English forms." On the other hand, absence of correction also does not seem to be desirable in the bilingual upbringing of children. Jiri Neustupny (1985:59) lists this as a reason why children with both Japanese parents resident in Australia quickly lose their competence in Japanese: "With no effective correction pattern on the side of the parents, the language of the children is quickly flooded with transfers from English and the next stage of abandoning Japanese in favour of English seems to be an inevitable conclusion." The secret of effective parental correction, therefore, as already alluded to, seems to be to do it, but to do it in moderation.

In my own study, an analysis of material taped regularly shows that there was a steady increase in the percentage of German words Thomas spoke to me, from a very low 28.0% at 3;5,3 to 59.0% at 3;5,22, 69% at 3;7,22, 74% at 3;8,8 and a very high 99.5% at 3;10,7. From 3;10,7 onwards the percentage of German words in Thomas's speech to me has never gone below 98%. The number of German lexical transfers present in his English to his mother has always been low. From age 3;10,7 he had about equal success in eliminating English words from his German as he did in avoiding transferring German into his English. In the 17 month period from 3;10,7 to 5;3,6 Thomas used an average of 99.4% German words to me and 99.6% English words to his mother.

It should be stressed that these statistics show only the degree to which the children used words from one language when speaking the other (called "lexical transference"). This and the transference of other features from one language to the other are discussed in detail in chapter 7.

Unlike her brothers, Katrina has never gone through a period of reluctance to speak German to me. The reason for this may be her position in the family. There is a gap of 5 years 4 months between her and Frank and a gap of 7 years 3 months between her and Thomas. She thus has two older brothers who serve as models of linguistic and other behaviour and whom she obviously tries to emulate in many respects. She hears them always speaking German to their father and does likewise; that is simply the done thing. Thomas, as the first child, had no such model to follow. Moreover, if she does use an English word in her German, she is often helped/ corrected by Thomas or Frank who find amusing such infringements of what they see as the rules of address in the family. Katrina also hears much more German, and a greater variety and complexity of German, than did her brothers at a similar age, simply because she is often present during conversations between her father and

Thomas and/or Frank. Another reason for Katrina's never attempting to address her father in English may be that from age 3;4,18 to 3;10,2 (which, as shown above, was a critical period for Thomas) she was in Hamburg in a predominantly German-speaking environment.

Thomas, Frank and Katrina usually receive parental linguistic assistance gratefully, providing it is offered in moderation and relatively unobtrusively. The children obviously wish to communicate with me in German and with their mother in English and naturally look to us for assistance if they are having difficulty expressing themselves. Consequently, this linguistic assistance is always given when asked for and also sometimes offered when there is no direct request for help expressed either verbally or by eye contact, but where a child is obviously struggling to find some expressions, e.g.:

Thomas (5;6,0) (showing me how he can jump over a chair): Jetzt mache ich das — without tripping. *(Now I'll do that —)*

The tone of voice with which the switch into English was uttered was somewhat hesitant and uncertain, and, together with the slight break in the flow of speech, marked it as an "intruder". As he made the switch, he looked directly at me, obviously seeking assistance. The difficulty Thomas has encountered here is not with vocabulary but with the syntactic construction required (which is different in German, literally "without to trip"). The conversation continued:

Father: Ohne zu stolpern. *(Without tripping.)*
Thomas: Hm, ich springe rüber, ohne zu stolpern. *(Hm, I'll jump over without tripping.)* (Satisfied, he proceeded to leap over the chair.)

The children's resorting to the other language in such predicaments is not discouraged, but when this happens both parents do ensure that they are provided with a suitable equivalent in the appropriate language.

The children began seeking linguistic assistance at an early age, around their second birthday, at a time when they were beginning to realize that there were two words, a German and an English one, for most things and that each word had its own particular function. To obtain information about the two language systems, the following strategies were used:

(a)   Mutti sagt ... *(Mummy says ...)*
       Daddy says ...

       Implying either:
       (i) "I don't know your word but I do know the other one."
       (ii) "I know your word and I can also tell you what Mummy/Daddy says."

An example of (i):

Father: Welche Farbe haben Susannes Füße? *(What colour are Susan's (a doll) feet?)*
Katrina: (2;3,5): Mutti sagt WHITE. *(Mummy says ...)*
Father: Oh, Mutti sagt WHITE. Bert sagt WEISS. *(Oh, Mummy says WHITE. Daddy says WEISS.)*
Katrina: Weiß.

(b) Was sagst du für ...? *(What do you say for ...?)*
     What do(es) you say for ...?

Example:

Thomas (3;9,22) (to mother): Dad drew me a — ah, what you say for LEUCHTTURM?
Mother: Lighthouse.
Thomas: He drew me a lighthouse.

(c) Was sagt Mutti für ...? *(What does Mummy say for ...?)*
     What does Daddy say for ...

(The word could be sought (i) just to satisfy the child's curiosity, (ii) as a conscious effort by the child to have German and an English word for every concept, (iii) because the word is needed for speaking to the other parent now or at a future time, or (iv) a combination of reasons (i)–(iii)).

Example:

Katrina (2;3,13) (pointing at a picture): Ist das ein Känguruh? *(Is that a kangaroo?)*
Father: Ja, das—oh, ist das ein Känguruh? *(Yes, that — oh, is that a kangaroo?)*
Katrina: Nein, das ist ein Eichhörnchen. *(No, that's a squirrel.)*
Father: Ein Eichhörnchen, ja. *(A squirrel, Yes.)*
Katrina: Was sagt Mutti? *(What does Mummy say?)*
Father: Was sagt Mutti für Eichhörnchen? *(What does Mummy say for EICHHÖRNCHEN?)* Ah, squirrel.

(d) Sagst du ...? *(Do you say ...?)*
     Do you say ...?

Implying (i) "I wish to confirm an assumption."; (ii) "I know the answer is 'no', but I want to know what you do say."; (iii) "I want to show you that I know the term in both languages."

Combinations of (a) and (b), as well as (a) and (d), have also been heard.

(e)   Sagt Mutti ...? *(Does Mummy say ...?)*
       Does Daddy say ...?

Heard only seldom. Used to check an assumption about what the other parent says, e.g.:

Katrina (2;1,10) (on walk at night with mother): Look! The moon! Does Daddy say **Mond**? *(Moon)*
Mother: Yes. Der Mond. *(The moon)*.

Since about age 4 direct requests for linguistic assistance have mostly taken the form "Wie sagt man ... (auf deutsch/englisch)?" (directed to their father), How do you say... (in English/German) (directed to their mother), with the actual names of the languages being used, e.g.:

Thomas (13;0,2) (telling me about an episode of the science fiction TV series *Dr Who*): Der Brigadier sagte: "Wenn solch eine parallele Welt existiert, dann können Sie mich dahin bringen und es beweisen." Und dann sagte der Doktor: "Nein, das würde ein, ah ... wie sagt man *temporal paradox* auf deutsch? *(The brigadier said: "If such a parallel world does exist, then you can take me there and prove it." And then the doctor said, "No, that would, ah — how do you say* temporal paradox *in German?)*
Father: Ah, ein zeitliches Paradoxon.
Thomas (continuing): Nein, das würde ein zeitliches Paradoxon machen. *(No, that would make a temporal paradox.)*

An alternative is to insert the word or expression from the other language, usually with a slight pause after, or particular emphasis on, the word to indicate that it is being used out of necessity, e.g.:

Frank (11;1,26): Unsere Lehrerin war gestern nicht da — sie wollte den *pope* sehen. *(Our teacher wasn't there yesterday — she wanted to see the* pope) (The word *pope* was emphasised.)
Father: Den Papst? *(The pope? — supplying the forgotten term.)*
Frank: Ja. *(Yes)*

If Wendy or I think a word asked about is one which the children do know we may prompt an answer rather than supply the desired information instantly, e.g.:

Katrina (5;5,7): Bert, Franks Ball ist über — wie sagt man "Fence"? (*Dad, Frank's ball went over — how do you say "fence"?)*
Father: (prompting) Z—
Katrina: — ist über den Zaun gegangen. *(Went over the fence.)*

Sometimes the children seek assistance with their German from each other before coming to tell or ask me something.

As already stated above, none of these strategies has been discouraged in any way as they are seen as an excellent means for the children to acquire vocabulary they do not know (or have forgotten), to check on assumptions about their two languages, and they enable them to say whatever they wish to in both languages.

However, this attitude is not universal. Jules Ronjat (1913:93) states that he never supplied German vocabulary to his son with whom he spoke only French, since this would be an "infraction of the rule 'one person, one language'." When Louis (3;7) asks him how to say "lizard" in German so that he can tell his mother what they have seen on a walk, Ronjat does not give him the information.

Werner Leopold (1970) shows a similar attitude towards helping his daughter, Hildegard:

At first she did not know the names of the languages. 'How does Mama say it?' was her question for an English equivalent *(which, however, she could not wheedle out of me.)*

No such refusals of information are made in our family, because it is felt that this would not foster learning. The child could become caught up in a vicious circle if both parents adhered rigidly to this principle, making the obtaining of a term in one of the languages a very tedious process.

If children hear an unfamiliar expression in one language they may use the other to seek verification that they have correctly decoded it, e.g.:

Thomas (5;5,16): Warum has du das benutzt? *(Why did you use that?)*
Father: Oh, nur zur Abwechslung. *(Oh, just for a change.)*
Thomas: For a change?
Father: Ja. *(Yes.)*

This sometimes happens even when the expression in question is clearly explained, e.g.:

Mother: In England there's a longer twilight than in Australia.
Thomas (6;8,1): What's that, Mum?
Mother: That's that sort of greyish, darkish time before it gets properly dark.
Thomas: Ah, DÄMMERUNG. *(dusk, twilight)*
Mother: Yes.

Werner Leopold (1949:146) reports on similar experiences with his daughter, Hildegard (8;0,6): "When she asks me for the meaning of an unfamiliar German word, which she does not do often, I give her as a rule not the English translation, but a simple explanation in German. Often she says then the more familiar English equivalent to show that she has understood."

Far from representing a danger to the maintenance of bilingualism, such requests for information demonstrate a desire on the part of the child to improve his or her knowledge of both languages, and as such they should be welcomed and every assistance given. These requests should be treated no differently from queries in and about one language (in fact, the type of request which would occur in a monolingual family), e.g.:

> **Frank** (10;3,8): ... Und ich hab auch sehr gute Bleistifte bekommen, die, ah, die Experten, ah, Leute, die malen, benutzen — wie nennt man sie? *(And I also got some really good pencils which, ah, experts, ah, people who draw, use — what do you call them?*
> **Father:** Oh, Künstler. *(Oh, artists.)*

Sometimes the parents can anticipate such difficulties and supply the children with vocabulary which may be unfamiliar in the other language, e.g.:

> **Thomas** (5;9,23): Ich werde Mutti sagen, was der Mechaniker gesagt hat. *(I'll tell Mum what the mechanic said.)*
> **Father:** Okay. Lichtmaschine heißt "generator" auf Englisch. *(O.K. "Lichtmaschine" is called "generator" in English.)*
> **Thomas:** Ah, gut. *(Ah, good.)* (Said appreciatively. Runs to mother.) Mum, the mechanic said he has to fix the generator. It's broken.

Or, if in our family a child is discussing a subject in one language and is using vocabulary which it is felt he or she would not know in the other language, the parent with whom he or she speaks this other language will often join in, using the vocabulary the child lacks. All this saves the chilren from a feeling of frustration which could lead them to avoid a particular topic in one language because they lack the appropriate vocabulary, which is often just one crucial word.

In the study of my children, the significant effect which emotional factors can exert on a child's acquisition of bilingualism became apparent. As can be seen in Figure 1 in chapter 7, in a speech sample recorded at age 6;3, Thomas made 3.6 errors per 100 words in his German, yet in a speech sample taken at age 6;6 there was a sudden upsurge in the number of errors, an all-time high of 7.5 errors per 100 words of German being made. This special sample was taped approximately one month after we had moved from Melbourne to Sydney. Although the whole family regretted having to make the move, it affected Thomas particularly. He missed his former friends and school greatly and had difficulty in adjusting to a much larger, more impersonal school where the other children unfortunately reacted aggressively to him as a newcomer. Since the move to Sydney had been made so that I could take up new employment, Thomas seemed for a while to blame me for the unhappiness he had been plunged into:

> **Thomas** (6;6,0) (agitatedly, after a day of bad experiences at school, to father): Warum hast du uns bloß zu dieser blöden, verflixten, verdammten Stadt gebracht? *(Why ever did you bring us to this stupid, damned, bloody town?)*

This time of upheaval and unhappiness clearly caused the decline in the accuracy of his German. Wendy and I did as much as possible to help him over this difficult period, for example by visiting his school and discussing the matter with his teacher (who proved very understanding and helpful), by giving him additional attention and sympathy at home, in short, by showing him that we understood his feelings and cared very much about his well-being.

These actions, plus the natural healing effect of the passing of time, helped him return to his normal cheery self quite quickly, so that one month later, at age 6;7 he was making only 3.5 errors per 100 words of German, having returned to his former accuracy. The whole experience demonstrates the more precarious position of a language relying on only one source of input and indicates the importance of a stable, secure environment for such language acquisition.

Susanne Döpke's (1986) research in Australia with young children being raised bilingually according to the "one person-one language" principle shows that the way in which the parent who speaks the minority language converses with the children can have a significant effect on how well they acquire the language.The most successful parents in her study are those who use "a child-centred mode of interaction", i.e. who actively work at sustaining a conversation with the children by being responsive to the children's contributions to the conversation, by working at maintaining a topic once it has been introduced, and by being more interested in conversing with the children than exerting control over them. This style of speaking with children has also been associated with faster language development in children in general, but it seems to be fairly crucial in the case of a language being acquired mainly from one person only. Even parents who are not naturally inclined to such a style of interaction can, with a little practice, increase their efforts to stimulate and sustain conversations with their children

Effect of the father's not being a native speaker of German

The most unusual aspect of the case of bilingualism described in this book is that I am not a native speaker of the language which I am passing on to the children. This, expectedly, has certain disadvantages, but there are also some advantages.

The main disadvantage is that in certain areas I do not feel as confident about vocabulary in German as I do in my native English. But in thirteen years fortunately only a few incorrect vocabulary items have been passed on to the children. If such errors are detected quickly they are easily eliminated. However, late detection can mean that the word or expression has already become firmly established and will be difficult to eradicate. For example, when Thomas was aged 3;10,14, I discovered, much to my chagrin, that the word *Wellenblech* for "corrugated iron", which Thomas and I had been using for nine months and which, to make matters worse, was one of Thomas's favourite words, should in fact be *Wellblech*. I had forgotten that whilst compound nouns formed with *Welle* (= wave) normally began with *Wellen* (e.g. *Wellenreiter,* "surfer", literally "wave rider"), they did not if the texture of materials was being described. It took much explanation and gentle persuasion before Thomas would accept *Wellblech.* After three days he would accept it as a synonym of his beloved *Wellenblech*, but still insisted adamantly:

> **Thomas** (3;10,17): Ich sage *(I say)* Wellenblech!

Fortunately, this resolve was quickly forgotten, and he was soon using the correct *Wellblech* in his own speech, apparently unconcernedly. Just how firmly entrenched the form *Wellenblech* had been, however, was demonstrated some thirteen months later when Thomas recalled that he and I had once said *Wellenblech.* However, it is some consolation to find documented in great detail in Michael Clyne's (1967 etc.) work that even native German speakers born in Germany and residing in Australia are often very uncertain about German vocabulary. For example, the following was heard in an interview on Radio 2EA, the multilingual radio station in Sydney:

> ... und wir haben den Hühnerstall aus CORRUGATED IRON gemacht.
> *(... and we made the chook-house out of CORRUGATED IRON.)*

As Clyne (1967:103) shows, second generation speakers consequently use many lexical and semantic transfers (see the glossary or chapter 7 for explanations of these terms) as well as neologisms which they have heard in their parents' speech and which they believe to be German. A non-native speaker is perhaps more conscious of this danger and takes greater precautions to avoid it.

The other few incorrect forms which I have passed on have been mainly minor pronunciation errors. These were words which I knew from reading but whose pronunciation I had not heard or learnt, e.g. *Kokosnuß* (=coconut), the first vowel of which I mistakenly pronounced short instead of long. Fortunately, errors like this were promptly detected by checking in a dictionary in cases of doubt. I then presented the children with the correct form in another conversation as soon as possible, explaining, if questioned, that I had unfortunately made a mistake and had pronounced the word wrongly when I had previously used it. Within a day or two the incorrect pronunciation would disappear from the children's speech. The children readily accepted that it was not possible for anyone, including their parents, to know what every word meant or how every word should be pronounced, be it in German or English. They knew from an early age that both parents frequently consulted books to obtain or verify information on various subjects. The following is a typical example:

> **Thomas** (3;11,1): Was sagt du für WALLFLOWERS, Dad? Sagst du Wandblumen? *(What do you say for "wallflowers", Dad? Do you say WANDBLUMEN?)* (A literal translation: *Wand* = wall, *Blumen* = flowers.)
> **Father** (scarcely a gardening expert in any language, but doubting that such a literal translation would be correct): Ah, ich weiß nicht recht. Ich muß das mal nachsschlagen. *(Ah, I don't really know. I'll just have to look that up.)* (He does so in a dictionary); Goldlack. *(Goldlack,* literally *gold varnish,* the German name for *wallflower.)*
> **Thomas:** Goldlack.

Another disadvantage of my being a non-native speaker of German is that in Australia I virtually represent the children's sole constant source of German; there are no German-speaking relatives to provide linguistic support through regular contact with the children. The children are used to communicating regularly in German with only one person, their father. My variety of German assumes, therefore, a much greater importance for the children than their mother's English, since they are constantly engaged in communication with other English speakers of various ages and speaking various types of English.

Katrina's situation is somewhat different from that of her brothers, since when she was beginning to talk she already had two brothers aged 6 and 8 whom she heard speaking every day to her father in German, so her exposure to German in the home was probably greater than that experienced by Thomas and Frank at the same age. Furthermore, she was exposed to an all-German-speaking environment (Hamburg) at a much earlier age (3;4 to 3;10) than her brothers.

Although Thomas and Frank had sporadic contacts with other German speakers in their first five years, it became apparent that during that time they tended to look on German as a unique family possession. An encounter with someone who addressed them in German, particularly if unexpected, was usually greeted with amazement, amazement that someone else spoke "their" language. In the following example, Thomas (3;10,7) and I are in a foreign-language bookshop looking at children's books in German. Thomas chatters on excitedly in German and eventually selects a book.

> **Thomas:** Kann ich das allein kaufen? *(Can I buy this by myself?)*
> **Father:** Ja, sicher. Hier ist das Geld. Bezahl den Mann da drüben. *(Yes, sure. Here's the money. Pay that man over there.)*
> **Thomas** (to shop assistant): I'll have this book.
> **Shop assistant:** Hm. (Takes book and money, wraps it and hands it back to Thomas.) Sag "Danke". *(Say "thank you".)*
> **Thomas** (astonished, turns and calls out to me): Dieser Mann kann Deutsch! *(This man can speak German!)*

Alvino Fantini (1978a:298) reports similar reactions from his children when a language was used which was unexpected for a given context, for example, when his daughter overheard two men speaking Spanish on a bus in Albuquerque:

> **Carla** (to father): ¡Esos hombres están hablando en español! *(Those men are speaking Spanish!)*

Frank even became, for a time, quite possessive about German, as evidenced by his reaction at age 4;3,26 when I told him that everyone spoke German in Germany:

> **Father:** Da sprechen all die Leute Deutsch. *(All the people speak German there.)*
> **Frank** (somewhat indignantly): Bert, sie sind Nachäffer! Das ist unsere Sprache! *(Bert, they're copycats. That's our language!)*

However, despite his indignation that the Germans were copycats for speaking German, an interesting and amusing point of view, this was not accompanied by any negative feelings towards them, quite the opposite. It seems that he considered that, as fellow speakers of German, they must be nice, as can be seen in the continuation of the above conversation:

> **Father** (amused): Nachäffer? *(Copycats?)*
> **Frank:** Ja. *(Yes.)*
> **Father** (jokingly): Diese blöden Nachäffer! *(These stupid copycats!)*
> **Frank** (defensively): Sie sind nicht blöd, sie sind nett! *(They're not stupid, they're nice!)*

My accent and way of speaking German were obviously seen as being "proper" German. My German was the familiar language of the home. German accents which differed from mine were considered quaint or amusing. This applied particularly to female voices, simply because the two boys rarely heard the language used by girls or women. I attempted to combat this feeling of strangeness about other German voices by purchasing and having made recordings of stories with a variety of voices and accents. This proved very successful, particularly as some of the stories were their favourites. Exposure to any German films which happened to be shown on television also helped. However, since most of the recordings and films were in a reasonably neutral sort of German accent, very similar to mine, they still found other German accents strange and sometimes difficult to understand. (see also chapters 9 and 10.)

Although exposing the children to a variety of German voices through recordings and on radio and television made them aware that mine was not the only kind of German, it still retained its strong emotional ties. Both boys expressed their preference for their father's German, e.g. Frank (4;9,30) while watching an episode of *Kontakte*, a BBC television course for beginners in German:

Frank: Sie sprechen gut Deutsch, Bert. *(They speak German well, Bert.)*
Father: Ja. *(Yes.)*
Frank: Aber du sprichst besser. *(But you speak better.)*
Father (surprised): Besser? *(Better?)*
Frank: Ja. Ich mag dein Deutsch. *(Yes. I like your German.)*

Not being a native speaker of German does have the psychological advantage that I do not have the same emotional attachment to the language as do most native speakers. I can maintain a more detached attitude towards my children's acquisition of German. After all, I know they are acquiring my own native language, English, at much the same rate as their monolingual peers. I am, therefore, perhaps more tolerant of aberrations in their German and of the fact that their ability in German may lag behind that of monolingual children in a German-speaking country. In addition, the fact that the children know that I, like themselves, can function in a way which is indistinguishable from monolingual speakers of Australian English, would seem to be a definite advantage. In families with immigrant parents the children often reject the home language and try to assimilate as much as possible, because, to use Michael Clyne's (1967:101) words, "the parents, with their fixed values and speech habits, will always remain 'different' from the community".

The question of whether their father is a native speaker of German or not has been of little interest to the children. Speaking German to me is simply a fact of life. What to outsiders might appear to be an artificial situation, does not appear so from within the family itself. German is the language naturally used for playing or arguing with me, seeking my advice, permission, consolation, telling me of their experiences, and so on. It is what Thomas once aptly called his *Vatersprache* (father tongue).

Thomas (7;4,5) (speaking about a former colleague of the father): Pavel spricht sehr gut Deutsch. *(Pavel speaks very good German.)*
Father: Ja, und auch sehr gut Tschechisch. Das ist seine Muttersprache. *(Yes, and also very good Czech. That's his mother tongue.)*
Thomas: Ja, ich weiß. *(Yea, I know.)*
Father (out of curiosity, since he does not think Thomas has heard the term "mother tongue" before): Was ist deine Muttersprache? *(What's your mother tongue?)*
Thomas (spontaneously): Deutsch. *(German.)* (But then pauses, thoughtfully): Nein, Englisch ist meine Muttersprache. Deutsch ist meine Vatersprache. *(No, English is my mother tongue. German is my father tongue.)*

In the linguistic literature, various definitions of "native language", "mother tongue", etc. can be found, e.g. the language one knows best, the language one uses most, the language in which one is acknowledged by other speakers of the language as a fellow native speaker, etc. (see Tove Skuknabb-Kangas, 1984:29ff). Richard Diebold (1961:99) regards a "native" language as one which must have been learnt in childhood without formal instruction. Jack Richards and Mary Tay (1981:53) define "native language" as one which is learned as a child and which the speaker continues to use regularly. According to these two definitions, at least, Thomas, Frank and Katrina are native speakers of both English and German.

The children did show some curiosity about the linguistic situation in the family. Just before his fourth birthday, Thomas began asking why I was his only German-speaking relative. At age 4;11,24 Frank began wondering how I came to learn German:

Frank: Bert, konntest du Deutsch sprechen, wenn du warst ein Junge? *(Bert, could you speak German when you were a boy?)*
Father: Nur ein bißchen. Ich habe Deutsch erst in der Schule gelernt. *(Only a bit. I didn't learn German until I went to school.)*
Frank: Was konntest du sagen? *(What could you say?)*

At the same age Thomas asked questions about his own bilingualism, e.g.:

Thomas (4;11,15): Not many people speak German in Australia, do they?
Mother: No, not many.
Thomas: Why do I speak German, Mum?
Mother: Well, so you can talk with your Dad, because he only speaks German to you.
Thomas (smiling): Yes.

Additional explanations to "so you can talk to your dad" were offered by Wendy and me, stressing the value of bilingualism in ways which would appeal to the children, e.g.: "One day we might spend some time in Germany and if you didn't know German you wouldn't be understood or be able talk to anybody, watch television, etc." This stay in Germany did, in fact, eventuate in 1984 (see chapter 10), and the children were able to see for themselves at first hand what an asset their proficiency in German was, enabling them to communicate and function well in an all-German-speaking environment. Since then there has been little need for us to stress the value of being bilingual, as this seems self-evident to the children and they are already looking forward to their next visit to Germany.

Even before Germany, Frank and Thomas themselves also independently mentioned aspects of their bilingualism which they perceived as advantageous, e.g. the fact that they had access to a much wider range of books, magazines, films, records, etc., than if they knew only one language.

Frank, whilst also recognizing the scarcity of German speakers in Australia, did see in this a certain advantage:

Frank (5;1,8): Nicht viele Leute hier können Deutsch. *(Not many people here know German.)*
Father: Nein. *(No.)*
Frank: Das ist gut, Bert. *(That's good Bert.)*
Father: Warum? *(Why?)*
Frank: Weil sie wissen unsere Geheimnisse nicht. *(Because they don't know our secrets.)*

Fantini's (1978:296) son, Mario (8;1), saw similar advantages in using his Spanish in a predominantly English-speaking environment.

Other explanations given to the children were based less on reason and more on the emotional ties between them and me, e.g.: "Ich spreche gern Deutsch mit dir/euch." (= "I like speaking German to you.") Even a circular argument such as "Wenn ich mit dir nicht Deutsch spräche, dann würdest du doch niemanden haben, mit dem du Deutsch sprechen könntest." (= "If I didn't speak German to you then you would have no-one to speak German to.") impressed Thomas at age 5;0,4. Whilst more sophisticated explanations were given as the children got older, it was this type of explanation emphasizing the bonds of affection between parent and child which particularly pleased them in the pre-school period. Jules Ronjat (1913:9) stresses the importance of this affection in maintaining his son's French in what was at the time a predominantly German situation:

The position of German is thus very strong, but the position of French also remains very strong: It is the language of papa who knows lots of

nice stories, who has taught him to pick out the good kinds of mushrooms, who knows how to fix broken toys, to glue back torn pages in picture books, etc ...
(Translated from the French)

And later, when Louis is exposed to much more French than German, Ronjat again remarks on the important role which mutual affection between child and parent plays in maintaining a language:

Since the 30th month everyone in constant contact with Louis, except his mother, has spoken French. Nevertheless, German maintains a very strong position. It never occurs to the child to abandon it and speak French to his mother, although he knows perfectly well that she understands and speaks this language very well. He continues to speak German out of affection for his mother for whom it is the preferred language ... (Translated from the French)

Thomas, Frank and Katrina usually just take it for granted that German is spoken between them and their father, although they all also know English. Their own opinion on the matter can be best summed up by quoting their (Thomas 5;9,29, Frank 3;11,6, Katrina 4;11,1) identical replies to separate questions from family friends as to why they spoke German to their father: "Because he speaks German to me", uttered in a tone of voice which suggested that the answer to the question was obvious.

Even at the time of writing, when Thomas is 13, Frank 11, and Katrina 5, there has been no departure from this attitude on the part of the children. Shortly before the boys' 13th and 11th birthdays, I asked, in a discussion with them about their thoughts on their bilingualism, if they would not prefer it if they spoke English to me and I English to them, since both they and I agreed that English was the language all three of us were more proficient in. Both boys rejected this suggestion: they obviously regarded German as an integral part of their relationship with their father. Frank (10;9,9) summed up his feeling with the comment: "Das wäre sehr komisch — als ob ich mit der linken Hand schreiben müßte!" (That would be very strange — as if I had to write with my left hand!)

The boys' close relationship with me has been established over many years through German, through their German — imperfections and all. The boys are now old enough to realize that a change to using English with me would — at least initially — be psychologically difficult and that whilst this might make communication marginally easier, it would mean the loss of an important part of our life.

There is now considerable evidence in the literature to show that bilinguals who have a choice of which language they can speak with each other do not necessarily always choose the one in which they are most proficient. There are other factors which influence this choice. For example, in her book *Language Death. The Life Cycle of A Scottish Gaelic Dialect*, Nancy Dorian (1981:107) discovered certain speakers of East Sutherland Gaelic (ESG), a dialect gradually dying out, who preferred to speak Gaelic to certain persons although English would have been "easier":

> It seems perverse that a group of people whose control of ESG is imperfect, and whose agemates have for the most part opted for English only, should continue to use a stigmatized language of strictly local currency when they are fully proficient speakers of a language of wider currency.

The factor most influencing this conscious choice was "a strong attachment to some kinsperson".

Although my children have always heard me speaking English practically every day to their mother and other people, and have even asked me questions about English, e.g. to explain difficult dialogue in a television show, etc. I was — until the children were about 6 — so strongly identified in their minds as a speaker of German, as someone to whom they always spoke German and from whom they always received German in return, that they at times forgot that I too knew English. Even at the age of 5;10,4, Thomas found it difficult to imagine his father in an English-speaking role. He had told me that his physical education teacher had been away for some time and he wished he would soon return. I jokingly suggested that I could fill in for the absent teacher:

> **Father**: Ich könnte euer Sportlehrer sein. *(I could be your sports teacher.)*
> **Thomas** (seriously): Aber du sprichst die falsche Sprache. *(But you speak the wrong language.)*
> **Father**: Oh. Ich könnte doch alles ins Englische übersetzen. *(Oh. I could translate everything into English, though.)*
> **Thomas**: Oh, ja, Bert. *(Oh, yes, Bert.)* (said in a tone of voice indicating "I hadn't thought of that!")

Perhaps the initial reaction here is due to Thomas's realization that he would be in the class to be taken by me if I became the sports teacher and that I would thus naturally speak German to him and his classmates would be excluded.

Another example with Frank (4;9,21) shows that whilst he considered German the appropriate language for me to use to him or, as in this case, for addressing myself in Frank's presence, he was aware that I did also use English. He also demonstrates his attachment to German as the only language to use to me.

Father (singing): Hey Mr. Tambourine Man, play a song for me —
Frank (amused): Du sprichst nicht Englisch! *(You don't speak English!)*
Father (a little taken aback): Oh. Welche Sprache spreche ich denn mit deiner
Mutti? *(Oh. Which language do I speak to your mum then?)*
Frank: Englisch. *(English.)*
Father: Aber nicht mit dir? *(But not to you?)*
Frank: Nein. *(No.)*
Father: Was würdest du machen, wenn ich Englisch mit dir sprechen würde?
(What would you do if I spoke English to you?)
Frank: Ich würde Deutsch zu dich sprechen. *(I'd speak German to you.)*
Mother (joining in father's laughter): You know the rules, don't you, Frank?
Frank (smiling): Yes.

No such objections were raised if my comments to myself were uttered in the presence of monolingual English-speaking friends or relatives. But within the family unit it was obvious that the children preferred me to address not only them but also myself in German, and, as a result, this became the established pattern and is what I still do today.

Another interesting result of the children's speaking only German with me was that, although aware that I was born and raised in Tasmania, until around age 6 they sometimes found it difficult to reconcile this knowledge with the fact that I spoke German to them. This was probably because most other fluent speakers of German they had come in contact with had been born outside Australia. For the children, the terms "German" and "German-speaking" seemed to be synonymous and interchangeable. *Deutschland*, literally "German Land", was consequently the place of origin of German-speakers. When the situation was explained to them, they did not seem to find it odd that I spoke a language to them which I had learned at school and university. They have never questioned the rationale for doing this.

The close association of their father with German in the children's minds becomes very evident when I have to be absent from home for any length of time. It has been observed that when they begin to miss me, they tend to speak a considerable amount of German among themselves and in monologues, much more than would normally be the case. The lack of German in the home is a tangible sign of their father's absence, and the desire to see me again and to speak "our" language, is given indirect expression through this increased use of German.

My use of only German to the children has had no adverse effects on the relationship between me and the children. In some ways it would even seem that this has enhanced the relationship. Because I, representing virtually the children's only contact with German, feel directly responsible for ensuring the children's contin-ued and unstressed progress in German, it has meant that I have perhaps given them more attention than would have been the case if I had spoken English to them. The children's favourable attitude towards their own particular bilingual situation could not be summed up more positively than in Frank's not exactly modest suggestion, at age 11, for a title for this book: "Bilingualism at its best"!

The children have even expressed the desire to perpetuate the use of German in the family, e.g.:

Mother (to Frank, aged 5;2,2): When you grow up and have kids, what language will you speak to them?

Frank (after pondering the question for a few seconds): German.

Mother: Oh. What will your wife speak to them?

Frank: German. She'll have to learn it. They'll have to learn it. I'll teach them.

Mother: Who'll be their granddad?

Frank: Daddy. That's why I'll teach them.

Although no longer expressing himself so forcefully, Frank (age 11) still holds this view, and it is shared by Thomas (age 13) and Katrina (age 5). Whether this comes to pass, remains to be seen, but the fact that it is being considered shows that German is obviously looked on very favourably and is regarded as an integral part of the children's lives.

The two boys have also expressed some concern about what will happen to their German when they eventually leave home, and at one stage Thomas (12;8,24) also asked: "Bert, was wird mit **deinem** Deutsch passieren, wenn alle Kinder weg sind?" *(Dad, what will happen to **your** German when all the children are gone?)* Their questions and comments led to interesting and helpful discussions about ways and means of maintaining their German when they are adults.

7 Measuring proficiency in both languages

Introduction

Except for six months spent in Hamburg from July to December 1984, the three children have been, and continue to be, exposed to much more English than German. Linguistic input in an average week would have been at least 3:1 in favour of English before each child started school, and probably as much as 6:1 in favour of English by 1986 when all three children were attending school. In view of this, it would be logical to assume that the children's dominant language would be English and that they would display greater proficiency in that language. A number of tests carried out over the years have shown this assumption to be basically true. But the results are still encouraging for any parents contemplating a similar bilingual upbringing for their children, as the gap between proficiency in English and German has been found to be not all that great.

Receptive vocabulary

A person's receptive (or hearing) vocabulary is the number of words he or she *understands*. (All people have a larger receptive vocabulary than an active vocabulary, i.e. they know more words than they actually use.) The receptive vocabulary of Thomas, Frank and Katrina has been measured at approximately two year intervals using the Peabody Picture Vocabulary Test (PPVT). The results of these tests give a good picture of the children's vocabulary development over the years and also permit some comparison between the children at similar ages.

The English-language version of the PPVT, which was standardized on 4,012 subjects, aged from 2;3 to 18;5 in Nashville (USA), is commonly used to assess verbal intelligence and scholastic aptitude through measurement of hearing vocabulary. The test consists of a series of plates, each with four pictures. A stimulus word is presented orally for each plate and the person doing the test is required to indicate which of the four pictures best illustrates the meaning of this stimulus word. The plates are graduated, that is, the stimulus words increase in difficulty, e.g. in Form A of the test item 1 is *car,* item 50 is *capsule,* item 100 is *amphibian.*

I prepared a German-language version of the PPVT, keeping in mind the dangers of test translation expressed by researchers such as Wiliam (1971) and Peña & Bernal (1978). Wiliam sums up the problem clearly when he writes:

> ... an ad hoc translation (of tests) creates a testing situation in which the discriminiation and difficulty values of the test items are not known; as standardization has not occurred in the ad hoc version, the validity of the items is uncertain ...while it is quite possible for an item to retain a degree of validity in translation, it is a hazardous procedure to rely on the original statistical data as an indication of validity in a new situation.

Since the stimulus words in the English-language version become progressively more difficult, an attempt was made to preserve this increasing degree of difficulty when preparing the German version. Simply translating the English stimulus words into German would, in some cases, produce items which, to use Nordberg's (1976) terminology, would have greater lexical transparency in German, e.g. if *bronco* were rendered as *Wildpferd* (literally *wild horse*). An attempt was made to approximate the difficulty of the English items, and where the German translation would be much easier because of its lexical transparency or greater frequency, it was replaced by a less common or more opaque item, e.g. *bronco* became *Hengst* (= stallion). Since the main aim of the test was a comparison of the children's receptive vocabulary in both their languages, such a procedure does not seem unreasonable.

In any case, even the use of the American English version of the PPVT to test Australian children could be seen as an example of what Peña & Bernal (1978) call "the historical malpractice of test importation". Taylor, de Lacey & Nurcombe (1972), in their investigation of the use of PPVT for Australian children, write: "It was apparent that the order of difficulty of items does not progress regularly at some points in the sequence for Australian children." They mention, for example, the word *pledging,* which occurs at item 47, as being very difficult for an Australian child, mainly because it reflects a cultural difference: Australian school-children are simply not seen facing the flag, hand over heart, and pledging. On the other hand, a term such as *marsupial,* known, for obvious reasons, to even very young Australian children, occurs at item 144, i.e. in that section of the test normally considered only within the capabilities of adults. In addition, some of the stimulus words, whilst known to Australian children, are used in a different sense. For example, the word *shining* is known to most young Australian children, but only in the sense of giving out light or brightness. The picture which is meant to depict this word shows a shoe resting on a last and being rubbed with a cloth. The usual Australian term for this activity is *cleaning* or *polishing*. Some other words, whilst common and easy for American children, e.g. *caboose* and *wiener,* are not used in Australian English. In fact, Taylor *et al.* (1972) recommend the use of *guard's van* and *sausage* instead of *caboose* and *wiener* respectively, as well as *engine driver* in place of *engineer*, when administering the test in Australia.

In some respects, therefore, the German version of the PPVT produced to test Thomas, Frank and Katrina is as valid as the American English test. Even if a German-language version of the test, standardized in one of the German-speaking countries were available, would it be any more valid for German-speaking Australians than the American English version for Australian English speakers? Peña & Bernal (1978) note a similar problem with the testing of Spanish speakers in the USA, pointing out the inadvisability and unreliability of using tests from other Spanish speaking countries for this purpose.

However, despite their limitations, it is is felt that in this case the tests have revealed much valuable information about the children's linguistic ability.

In the normal administration of the PPVT, the person being tested proceeds until he or she makes six errors in any eight consecutive presentations. At age 3;7, for instance, Frank was given Form A of the test in English and Form B in German. His raw score for English was 50, for German 46.

From shortly after their fifth birthdays the children have also been tested on the first 100 items of both the English and German versions of both Forms A and B of the test. (The PPVT Manual asssumes that persons aged 17;6 and above would know the first 100 items.) The results can be seen in Table 2. (At a much younger age, namely 2;4, Katrina was tested in both languages on the first 50 items of both Forms: on Form A she scored 35/50 in English and 34/50 in German, on Form B 32/50 in English and 29/50 in German.

The results shown in Table 2 may be slightly biased in favour of German because of the non-standardized nature of the German version of the tests. However, it is felt that the difference in difficulty between the English and German versions is quite small and that they do provide a useful means of comparing the children's vocabulary development in their two languages. As can be seen in the table, overall the children performed approximately equally in English and German. This is interesting and encouraging, because it suggests that the considerable imbalance in favour of English in the linguistic input which the children receive is not as significant a factor in the acquisition of a receptive vocabulary as, as will be seen, in the acquisition of oral fluency and grammatical accuracy.

TABLE 2

	Number of items correct out of the first 100 (PPVT)			
	English		*German*	
Child and age	*Form A*	*Form B*	*Form A*	*Form B*
Katrina 5;3	66	66	61	65
Frank 5;5	66	70	70	74
Thomas 5;5	76	69	75	80
Frank 7;9	78	81	75	83
Thomas 7;3	80	79	82	92
Frank 9;7	86	86	85	87
Thomas 9;7	92	97	90	99
Thomas 11;7	94	97	96	97

Merrill Swain (1972) suggests that when both a bilingual's languages are examined, his or her total conceptual vocabulary may exceed that of a monolingual child. This would seem to be so in this case, for, as can be seen in Table 3, the vocabulary items not known by each child were not exactly the same ones in each language.

TABLE 3

	Forms A (100) + B (100) = 200 vocabulary items in each language		
Child and age	*Items known in English*	*Items known in German*	*Items known in either English or German*
Katrina 5;3	132	126	152
Frank 5;5	136	144	163
Thomas 5;5	145	155	169
Frank 7;9	161	158	173
Thomas 7;3	159	174	182
Frank 9;7	172	172	191
Thomas 9;7	189	189	196
Thomas 11;7	191	193	198

As can be seen, in every case the total number of concepts known by the children *in at least one* of their languages exceeds the number known in each language individually by quite a significant margin. A look at one example will make this clear. At age 9;7 Frank scored 172/200 for both English and German. However, out of the 28 concepts which he did not know in each language, only 9 were the same in *both* languages, e.g. he missed both *coil* and its German equivalent *Spirale*. This means that there were also 19 concepts which he missed in English but knew in German (e.g. he knew *Kelch* but not its English equivalent *goblet*), and another 19 *different* concepts which he missed in German but knew in English (e.g. he knew *beam,* but not its German equivalent *Balken*). This means that if *all* Frank's correct answers were counted, irrespective of language, the total number of concepts known would rise quite dramatically to 191/200. Similar comments could be made about both the other tests done by Frank and also about the tests done by Katrina and Thomas.

Such results suggest the unfairness of assessing bilinguals for verbal intelligence as if they were simply two monolinguals. Since a bilingual's linguistic input is divided between two languages, it is most unlikely that the range of vocabulary heard or acquired will be identical in both languages. For example, in his test done at age 5;5, Thomas showed that he did not know the term *soldering* in English, but he responded instantly and accurately to the German equivalent, *löten*. The explanation for this is that his only experiences with soldering to that time had been with me (and hence in German), and he had had no cause to talk about the subject in English.

A comparison of the children's performance over time shows an expected increase in knowledge of vocabulary in both languages. If we compare Thomas's results at age 5;5 and 7;3 for example, we find that words previously not known (e.g. English *archer,* German *errichten (=* erect) have been added to his receptive vocabulary. However, it is not only a question of gains: some words known in the first test have in the meantime been little heard and as a result are no longer recognized (e.g. English *erecting,* German *hissen (=* hoist). In fact, 32.5% (N = 13) of the English items and 50.0% (N = 15) of the German items missed by Thomas at age 7;3 were correctly identified by him at age 5;5. Whilst this may be partly due to the differences in guessing on the more difficult items at each testing, it does show that through disuse and lack of reinforcement items can be lost from a child's receptive vocabulary. For instance, in his test at age 5;5, Thomas easily identified the German *Profil,* but failed to recognize the corresponding English *tread* (i.e. on tyres). In the months preceding that test he had been very interested in parts of cars and had acquired most of his car terminology in conversations and play with me (in German). His knowledge of vocabulary in this area was consequently greater in German. When tested again at age 7;3, Thomas not only did not know *tread* but now also did not recognize *Profil.* This can be explained by the fact that soon after the first test his interest in car parts had waned and this vocabulary was seldom used in the 22 months until the second test.

The children were invited to make comments during the administering of the tests. These comments revealed that in two cases the children's bilingualism assisted them in correctly responding to the stimulus words. Frank did not know English *walrus* but identified it from the German cognate *Walroß* which he knew well from a favourite story. Thomas (7;3) similarly successfully identified English *angling* with the comment: "That's like German *angeln*. Just as well I know the German word." (*Angling* is considered a less frequent, more technical word in English than *angeln* is in German.) Yet in other cases the existence of cognates did not help; Thomas (5;5) knew *Stadion* in German, but could not connect it with English *stadium*. Frank (5;5) and Katrina (5;3), on the other hand, knew *stadium* but not *Stadion*.

Since researchers such as Doyle *et al.* (1978) have found that bilingual children have a vocabulary lag in each of their languages, Thomas's, Frank's and Katrina's performances on the PPVT in English were assessed to see how they compared with monolingual children of the same age in the USA. Using the Manual, raw scores were converted into mental age scores, percentiles, and standard score-type intelligence quotients (IQs). Full details are given in Table 4.

As can be seen, the percentile scores for the children at various ages are quite high. Percentile norms provide an index of brightness, as do IQs, indicating how an individual compares with others of his or her own age. A percentile of 98 (as scored by Thomas at age 7;3), for instance means that for every 100 children of the same age doing the test only 2 would score above him. Even the lowest percentile in the table, 71 scored by Frank (at age 9;7) on Form B, indicates that his performance is better than 71% of children in that age category. The children's English vocabulary, therefore, compares very favourably with that of their monolingual American peers. It could be argued that the children's scores on the PPVT might have been even higher if they also had been monolingual English speakers, but such a claim is impossible to prove or to refute. It is, however, possible that in a few cases, where the children knew German vocabulary items but not the English equivalents (e.g. both Thomas [5;5] and Frank [5;5] knew *Kunststück* but not *stunt*), they would have acquired the word from me if I spoke English to them (*Kunststück* being regularly used in circus games we played together). In any case, having a possibly slightly smaller vocabulary in English would seem to be a small price to pay for possessing, in addition, a similar vocabulary in German.

TABLE 4

PPVT — Standardized English-language version

		Form A				Form B		
Child and age		Raw score	Per- centile	Mental age	IQ	Raw score	Per- centile	Mental age	IQ
Katrina	2;4	36	93	3;6	128	32	89	3;2	121
Katrina	4;3	52	80	5;5	111	55	91	5;11	119
Katrina	5;3	62	95	7;3	122	55	76	5;11	110
Frank	3;7	50	94	5;1	122	—	—	—	—
Frank	5;5	56	75	6;1	111	60	91	6;10	119
Frank	7;9	78	94	10;5	121	73	78	9;4	112
Frank	9;7	84	82	11;9	113	81	71	10;9	108
Thomas	5;5	60	93	6;10	118	63	95	7;5	125
Thomas	7;3	78	98	10;5	133	76	97	10;1	130
Thomas	9;7	95	97	14;6	130	99	97	14;11	137
Thomas	11;7	117	99+	18;0+	147	100	98	14;8	134

In his book *Second Language Acquisition in Childhood*, Barry McLaughlin (1978:172) suggests monitoring children's IQ over time to see whether their bilingual experience has had any effect on their intelligence. However, to make valid claims in this regard, it would be necessary to compare two groups of children who differed in only *one* respect, i.e. in that one group was monolingual, the other bilingual. In the case of Thomas, Frank and Katrina, certain changes in IQ, as measured by the PPVT, have occurred from test to test, sometimes an improvement in IQ, sometimes a decline, but it is not possible to attribute these changes to their bilingualism as, obviously, many other factors could be involved. In most cases the differences recorded from one testing to a subsequent testing two years later are no greater than those noted between Forms A and B of the PPVT at the same testing.

Estimating fluency and accuracy

Over the years a number of methods have been employed to measure and compare the children's fluency and "accuracy" in both languages, with "accuracy" being taken to mean conformity to the grammatical norms of the adult standard language. The children have been taped in a variety of situations in both languages, e.g. spontaneous conversations, story-telling etc. Considering the fact that they live in an English-speaking country and go to English-language schools, it is natural to expect that their English would be superior to their German as far as fluency and "accuracy" are concerned. As will be seen, this assumption is, and has been, basically correct for all the children. It may seem a little negative to look closely at deficiencies in the children's two languages, particularly in their German, but this is done to point out to parents that under similar circumstances it is highly unlikely that their children will speak their home language as well as children in the linguistic homeland or as well as they speak the dominant language of the country in which they now live. At the same time it is hoped that readers will look beyond the deficiencies in the speech of Thomas, Frank and Katrina (and in the speech of their own children!) and consider their considerable achievements, e.g. that not only can they function in English in a way indistinguishable from monolingual English speakers, but that, as a bonus, they can also function very well in German, mistakes and all! (How well their "home German" served them during their first visit to Germany is documented in Chapter 10.)

Storytelling

Tapes of the children telling stories at approximately the same age were analysed to permit some comparison of their proficiency in both languages. Table 5 shows how Thomas (age 5;7) and Katrina (5;4) performed telling *Little Red Riding Hood* and Frank (5;5) telling *The Three Little Pigs*.

TABLE 5

	Errors per 100 words	Words per minute	Filled pauses with 100 words	Repeats per 100 words	Length in words	Time (min:sec)
Katrina						
English	1.2	90.1	4.0	2.3	347	3:51
German	8.2	53.0	11.0	4.1	292	5:33
Frank						
English	0.3	114.0	1.4	2.8	359	3:09
German	8.8	85.0	0.0	5.6	125	1:28
Thomas						
English	2.1	100.0	6.7	9.2	195	1:57
German	5.5	68.5	25.8	5.0	225	3:17

When calculating the number of words (tokens), repeats are excluded (e.g. "I,I,I did it" is counted as three words, not five), as are filled pauses (e.g. ah, um, and the like). However, repeats and filled pauses are listed separately, since a speaker presumably produces less of these in the language in which he or she is most fluent. Similarly, the number of words uttered per minute are listed, the assumption being that one's speaking speed will be faster in the language in which one is more proficient.

These samples of the children's English and German are fairly representative of each child's languages at five years of age. As can be seen from Table 5, in English each child had a faster rate of delivery, less repeats and made less errors than in German; Thomas and Katrina also made less filled pauses in English; in other words their English was more fluent and more grammatically accurate. However, despite this, the German versions of the stories are easily understandable.

When Thomas was aged 7;5 and Frank 5;5 (April 1980), they were recorded telling in German *Ootahs Glückstag* (= Ootah's Lucky Day) (written by Peggy Parish, trans. Ursula Bahn, and published by Carlsen Verlag, 1976), a German story which had been read to them a number of times. Katrina was taped telling the same story at age 5;4 (June 1986). Table 6 shows how they performed.

TABLE 6

	Errors per 100 words	Words per minute	Filled pauses with 100 words	Repeats per 100 words	Length in words	Time (min:sec)
Katrina (Age 5;4)	7.3	62.7	13.5	5.5	387	6:10
Frank (Age 5;5)	8.9	65.0	0.3	3.2	315	4:51
Thomas (Age 7;5)	4.5	62.8	0.6	3.7	513	8:10

Since it is the children's German which deviates most from the adult standard language (their English being very close to the adult standard), it is interesting to examine a segment of their German produced in the narration of *Ootah's Lucky Day*. The following excerpt, describing one incident from the story, gives an idea of the quality of their German at this particular stage in their linguistic development. The original text of the story is also given for comparison.

Frank (5;5) German (March 1980)	*Thomas (7;5) German* *(April 1980)*	*Katrina (5;4)* (June 1986)	*Original text*
Ootah seht einen grauen Flecken. *(Ootah sees a grey speck.)*	Ootah sieht ein schwarzer Fleck. *(Ootah sees a black speck.)*	Und dann hat er ein schwarzen Fleck geseh—, gesehen, und, und ihn—seine Hunden auch. *(And then he saw, saw a black speck, and, and him— his dogs too.)*	Dann blickt Ootah über das gefrorene Meer. Weit hinten sieht er einen schwarzen Fleck. Der Fleck bewegt sich nicht. *(Then Ootah looks across the frozen sea. In the distance he sees a black speck. The speck does not move.)*
„Vielleicht ist das ein Seehund!" *("Perhaps it's a seal!")*	„Vielleicht ist das ein, ein Eis—, ein Seehund," sagt er. „Seehundfleisch schmeckt gut." *"Perhaps it's a, a polar—, a seal," he says. "Seal meat tastes good.")*		„Vielleicht ist es ein Seehund," sagt Ootah. „Seehundfleisch schmeckt gut. Seehundtran gibt ein gutes Feuer. O bitte, laß es einen Seehund sein!" *("Perhaps it's a seal," says Ootah. "Seal meat tastes good. Seal oil makes a good fire. Oh please, let it be a seal!")*
Er kommt NEAR Das „Nein! Das ist ein Walroß. Walroßtran ist sehr gut. Walroßfleisch ist sehr gut." *(He comes near to it "No! That's a walrus. Walrus oil is very good. Walrus meat is very good.")*	Der Fleck wird größer und größer. „Das ist ein Walroß," sagt er. *(The speck gets bigger and bigger "That's a walrus," he says.)*	Und als sie näher war, war das Fleck, ahm, größer geworden, und dann war es ein Walroß. *(And when they were closer, the speck had um, got bigger, and then it was a walrus.)*	Ootah fährt mit seinem Schlitten auf das Eis. Der Fleck wird größer. „Ein Walroß! Es ist ein Walroß!" denkt Ootah. „Ein Walroß ist noch größer als ein Seehund." *(Ootah drives his sled on to the ice. The speck gets bigger and bigger. "A walrus! It's a walrus!" thinks Ootah. "A walrus is even bigger than a seal.")*
Das Walroß gleitet zurück in Eis. Ootah war—, Ootah wartet sehr still. *(The walrus slides back into ice. Ootah wai—, Ootah waits very quietly.)*	Das Walroß darf ihn nich sehen und nicht hören. Er war—, er wartet bis er raus das Eis kommt, aus das— der Tümpel kommt. Er, er schneidet ein Loch in das Eis und steckt die Schnur von seiner Harpune rein, und, und gießt Wasser	Ah, ah, und es war, ahm, sehr still. Und dann hat er eine Idee gehabt, wie er konnte es fangen. Zuerst hat er ein, ah, Loch in die, ahm, Eis gemacht, und dann hat er die Leine von seiner Harpune reingesteckt, Und dann hat er es rausgeholt,	Ootah weiß, was er tun muß. Er bohrt ein tiefes, enges Loch in das Eis. Er steckt das Ende seiner Harpunenleine in das Loch und gießt Wasser darüber. „So," sagt er. „Das Wasser wird frieren. Wenn ich meine Harpune werfe, wird die

Frank (5;5) German	Thomas (7;5) German	Katrina (5;4)	Original Text
über das, damit wenn der Walroß getötet ist, kann er nicht rausbrechen. *(The walrus mustn't see or hear him. He wai—, he waits till he comes out of the ice, comes out of the, the pool. He, he cuts a hole in the ice and puts the cord of his harpoon in it, and, and pours water over it, so that when the walrus is killed, he can't break out.)*	und dann hat er sehr still, ahm, ges—, gesitzt. *(Ah, ah, and it was, um, very still. And then he had an idea how he could catch it. First he made a, um, hole in the ice, and then he put the line of his harpoon in. And then he took it out and then he, ah, sa—, sitted very still.)*	Leine festsitzen. Das Walroß kann nicht fliehen." Ootah hockt sich hin und wartet. Ootah sitzt still, ganz still. Das Walroß darf ihn nicht hören. Ootah wartet und wartet . . . *(Ootah knows what he has to do. He puts the end of his harpoon line in the hole and pours water over it. "There," he says. "The water will freeze. When I throw my harpoon, the line will stick fast. The walrus won't be able to get away." Ootah crouches down and waits. Ootah sits quietly, very quietly. The walrus must not see him. The walrus must not hear him. Ootah waits and waits.)*	

Plötzlich hört er ein Platschen. Das Walru—, das Walroß kommt raus das Eis. „Jetzt!" sagt Ootah. Er schmeißt sein Harpune und das geht in das Walroß. *(Suddenly he hears a splash. The walro—, the walrus comes out of the ice. "Now!" says Ootah. He throws his harpoon and it goes into the walrus.)*	Plötzlich kommt er aus das Wasser, und er— Ootah wartet bis der richtige Moment—und dann mit aller Kraft. Ah, zielt er auf der, ah, auf der Walroß, und das Walroß kommt immer weiter aus das Wasser. Dann, dann, ah, zielt er mit seiner Harpune, und, und, dann wartet er bis der richtige Moment. Mit aller Kraft schmeißt er seine Harpune sehr weit, und sie trifft das Walroß.	Und dann, ah, hat die Walroß, ah, sehr, ah, leise, ah, rausgekommen, und dann hat er seine Harpune, ah, geschmiss—, geschmissen, und er hat es ge—, getroffen. *(And then, ah, the walrus, ah, came out very, ah, quietly and then he, ah, thr—, threw his harpoon, and he hi—, hit it.)*	Plötzlich hort er ein Plätschern. Er sieht eine schwarze Nase aus dem Loch hervorkommen. Ein runzliger Kopf folgt. Ootah packt seine Harpune fester. Er hält den Atem an. Er muß genau den richtigen Augenblick abwarten. Das Walroß kommt immer weiter aus dem Wasser heraus. „Jetzt!" denkt Ootah. Mit aller Kraft wirft er die Harpune. Die Harpune trifft das Walroß. Das Walroß stürzt auf das Eis.

Frank (5;5) German	*Thomas (7;5) German Katrina (5;4)*	*Original text*
	Ootah sagt: „Ich habe ein Walroß getötet!" *(Suddenly he comes out of the water, and he—Ootah waits until the right moment—and then with all his strength, ah, he aims at the, ah, at the walrus, and the walrus comes further out of the water. Then, then, ah, he aims with his har- poon, and, and, and then he waits until the right moment. With all his strength he throws his harpoon very far and it hits the walrus. Ootah says, "I killed a walrus!")*	Ootah starrt das große Tier an. „Ich habe es geschafft!" flüstert er. „Ich habe ein Walroß getötet!" *(Suddenly he hears a splash. He sees a black nose come out of the hole. A wrinkly head follows. Ootah holds his harpoon more tightly. He holds his breath. He must wait for precisely the right moment. The walrus comes further out of the water. "Now!" thinks Ootah. With all his strength he throws the harpoon. The harpoon hits the walrus. The walrus falls onto the ice. Ootah gazes at the huge animal. "I did it!" he whispers. "I killed a walrus.")*

The German of Thomas and Frank was delivered confidently and fluently. Katrina was less confident, as at that age (5;4) she was somewhat reluctant to tell stories in German. Although the children's German contains more errors than would usually be found in the speech of monolingual German-speaking children, it is still quite clear and comprehensible. In view of the particular circumstances in which the children had acquired their German, this would seem to be a significant and worthwhile achievement.

Of course, the above samples of the children's languages are somewhat out of date for both Thomas and Frank who, at the time of writing (late 1986) are aged 13 and 11 respectively. English is still the language they operate in most accurately and fluently, although their ability to comprehend and to express themselves easily in German on a wide range of subjects is impressive.

The following samples of Frank's speech at age 11;1,8 are a good demonstration of his proficiency in both his languages. The German sample was recorded shortly after he had taken part in a 12 kilometre fun run and was telling me how he had performed. The English sample was taped later the same day as he was making a cassette for his grandparents to tell them about the same event.

GERMAN	ENGLISH

. . . und man muß zwölf Kilometer laufen. Und, ah, am Anfang war es sehr e—, eng, weil es gab sehr viele Leute, und ich bin beinahe ins Bach gefallen, aber dann mußte ich ziemlich— sehr schnell laufen, um all—, durch all die Leute zu kommen, und, ah, dann war es leicht. Und, ah, man mußte ein' sehr steilen Hügel hinauflaufen, aber dann gab es Getränke und so weiter. Ich habe viele Männer und Frauen, ah, überholt. Und, ah, dann war der Hälfte des Wettbewerbs, ah— hat der Mann ge—, mir mein—, meine, ah, Zeit gesagt, und er hat gesagt: „Neunundzwanzig Minuten und fünfzig Sekunden." Und ich hab gedacht: „Sehr gut. Jetzt muß ich, ahm, schnell auf den Heimweg laufen." Und, ahm, ich bin den Hügel ziemlich schnell hinaufgelaufen, und dann noch ein Getränk geholt. Und es gab ein Mann in einem roten, ah, Hemd vor mir, Bert, und ich wollte ihn besiegen, und, ah, ungefähr die letzten zwei Kilometer hab ich ihn überholt. Und dann bin ich sehr schnell gegangen, und ich konnte die Brücke sehen—weißt du diese Brücke?— Ja, und ich fühlte mich krank in den Kopf, aber ich wollte immer noch—ich mußte immer noch laufen. Und dann, ein paar Minuten später bin ich angekommen. Undich wollte meine Zeit kriegen, und, ah, ich bin zur Frau gegangen, und dann hab ich mich erbrochen. Und die Frau hat mich gesagt, was meine Zeit war: es war sechzig Minuten und achtzehn Sekunden.

. . . *and it's twelve kilometres. And when we got there we lined up and the bloke, um, and the bloke sounded the gun and we were off. And I— I nearly ran into the creek because you get almost crushed, 'cause there's a— over two thousand people running in it. And then gradually you make your way through the people and they get dropped back. And, um, and I overtook, um, all these men and that. And I was aiming to overtake this bloke in this red, um, shirt and all the way I was behind him— most of the way I was behind him— and then he ran up the hill, and you could get drinks, and I washed myself down with a sponge . . . And when I got to the half-way point I, um, I started— the bloke there said that I did the six kilometres in twenty-nine minutes and fifty seconds, and I thought, "Oh, that's pretty good." And the on the way back I overtook that bloke in the red shirt, and I overtook all these people. And then on the last bit where I could see the bridge near the end— and then, um, I ran real fast, and I was feeling sick in the head, but I kept on going. And then when I got to the finish my time was sixty minu— , my time for twelve kilometres was sixty minutes and eighteen seconds, and I was real pleased. And after— ah, when I went to get my time I was sick, because I felt sick in the head, and I vomited up. Yeah, yeah, it was a real good run . . .*

(Translation of the German version:
. . . and you have to run twelve kilometres. And, um, at the start it was very cr—, cramped, because there were lots of people, and I nearly fell into the creek, but then I had to run fairly— very fast to get through all the people, and then it was easy. And, ah, you had to run up a very steep hill, but then there were drinks etc. I, ah, overtook lots of men and women. And, ah, then half of the competition was, ah— the man to—, ah, told me my— my time, and he said: "Twenty-nine minutes and fifty seconds." And I thought: "Very good. Now I'll have to, ah, run fast on the way home." And, um, I ran up the hill fairly quickly and then got another drink. And there was a man in a red, ah, shirt in front of me, Dad, and I wanted to beat him, and, ah, about the last two kilometres I overtook him. And then I went very fast, and I could see the bridge— you know that bridge? — Yes, and I felt sick in the head, but I still wanted to — and I had to keep on running. And then, a few minutes later I arrived. And I wanted to get my time, and, ah, I went to the lady, and then I vomited. And the lady told me what my time was: it was sixty minutes and eighteen seconds.)

If we compare the German and English versions we find the following:

TABLE 7

	Errors per 100 words	Words per minute	Filled pauses with 100 words	Repeats per 100 words	Length in words	Time (min:sec)
English	0.4	151.2	2.3	1.9	258	1:42
German	4.7	129.4	3.8	1.7	235	1:49

The two versions are remarkably similar both in content and the fluency with which they are told. The similarity in rate of delivery is even more striking if, instead of counting words (on average English words are shorter than German words), we count *syllables*: in the German version Frank speaks at a rate of 179.4 syllables per minute, and in the English version at a rate of 182.9 syllables per minute. The speech samples are reasonably typical of the way he speaks both his languages, although on some topics he may sometimes strike a few vocabulary problems in German which slow down his rate of delivery. The number of errors is higher in German, but none of them hinders understanding. (*Real* used as an adverb instead of *really* e.g. "I was *real* pleased" has been counted as an error here in the English version, although it is acceptable in colloquial English, since in the German version the *weil* sentence without the verb at the end of the clause, has also been counted as an error, although, as discussed below, it is probably acceptable colloquial German.)

We now see two samples of Thomas's speech which show a slightly diffe-rent picture. Overall, Thomas has a better grammatical knowledge of German than his brother and sister (and this is reflected in the accuracy chart in Figure 1). However, like his father he speaks more slowly and deliberately. This is more noticeable in his German, where he sometimes becomes concerned with *how* he is expressing himself rather than just conveying a message — this tends to slow the speed of his speech. Frank, on the other hand, has usually been just the oppo-site — what he has to say is much more important than how it is said. In the speech samples, Thomas (13;0,20) is describing part of the popular Australian film *Crocodile Dundee,* first to me in German, and later the same day to his grandparents in English.

GERMAN	ENGLISH
Letzten Sonntag sind wir ins Kino gegangen, und wir haben einen Film gesehen, und er hieß *Crocodile Dundee.* Und, ahm, es handelte von eine junge Amerikanische Reporterin, und sie ist zum Nordterritorium in Australien geflo-gen, weil sie hat Geschichten von einem Mann	*Last Sunday we went to the pictures and we saw a film called* Crocodile Dundee, *and it was about this young American reporter. And she went to the Northern Territory in Australia because she'd heard of— stories of this bloke who'd been attacked by a crocodile and his leg*

gehört, dessen Bein von ein' Krokodil abgebissen worden war. Und— ah— sie wollte wissen, wo, ah, es passiert ist, und sie hat ihn kennengelernt, aber echt— echt— sein— er hatte noch zwei Beine— aber echt, ahm, hatte er nur ein paar große, ahm, Narben auf sein— auf seinem Bein. Und, ahm, sie sind durch den Busch gegangen— in einem Jeep, weil er wollte ihr zeigen, wo es passiert ist. Und dann sind sie auf einem— mit einem Boot über einen Fluß gefahren, und, ahm, sie sind an die Stelle, wo es passiert ist, übernachtet. Und am, ah, Morgen ist sie ins Wasser gegangen, um Wasser zu holen, und dann hat ein großes Krokodil sie angegriffen. Es hatte sehr große Zähne und war ungefähr fünf Meter lang. Ahm, aber zum Glück hat Crocodile Dundee ihr zum Wasser gefolgt, und er hat— mit seinem Messer ist er aus die Büsche gesprungen, und er hat das Kro—, Krokodil getötet. Und dann sind sie wieder zurück zur Stadt gegangen, und sie hat gesagt: "Willst du mit mir nach New York kommen?" Und er hat gesagt: "Ja."

had got bitten off, and, um, his name was "Crocodile" Dundee. And, um, she wanted to know where it happened. And she met up with him and, um, the, they— the stories were just, um, lies bescause he'd, he'd only had a few big scars on his leg from the crocodile attack. And, um, they, they went— they went through the bush because he wanted to show her where um, he got attacked by the crocodile and, um— in this jeep. And they crossed this river in— in this boat, and then they camped the night. And next morning — that was where, that was where he got attacked. Next morning she went to get some water and he followed her. And, um, this real massive crocodile came out of the water and it started to attack her, and it was a real big one with sharp teeth, and it had—, ah, it was about five metres long. And he got his knife, and, um, he killed the crocodile. And then, um, they went back to the city— the town, where they'd left from, and, um, she said, "Do you want to come back to New York with me?" And he said, "Yes."

(Translation of the German version:

Last Sunday we went to the pictures and we saw a film, and it was called *Crocodile Dundee*. And it was about a young American reporter, and she flew to the Northern Territory in Australia, because she had heard stories of a man whose leg had been bitten off by a crocodile. And— ah— she wanted to know where it happened, and she met him, but really— really— his— he still had two legs— but really, um, he only had a few big, um, scars on his— on his leg. And, um, they went through the bush— in a jeep, because he wanted to show her, where it happened. And then they crossed a river on a— in a boat, and um, they spent the night at the spot where it happened. And in the, ah, morning she went into the water to fetch some water, and then a big crocodile attacked her. It had very big teeth and was about five metres long. Um, but fortunately Crocodile Dundee followed her to the water, and he— he jumped out of the bushes with his knife and he killed the cro—, crocodile. And then they went back to the town again, and she said, "Do you want to come to New York with me?" and he said, "Yes.")

A comparison of the two versions shows the following:

TABLE 8

	Errors per 100 words	Words per minute	Filled pauses with 100 words	Repeats per 100 words	Length in words	Time (min:sec)
English	0.4	134	5.2	3.9	230	1:43
German	4.2	96	5.1	2.3	213	2:13

The information conveyed in each language is very similar. As with Frank, the number of *words* uttered per minute gives the impression that Thomas speaks German much more slowly than English than is in fact the case, since German words are on average longer and contain more syllables. In the above speech samples, for instance, Thomas uttered 167 syllables per minute in English and 147 syllables per minute in German, i.e. his German was 88% as fast as his English. The speech samples are fairly typical of both his languages at age 13;0.

A look at the children's accuracy over time

To obtain a clearer picture of the frequency and type of errors made by the children over time, an analysis was made of taped material covering for Thomas the period from age 3;10 to 13;0, for Frank the period from age 3;0 to 11;1, and for Katrina the period 2;6 to 5;9. The starting points for each child represent the ages at which over 95% of utterances directed at me were in German (see Chapter 6). Each speech sample contained approximately 400 words and was considered to be representative of the children's speech in each language at that particular point in time. The results are given in Figure 1.

The average number of errors in Thomas's German for the period from age 3;10 to 8;0 was 4.7 per 100 words (Standard Deviation 1.0), compared with 0.7 per 100 words (SD 0.8) in his English; in the following five years, from age 8;0 to 13;0, he averaged 4;3 errors per 100 words (SD 1.4) in his German and 0.2 per 100 words (SD 0.2) in his English. Frank's German from age 3;0 - 6;0 contained an average of 8.3 errors per 100 words (SD 1.0), whereas his English contained only 1.5 errors per 100 words (SD 0.8); in the subsequent five years, from age 6;0 - 11;1, Frank averaged 6.8 errors per 100 words (SD 1.6) in German and 0.3 errors per 100 words in English (SD 0.2). In the period from age 2;6 - 5;9 Katrina averaged 7.6 errors per 100 words in German (SD 0.8) and 0.7 errors per 100 words in English (SD 0.4).

As can be seen in Figure 1, Thomas's German has, on the whole, been more accurate over the years than Frank's and Katrina's. A partial explanation for this difference may be Thomas's position in the family and the different circumstances arising from this.Being 22 months older than Frank, for instance, means that at the time Thomas was beginning to speak, he could virtually have my undivided attention, that is, without, as was the case with Frank, having to compete for speaking time with an already quite voluble brother. This was probably even more the case when Katrina was beginning to speak; she also did not have my exclusive attention, since her brothers, then aged 8 and 6, naturally also demanded a considerable amount of my time.

However, whilst Frank and Katrina may have had less opportunity to *speak* German with me on a one-to-one basis, they may have had more opportunities to

FIGURE 1

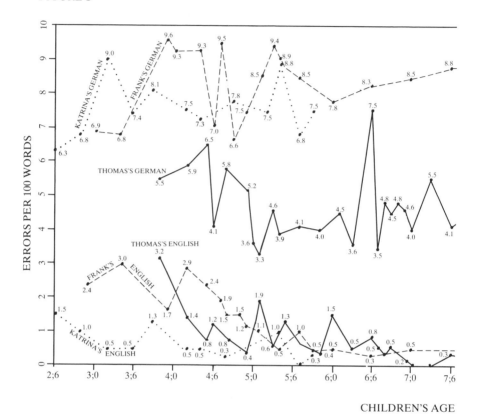

CHILDREN'S AGE

hear the language in the early stages of their speech development. Whilst Thomas initially heard only the German which I spoke to him, Frank could also listen to conversations between Thomas and me, and Katrina heard conversations between her two brothers and me. One would therefore assume that Frank's and Katrina's *understanding* of German would be at least equal to that of Thomas. But, as was seen earlier in this chapter in Tables 2 and 3, a comparison of the three children's receptive vocabulary at age 5 shows Thomas's to be a little superior and Katrina lagging a bit behind both brothers. Nevertheless, Katrina's receptive vocabulary in German is of a good standard, and she always speaks German to me, even if at times it is somewhat of a struggle for her to express more complicated matters fluently in German. Her active command of German thus exceeds, for example, that of Karla Leopold (Leopold, 1949b:155ff), whose position in her family was similar to that of Katrina. Karla was born six years after her sister Hildegard and, unlike her sister,

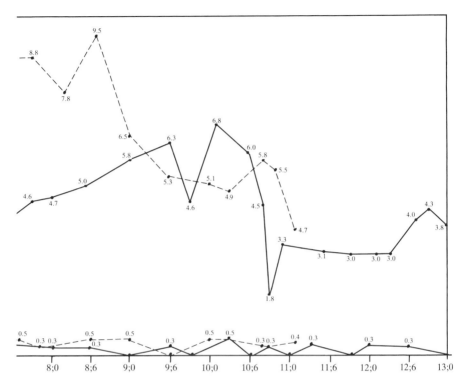

(years;months)

became a receiving bilingual only, able to understand most of what her father said to her in German, but always replying in English; her spoken German was very limited. This is one of the disadvantages of one parent representing practically the only source of one of a child's languages. Depending on family circumstances, it may be possible to combat this to some extent by arranging certain times when the younger child can be alone with the particular parent and can speak unhampered by sibling competition. I have been able to do this occasionally, first with Frank, then with Katrina.

Differing attitudes on the part of the children may also have something to do with their differing accuracy in German. Thomas has, on the whole, been more concerned with the correctness of his speech and more interested in and observant of any corrections which I suggest than Frank and Katrina.

Figure 1 also provides evidence of the linguistic benefits which can be derived from a stay in a country where the children's home language is the national language. Shortly before arriving in Hamburg at age 8;9,0 for a six month stay, his first in an all-German environment (see chapter 10 for further details), Frank was making 9.5 errors per 100 words in his German. After three months, his error rate had dropped to 6.5 errors per 100 words. Similarly, a month before Thomas's arrival in Germany at age 10;7,22 he was making 6.0 errors per 100 words in his German; after three months this had dropped to 4.5 per 100 words.

Most of the errors made in English and many of those made in German are the type made by monolingual children in either language as they progress towards mastery of the adult form, e.g.:

Thomas (3;9,21): What else Grandma said? (i.e. What else did Grandma say?)
Thomas (3;10,7): Was diese Männer machen? *(What these men do?)* (i.e. What are these men doing?)

(This utterance was not an echo-question, in which case Thomas's word order would be correct, but simply an initial enquiry, where normal German would require *"Was machen diese Männer?"*)

Other types of errors seem to arise specifically because the children have two languages, the grammatical systems of which influence each other to a certain degree, in other words, because of what Uriel Weinreich (1953:1) calls "interference", and what Michael Clyne (1967) prefers to refer to by the more neutral term "transference". As will be shown in the following discussion, it is not always possible to decide whether an error in one language is due to the influence of another language. Nevertheless, it does seem clear that a certain proportion of the errors made by Thomas, Frank and Katrina can be attributed to this influence.

Types of errors and reasons for their occurrence

In the *English* of the three children the most common type of error until age 6;0 was the use of incorrect verb forms, usually analogical past tenses, e.g.:

Katrina (4;4,23): Graeme *catched* the ball.
Frank   (4;4,28): I *drawed* a big goanna.
Thomas (4;2,16): Peter *throwed* the clay pigeon real high.

Errors in verb forms account for an average of 40.7% of Thomas's, 35.3% of Frank's, and 51.9% of Katrina's errors in that period.

The next easily definable type of error in English until age 6 was, for Thomas, word order, although this made up an average of only 4.9% of all errors. For Frank and Katrina, the second most common type of error was semantic transference (explained a little later in this chapter), comprising 13.7% and 14.8% respectively of their errors. Other types of errors in the children's English were so varied that no one type constituted more than 2% of the total errors. After age 6, errors in the children's English have been minimal, with few deviations from the adult standard language. Their English is practically indistinguishable from that of their monolingual peers; it is only the observant listener who can very occasionally detect some slight influence from German in their English.

The main types of errors made by the children in their German are show in Table 9. These different types of errors will be explained and discussed below.

Syntactic transference

Syntactic transference is defined by Michael Clyne (1967:19) as "the taking over by one language of a sentence pattern or system of inflections of the other language".

(a) Case and gender

The majority of errors made by Thomas, Frank and Katrina are errors of case and/or gender; in most speech samples such errors make up over 50% of the errors made. Indeed, the gap between the children's accuracy in English and German would be reduced considerably if German did not have three genders and a complicated case system (compare, for example, German's much simpler Germanic cousin, Afrikaans).

The following sketch, though a simplification of the situation, will give an idea of how complex the German system is in comparison with English: German has 6 words for English *the,* and the decision as to which is required in a particular instance is made on the basis of whether the following noun is *masculine, feminine, neuter* or *plural* (and gender, as a rule, follows no logical system, e.g. *Löffel* [=spoon] is masculine, *Gabel* [=fork] is feminine, *Messer* [=knife] is neuter), and in which of four cases (nominative, accusative, genitive and dative) the noun is. The six words for *the* are: *der* (masculine nominative singular, feminine dative singular, feminine genitive singular, genitive plural), *die* (feminine nominative/accusative singular, nominative/accusative plural), *das* (neuter nominative/accusative singular), *den* (masculine accusative singular, dative plural), *dem* (masculine/ neuter dative singular), *des* (masculine/neuter genitive singular).

TABLE 9

Child/ (Age)	Types of errors in German				
	Gender/ Case	Verb form	Word order	Semantic transference	Lexical transference
Katrina (2;6–5;9)	63.3% (SD 12.5)	9.8% (SD 10.3)	8.5% (SD 7.0)	5.5% (SD 12.9)	4.0% (SD 4.6)
Frank (3;10–6;0)	37.8% (SD 9.1)	14.1% (SD 7.0)	13.5% (SD 7.9)	9.2% (SD 5.1)	7.1% (SD 6.4)
Thomas (3;10–6;0)	52.8% (SD 14.8)	12.8% (SD 10.3)	4.8% (SD 5.1)	11.6% (SD 7.4)	6.8% (SD 7.9)
Frank (6;0–11;1)	61.0% (SD 12.8)	13.4% (SD 10.6)	8.4% (SD 5.0)	10.0% (SD 8.9)	0.8% (SD 1.2)
Thomas (6;0–13;0)	58.9% (SD 12.5)	6.4% (SD 6.0)	9.3% (SD 9.5)	10.0% (SD 7.7)	1.6% (SD 3.0)

Thus in each of the following four simple sentences English has *"the* man",
whereas German requires four different words for *the*:

The man is old.	*Der* Mann ist alt.
I know *the* man.	Ich kenne *den* Mann.
I help *the* man.	Ich helfe *dem* Mann.
Despite *the* man.	Trotz *des* Mannes.

Monolingual German-speaking children obviously require much more time
to master such a system than English speaking children to acquire the very simple
English system. Could it be that Thomas's, Frank's and Katrina's difficulties with
this aspect of German are partly an attempt to "rationalize" the German system, to
make it more like English? After all, use of the wrong word for *the* rarely interferes
with comprehension in German. However, it is probably not plausible to attribute
the children's difficulties here to the influence of English. If that were the case, we
would perhaps expect at least one of the children to have gone through a phase of
using only *one* word for *the* in their German, but this has never happened.

In Thomas's case, until age 6;0 he assigned masculine gender to most neuter
nouns (but usually correctly marked feminine, masculine and plural), and ignored
most of the case distinctions. Frank "simplified" the system even further, generally
using *das* as singular (for all genders and cases) and *die* for plural *the*. Katrina's
system is different again: she uses all the German forms of "the", but not always
appropriately and with a certain amount of free variation (e.g. "the car" may
occur correctly as "das Auto" in one utterance and incorrectly as "der Auto" in
another); *den,* which is appropriate for *masculine* accusative only is often used as
an accusative marker for feminine and neuter as well.

I have made some attempts to bring the children's case and gender system
more into line with my own and that of Standard German. Between Thomas's sixth
and eighth birthdays, for instance, he was made aware of neuter nouns (e.g. through
play, such as quizzes, and through short writing exercises), so that by age 8;0 he
knew approximately the hundred most common neuter nouns, and, more often than
not, used them correctly in his speech. Similar methods had some success with
Frank, so that by his eighth birthday the three genders were present in his German.
The boys' six month stay in German (see chapter 10) also had a very beneficial
effect on modifying their gender and case systems in the direction of the standard
language.

(b) Word order

The word order of German and English differs in many respects, so that it is
likely that some influence of the one on the other will be evident in bilinguals'

speech. (This is confirmed by Clyne (1967)). The main ways in which German word order differs from that of English are as follows:

(i)   In a German statement sentence the verb occupies second position. This means that if the first word is not the subject, the subject then follows the verb, e.g.:

   Frank (4;4,28): Vielleicht ist er verletzt. (Literally: Perhaps *is he* hurt.))

(ii)   Certain German conjunctions (such as *weil* [because], *wenn* [when, if], *damit* [so that], etc.) require the verb to be placed in the final position in a clause, e.g.:

   Thomas (4;1,14) (looking at a life-buoy on a ship): Wenn jemand in der Wasser *fällt,* dann kommt ein Seemann raus und schmeißt das in die Wasser! (Literally: If someone in the water *falls,* then comes a sailor out and tosses that in the water!)

(iii) Certain German verbs (e.g. the so-called modal verbs such as *müssen* [must, have to], *können* [can, be able to], and *werden* [will] used to form the future tense) require a following infinitive to occupy the final position in the clause, e.g.:

   Katrina (2;5,2): Ich kann der Hund nicht sehen. (Literally: I can the dog not *see.*)

(iv)   German past participles come not after the auxiliary verb as in English, but at the end of the clause, e.g.:

   Frank (7;5,1): Eine große Tigerschlange hat Peters Hund gebissen! (Literally: A big tiger snake has Peter's dog *bitten* !)

(v)   Relative pronouns (*who, which, that*) cause the verb to occupy the final position in a clause, e.g.:

   Thomas (4;3,23): Ein Dolmetscher hilft Leute, *die* nur eine Sprache *sprechen.* (Literally: An interpreter helps people *who* only one language *speak.)*

(vi)   German has verbs which have a separable prefix which occupies the final position in the clause, e.g. *aufwachen* (= wake up):

   Frank (5;5,22): Er wacht sehr früh *auf.* (Literally: He wakes very early *up.)*

(vii) The normal order of adverbs or adverbial expressions in a German sentence is time-manner-place, whereas in English adverbs of place usually take precedence, e.g.:

Katrina (5;9,16): Wir fliegen am 19. Dezember nach Tasmanien. (Literally: We fly on 19 December to Tasmania, cf. normal English: We're flying to Tasmania on 19 December.)

Of course, various combinations of the factors mentioned in (i)–(vii) may also occur. For example, the following utterance combines the rules of (ii), (iii) and (iv):

Thomas (4;7,21): Ich habe Frankie gesagt, er muß das hier halten, damit das warm bleibt. (Literally: I have Frankie told, he must this here hold, so that this warm stays.)

As can be seen, the potential for the word order of one language to influence that of the other in a bilingual's speech is quite large. In the speech of both Thomas and Frank, the transference of word order patterns is predominantly in one direction, namely from English to German. However, as can be seen in Table 9, errors in German word order make up only a very small proportion of the errors the children make.

Occasional influences of German word order on the children's English are also observed, and these can be attributed *exclusively* to types (vi) and (vii) outlined above, e.g.:

Thomas (5;5,2): Mum, I had my school jumper all day **on**.

Frank (5;5,23): Shane, Dad comes at eight o'clock **home**.

The children have not mastered German word order as well in German as in English, and most deviations from normal German word order seem to be word order patterns transferred from English. Thomas's one persistent word order mistake over the years, which is also made by Frank and Katrina, and which is still present in his speech, is in type (ii) above, but only in clauses beginning with *weil* (=because); instead of putting the verb at the end of the clause as required, he usually gives the clauses the same word order as English, e.g.:

Thomas (12;8,29): In Hamburg ist mein Deutsch besser geworden, weil ich **benutzte** es viel mehr. (In Hamburg my German improved because I **used** it a lot more.)

Interestingly, Thomas went through a period (about age 4;2–5;0) when he did consistently produce such *weil* - sentences with correct word order. Later, from age 10;7 to 11;1, during his stay in Hamburg the frequency of *weil*-sentences with correct word order also increased. If any of the children have to write a *weil*-sentence, they almost invariably use correct word order. They can also correct, without difficulty, one of their spoken *weil*- sentences, if requested to do so. A problem with *weil*-sentences, though, is that it is debatable whether not putting the verb to the end of the clause should be considered an error. There has been a noticeable tendency over the last few years for native German speakers in Germany to do this, too, at least in speech, if not in writing. This phenomenon has been commented on by Geoffrey Perrin (1982) and Wolfgang Butzkamm (1982). It is particularly likely to occur if there is a slight pause after the word *weil* is uttered. The present writer has also noticed that in some Germans' speech this is also happening in clauses introduced by *obwohl.* (=although) which traditionally also sends the verb to the end of a clause. An interesting example of a *weil*-sentence with non-standard word order occurs in a photo of a section of a 14-year-old girl's letter to the teenagers' magazine *Mädchen (=*GIRLS), 28 September 1983, p.12: "Mein Problem ist ganz schwierig zu beschreiben. Weil eigentlich *ist* noch gar nichts passiert ..." *(My problem is quite difficult to describe. Because really nothing at all has happened yet ...).* The whole letter is also *printed,* but in the printed version the editor has moved the verb *(ist)* to the end of the clause.

Nevertheless, until the children's six-month stay in Hamburg in 1984, the children's principal model of German was that spoken by me, and I use traditional word order in *weil*-sentences. Still, it does mean that their spoken *weil*-sentences are no longer conspiciously deviant and would be quite acceptable to many native German speakers.

Frank's and Katrina's word order is a little more deviant than Thomas's, but even so, mistakes in sentence types (i), (iii), (iv) and (vi) mentioned above are rare. Most of their errors occur in sentence type (ii). Apart from *weil* (= because) sentences, Frank at present (11;1) has problems really only with *daß* (= that) clauses. In the following example, which combines the two, he gets the *weil* part "right" and the first *daß* part wrong, the second *daß* part right, demonstrating neatly the fluctuation which occurs in his speech:

> **Frank** (10;0,0) (telling me what his maternal grandmother has just told him on the telephone): Oh, sie hat nur gesagt, daß sie *hat* ihr Programm verpaßt, weil sie am Schlafen *war,* Bert, und, ah, daß Opa ein Eis *macht. (Oh, she just said that she missed her program because she was asleep, Dad, and, ah, that Grandpa is making an ice-cream.)*

Katrina at present (5;9) has problems with word order in most of the types of sentences possible in (ii) above, i.e. with other conjunctions, too (e.g. *wenn* (when, if); they are often deviant, but not invariably so.

(c) Plurals

One area where errors would be expected to be quite frequent in the children's German is in forming the plural of nouns, yet in this respect their German is surprisingly accurate. In English, forming the plural is relatively simple, it being in most cases phonologically conditioned, that is, the final sound in a noun determines whether the plural is pronounced /z/, /s/ (both spelt -s) (e.g. dog—›dogs, cat—›cats) or /∂z/ (spelt -es) (e.g. bush—›bushes). There are not many exceptions: sheep—› sheep, goose—›geese, plus a few others. In contrast, the formation of the plural in German is quite complex and is not phonologically conditioned. There are, depending on the criteria for classification, about a dozen different ways of making nouns plural, e.g.:

1. +e	: Hund	→Hunde	(dog[s]);	2. +¨e	: Hut	→Hüte	(hat[s]).
3. +er	: Rind	→Rinder	(cow[s]);	4. +¨er	: Loch	→Löcher	(hole[s]).
5. +en	: Uhr	→Uhren	(clock[s]);	6. +n	: Eichel	→Eicheln	(acorn[s]).
7. +—	: Zimmer	→Zimmer	(room[s]);	8. +¨	: Vogel	→Vögel	(bird[s]).
9. +ien	: Reptil	→Reptilien	(reptile[s]);	10. +s	: Pulli	→Pullis	(sweater[s]).

Thomas, Frank and Katrina did make errors on their way to mastering German plurals, but, in view of the complexity of the German system, the number of errors was surprisingly low — in most of the speech samples analysed they simply do not occur. Most of the errors which are made are due to the addition of an -n to the plural forms 1–4 and 7,8 given above, e.g.:

Frank (5;0,3): Sie haben keine Kleidern (instead of Kleider). *(They have no clothes.)*

But this is most probably because the children do sometimes hear an -n added to these plural endings, but *only* in the dative case, e.g. in diesen Kleidern (in these clothes), and are still uncertain as to when the -n should be added and when not. Such errors are thus more errors of case than of plural formation. Influence from the English plural ending -s has also occurred, e.g.:

Thomas (3;10,7): Brauchen Straßenbahns (instead of Straßenbahnen) ein Gleis? *(Do trams need a track?)*

But such occurrences have been negligible.

Semantic transference

Clyne (1967) introduced this term to refer to the transference of the sense, but not the word-form, of a word in one language to a *cognate* (a word in one language related in origin and meaning to one in the other), *partial equivalent*, or *(near)-homophone* (a word sounding [nearly] the same in another language). He found three types of semantic transference in the speech of his informants, and these were also present in the speech of Thomas, Frank and Katrina:

(i)	the literal translation of an idiom or compound (also called a "calque" or a "loan translation"), e.g.:

> **Frank** (4;9,2): The peppermint is *all*. (From German *alle* which, besides meaning "all", also means "all gone", "finished".

> **Katrina** (5;4,2) (telling her grandparents a story): He cut off a bit of ice with his knife and then he threw it at the *ice bear*... ("Ice-bear" is a literal translation of *Eisbär*, German for "polar bear".)

(ii)	the transference of the meaning of a word in one language to a word in another which is *sometimes* an equivalent (also called a "loan meaning" or a "semantic extension"), e.g.:

> **Frank** (8;0,0)(telling what happened when he came too close to a cockatoo's cage): Mum, he tried to get my finger, and he *chopped* it! (The meaning of English "chop" has been extended to include "peck", presumably modelled on German *hacken* which is used to describe both what an axe does to wood and what a bird's beak does to unwary human fingers.)

(iii)	the transference of the meaning of a word in one language to a word form in the other language which sounds the same or similar but which is never an equivalent. Only a few instances of this type have occurred, e.g.:

> **Thomas** (4;4,9): I like this bread *while* it's very nice. (From German *weil*, which means "because", the sense intended in this sentence.)

> **Thomas** (5;4,20): Oh! Ich kann nicht sehen. Die Sonne ist sehr *breit. (Oh. I can't see. The sun's very BRIGHT.)* (The German word *breit*, whilst very similar in sound to English "bright", means "broad", "wide". The German sentence would require *grell* or *hell* to convey this meaning.)

On rare occasions the semantic transference may be made not by the speaker but by the listener, i.e. by decoding a word incorrectly because he or she thinks of a similar sounding word in the other language:

> **Mother** (reading *Puss in Boots* to Frank): "Good day, your Majesty, my master, the Marquis of Carrabas sent me with this *gift*."
> **Frank** (4;0,16) (highly amused): Why did he send that? Why did he send poison?
> **Mother** (also amused): Not poison. *Gift* means poison in German, but in English gift is another word for present.

In each of the children's languages, examples of semantic transfers are to be found, although they are far less common in English. (Tapes show, for example, that from age 3;10–6;0, Thomas made an average of 1 semantic transfer per 1,000 words of English, and 7 per 1,000 words of German; for the same age range, Frank averaged 2 semantic transfers per 1,000 words of English, and 9 per 1,000 words of German and Katrina averaged 2.5 per 1,000 words in English and 8.5 per 1,000 words in German. As the boys have got older the number of semantic transfers in their English has decreased even further, whilst the number occurring in their German has decreased less noticeably.

Most of the semantic transfers which occur in the children's English do not attract the attention of monolinguals because, whilst they may sound quaint, they are easily understandable and resemble deviations from the adult norm heard from monolingual children, e.g.:

> **Thomas** (5;0,6): He *goes me* on *the* nerves! (cf. German "Er *geht mir* auf *die* Nerven!" and Standard English "He gets on my nerves!")

> **Frank** (11;2,28): And then a massive big eel *bit on*! (cf. German : "Und dann hat ein riesengroßer Aal *angebissen*!" and Standard English "And then a massive big eel took the bait!")

Very few of the semantic transfers occurring in their English have been misunderstood by monolinguals. Many of the semantic transfers in the children's German likewise sound odd, but are readily intelligible to monolinguals, e.g.:

> **Frank** (11;2,3): Flötenvögel haben die Zikaden mit ihrem Schnabel GESPEERT. *(Magpies were SPEARING the cicadas with their beaks.)* (The English word "spear" can be used as both a noun and a verb, whereas its German cognate *Speer* is a noun only. Here, Frank has formed a German verb **speeren* (to spear) to match the English system; German would require *aufspießen.*)

But in their German there are more semantic transfers which would probably cause comprehension difficulties for a monolingual speaker, e.g.:

> **Frank** (10;3,8) (recalling an incident with our car): ... und du hast deine Lichter angelassen, und der Batterie war **PLATT**, und ... *(... and you left your lights on and the battery was FLAT, and ...)* (Frank is using German *platt* like English "flat". *Platt* can mean "flat", in the sense "having a level, even surface" (e.g. land), and also in the sense "deflated" (e.g. tyre), but it cannot be used to mean "drained of electricity"; in that sense of "flat", German requires *leer* (= empty).)

There are a number of possible reasons for the occurrence of semantic transfers in the children's two languages. Firstly, they may occur because of a vocabulary gap in one language. For example, Thomas, at age 3;10,24 used

Geleefisch, a literal translation of *jellyfish*, the correct *Qualle* being not yet known. Or the word may be known but not come readily to mind, e.g. Frank's (5;3,11) use of *Sternfisch*, a literal translation of English *starfish*, although the correct German *Seestern* (literally SEA STAR) had been used frequently in conversations the previous day.

Secondly, the type of semantic transfer described in category (ii) above is difficult to avoid completely, since it is quite rare that one language has a word which has a single equivalent covering exactly the same semantic range in another. Often one word in one language may have several meanings, each of which requires a different word in the other language.

There is also considerable motivation for the children at times to resort to the use of semantic transfers, particularly in their German. Firstly, they are a means of avoiding lexical transfers which I discourage and which they do not like particularly themselves. Secondly, the chances of success between two languages such as English and German are quite good, e.g. at age 5;0 Thomas first heard *Teppichschlange (Morelia argus)* in German and "rock kangaroo" *(Petragale)* in English and simply translated them literally as "carpet snake" and *Felsenkänguruh*, which, in this case, happened to be the correct terms in the other language.

The unique flora and fauna of Australia present a particular vocabulary problem which is conducive to loan translation. Only half a dozen of the best-known animals have common German names, some using, as does English, a form taken from one of the Aboriginal Australian languages, e.g. *Dingo, Känguruh, Koala*, others a specially created German word, e.g. *Schnabeltier* (literally "beak animal") for platypus *(Ornithorhynchus anatinus)*.

But once one gets away from these well-known terms, the situation is more difficult, as can be seen in the following incident. Thomas (5;1,30), playing outside near the wood-heap at his grandparents' holiday home, had been warned by his grandfather to watch out for jackjumpers. (Jackjumpers [*Myrmecia pulosa*], also called jumping jacks and well-known to Australians, are quite ferocious ants, about 1.3 cm long, which are capable of inflicting a very painful sting. They are aggressive and will attack anything or anyone that disturbs them, sometimes jumping through the air to make their attack, hence their common name in Australian English. Since, with their larger relatives, the bull ants [*Myrmecia forficata*, etc.], they belong to a distinct subfamily of ants, the Myrmeciinae, which is confined entirely to Australia, no common name exists in German.)

> **Thomas**: Bert, ich habe ein paar—ah, ein paar Ameisen gesehen. *(Bert, I saw a few—ah, a few ants.)*
> **Father:** So? Wo? *(Did you? Where?)*
> **Thomas:** Draußen, wo Opa Holz hackt. Man muß aufpassen, weil sie beißen. *(Outside where Granddad's chopping wood. You have to be careful because they bite.* Then, thoughtfully: Wie heißt, "jackjumper" auf deutsch? *(What's "jackjumper" called in German?)*
> **Father** (stalling for time, as he does not know): Ah—
> **Thomas** (spontaneously suggesting a literal translation of jackjumper): Johannspringer?
> **Father** (amused): Johannspringer? Das klingt gut. *(JOHANNSPRINGER? That sounds good.)*
> **Thomas**: Ja, Johannspringer. *(Yes, JOHANNSPRINGER.)*

From that time on, this loan translation *Johannspringer* became the family's German word for this fierce little ant. Another term formed in the same way and also suggested by Thomas was *Peitschenschlange* (literally "whip snake") to refer to a small snake *(Denisonia coronoides)*, known commonly in Tasmania as a whip snake.

This type of loan translation is an alternative to using the English word and is a procedure often followed by writers in German-language publications when referring to Australian fauna. Villwod, the translator of Bergamini's *The Land and Wildlife of Australia* into German, in which it appeared as *Australien, Flora und Fauna,* for example, translates tiger snake *(Notechis ater)* literally as *Tigerschlange.* Similarly, Rukshio translated *Magpie Island,* the title of a children's book by popular Australian author Colin Thiele, into German as *Die Insel des Flötenvogels* (= The Island of the Flute Bird). The bird referred to, *Gymmorhina tibicen,* is known generally in Australia as a magpie, although it is quite distinct from the European magpie *(Pica pica).* But in some parts of the country the Australian magpie is known, because of its singing ability, as a "flutebird", a literal translation of which the German translator has cleverly used rather than *Elster* (=*magpie*), which readers outside Australia would associate with the European magpie.

When referring to Australian wildlife, I normally use a German term, preferably one which seems to have gained some acceptance in German writings, e.g. *Hühnergans* (literally "hen goose") for Cape Barren goose *(Ceropsis novaehollandiae)* or *Beutelteufel* (literally "pouched devil") for Tasmanian devil *(Sarcophilus harrisii).* Although some Australian German speakers would find my attitude very puristic and unnecessary (e.g. Michael Clyne (1985:46) even refers to it a little exaggeratedly as an "obsession with purism"!), I still consider it an advisable procedure, as it gives the children a vocabulary which enables them to understand German publications and broadcasts about Australian animals and to converse about them with monolingual German speakers. This indeed proved to be the case during our six month stay in Germany in 1984: a small survey of friends and acquaintances revealed that using English words such as *echidna (Tachyglossus aculecitus)* (also known as 'spiny anteater') meant *nothing* to the average German without an extensive knowledge of English, whereas the existing German terms, e.g. *Ameisenigel* (literally "ant hedgehog"), *were* understood.

Communication is not hampered with Australian German-English bilinguals, many of whom refer to Australian wildlife by the English names, e.g. der *Platypus,* and may not be familiar with the available German equivalents, since the children know the English terms, too, and can use these if they see the German terms are not being understood. This also applies to the few family loan translations such as *Johannspringer* for "jackjumper".

Of course, finding an acceptable German term for certain Australian animals, etc., has at times involved lengthy, albeit interesting, searches of German books and articles referring to Australia, since English-German dictionaries deal only with those Australian animals which are reasonably well-known to Europeans. When such searching proves fruitless, and the particular word has no readily translatable parts to enable the creation of a loan translation (such as *Plattkopf* for the Australian fish "flathead" [*Platycephalus fuscus*]), the English term is used out of necessity, e.g. another Australian fish, the "trevally" [trɔˈvæli] *(Caranx georgianus)*, is called *Trevally* [trɔˈvali] in the family's German.

Another source of semantic transfers of the loan translation type are proper nouns. Shortly before his fourth birthday, Thomas showed a strong desire for there to be a separate word for everything in his two languages. He began translating English proper nouns into German and even insisting that I supply him with an equivalent if he could not think of one himself. If this could not be done, he contented himself with giving a German pronunciation to the English word, e.g. Hobart. This desire is understandable. After all, he already knew, for example, that London was said differently in English and German, and that Köln was Cologne in English. Thomas gave the Melbourne suburb Pinewood the name *Tannenholz*, a literal translation, and referred in German to his kindergarten teacher as Frau Niedrig *(Mrs Low)*. (Actually her surname was Chinese – Loh!)

Whilst at that stage such translations were made and accepted to satisfy Thomas's strong feeling that this should be done, they have, to a certain extent, carried on in the family as a kind of linguistic game from which the children (and their parents) have gained considerable amusement.

Michael Clyne (1967:112), in his study of Australian German-English bilinguals, refers to the translation of proper nouns as "hypercorrectness", and reports that 5% of his informants do this in an attempt to keep their German free of English lexical transfers. He cites words such as *Collinsstraße*, instead of Collins Street, as examples of hypercorrectness. However, every language does this to a certain extent, and many examples can be found in German and English publications meant for a monolingual readership. For example, in the German version of *Magpie Island* mentioned above, the Eyre Peninsula is referred to as *"die Halbinsel Eyre"*, and the well-known German zoologist Bernhard Grzimek (1971:13), in his book *Mit Grzimek durch Australien* (= Around Australia with Grzimek), uses a German translation for Kangaroo Island, an island situated off the South Australian coast:

> *Die Känguruhinsel* ist 144 Kilometer lang und durchschnittlich 40 Kilometer breit. *(KANGAROO ISLAND is 144 kilometres long and has an average width of 40 kilometres.)*

Some loan translations of proper nouns have a long history, e.g. most English-speakers when speaking English refer to the Black Forest rather than the *Schwarzwald*. However, this type of translation does not extend to the translation of people's surnames, although first names may be translated. In the case of my children there seems little harm in the use of loan translations for proper nouns, even of people's names. If not understood, they can give the name in the original language.

It has been seen that there is a good chance of what is in fact a semantic transfer turning out to be the correct word or expression in the other language. It is usually only when such direct translations fail that they attract attention.

In a small number of cases, although the children know the correct word, they continue to use a semantic transfer by preference, considering it a better way of expressing the concept in question, e.g.:

> **Thomas** (6;11,12): I use a knife to eat *mirror eggs.*
> **Mother**: Yeah— mirror eggs? What are they called? Fried eggs.
> **Thomas**: But I call them mirror eggs because they've got an orange mirror in the middle.

He persisted with "mirror eggs", a direct translation of *Spiegeleier*, until shortly after his eighth birthday because he considered it more descriptive than "fried eggs" which refers to the process by which they are cooked rather than to their appearance. Again this is harmless enough. Monolinguals find the few semantic transfers used consciously in this way quaint and, if they do not understand them, the children know and can provide the normally used term.

The actual number of semantic transfers employed by Thomas, Frank and Katrina is difficult to assess accurately. Most of the successful semantic transfers in their German are detectable because it is possible to monitor their linguistic input quite closely. With regard to their English, however, there is such a variety of input that it is often impossible to judge with certainty whether some words and phrases are semantic transfers from German or are due to the influence of other types of English heard by the children, as in the following example:

> **Thomas** (4;9,13) (at airport): Mum. The plane's *lifting off!*

In the children's family, and generally in Australian English, if "lift off" is used, it is used in reference to craft such as rockets which leave the ground vertically, "take off" being used for aeroplanes. Thomas's utterance could thus be regarded as semantic transference from the German "Das Flugzeug *hebt ab*." However, "lift off" is used in aviation language, particularly in American English, and the expression is beginning to appear in Australian English, e.g.:

> ... the plane suffered an electrical fault as it was about to *lift off.*
> *(The Herald,* 28.5.1979, p.1)

It cannot, therefore, be discounted that Thomas had already heard the expression at some stage.

A word of caution is thus perhaps appropriate here with regard to determining what is a semantic transfer from one language to another, particularly in children's speech. Some constructions which seem to be due to the influence of the other language may in fact also occur in the speech of monolingual children before they acquire the adult norm. Consider two examples from Thomas's speech:

Thomas (5;9,29): Jim, I've seen the man who changes into the Incredible Hulk.
Jim (a family friend): Oh, where did you see him?
Thomas: *In* TV.

Mother: How do you know how to make chocolate? Did you see it somewhere?
Thomas (5;5,4): Yes, *at* television.

In both cases English requires "*on* TV/television". But can it be said that the first example ("In TV.") is a case of semantic transference from German *im Fernsehen*, whereas the second example, "at television", is merely a deviation from the norm, an example of the correct usage not yet having been established? However, if Thomas's other language were French, a semantic transfer from "à la télévision", could be suspected for "at television" and "in televison" regarded as a mere deviation from the adult norm.

Semantic transfers, particularly in the speech of young children and espe-cially with regard to prepositions, can perhaps only be identified with any degree of certainty if the particular expression is used frequently over a period of time. Grimm (1975) shows, for instance, in experiments with 115 monolingual German pre-schoolers aged 2;7 to 5;11 and 22 first-graders, that 17.9% of all utterances containing locative prepositions were irregular in the sense of incorrect word choice. For example, the childen aged 2;7 to 3;6 produced such constructions as "in Straße laufen" (= run into street — German requires *"auf* die Straße laufen", literally "run on to the street"), "*im* Stuhl sein" (= to be in the chair — German requires "*auf* dem Stuhl", i.e. "on the chair"). A child aged 5;6 even said "geben *zu* dir" (= give *to* you — where German does not use a preposition at all), cf. Thomas (4;1,2): Wer hat das *zu* dir gegeben? (= Who gave that *to* you?). If these particular constructions had been produced by German-English bilingual children, there is a strong likelihood that they would have been classified as semantic transfers from English.

Similarly, Horgan (1978) gives examples of passives produced by 5–13 year-old monolingual speakers of English which contain the prepositions *of* and *from*, instead of *by* to denote the agent, e.g.: "They got shot *from* Japanese". If the sentences had been produced by an English-German bilingual, the deviant propositional usage would probably have been attributed to interference from German *von*, the preposition used to denote the author or doer of a deed in German passives, but which is also used in other constructions where English would require *from* or *of*.

Semantic transference, particularly in the form of loan translation, is one way in which German, English and other languages deal with new concepts originating in another language. Broder Carstensen (1965:237) states, for example, that both English *brain washing* and German *Gehirnwäsche* are literal translations of a term first used in Chinese, namely *hsi-nao* (literally "wash brain"). Carstensen documents many examples of semantic transfers from English which are now used and accepted in the German-speaking countries. A problem with attempting to avoid semantic transfers is that one can be too vigilant, rejecting, for example, words and expressions which seem to be, or in fact are, direct translations from English, but which are, or are becoming, acceptable usage. One example from a German childen's book will illustrate this. Michael Clyne (1967 and 1981) lists the following among his examples of semantic transference:

> **Student**: Das neue Flugzeug geht ... einfach in die Luft. *(The new aeroplane simply goes up in the air.)*

He explains that the German expression *"in die Luft gehen"* means not "to go up in the air" (i.e. "take off") but "to blow up", "explode". Dictionaries support this interpretation. However, consider the following extract from *Das wunderbare Bettmobil* (= The Wonderful Bedmobile) by Achim Bröger and Gisela Kalow (Stuttgart: Thienemanns Verlag, 1975:13):

> Herr Hinzel schmunzelte nur, warf den Propeller an und GING mit dem Bett IN DIE LUFT. Über den Hausdächern flog er spazieren. *(Mr Hinzel just smiled, swung the propeller and WENT UP IN THE AIR on the bed. He went for a joyride over the roofs of the houses.)*

Here the expression *"in die Luft gehen"* obviously does not mean "explode", but is used in the same way as English "go up in the air".

However, there is no denying that some vigilance is required by parents to detect semantic transfers in their own and their children's speech, particularly those which would lead to misunderstandings with monolingual speakers of the language (e.g. using *breit* in German in the sense of "bright", when it means "wide"). This has remained the goal in my family.

Of the various semantic transfers which have occurred in the speech of Thomas, Frank and Katrina, most have been short-lived, either because they represent a momentary lapse, the correct form already being well-known, or because the children have then heard the correct term and adopted it. However, some semantic transfers have proved difficult to budge. In English, the two most persistent have been the use of *from* to include the meaning of *of* (as with German *von*), and the expression "Good that ..." from German *"Gut, daß ...",* as in "Good that I noticed it" (meaning "[It's] a good thing [that] I noticed it"). In the children's German, there are, as has been seen, many more instances of semantic transference, the most persistent being undoubtedly the following: *auf* + vehicle, modelled on English *on* + vehicle (e.g. *on* the bus) where German requires *in* (= in) or *mit* (= with) (e.g. *mit* dem Bus); the use of a preposition + adverb of place, e.g. *in da* from English "in there") where German requires *(da) d(a)(r)* + preposition (e.g. *d(a)rin* or *da drin*) as in older English *therein*; the use of *mich* or *mir* (= me) instead of *ich* (= I) in cases where English now prefers the object pronoun *me*, e.g. Who did it? *Me.*; difficulties with expressing *when* in German. English *when* can be translated in three ways: *wann* (used interrogatively and conjunctionally in the sense "at what time"), *als* (used to refer to a single occurrence or state in the past tense), and *wenn* (used to refer to the present and future and, if used in the past tense, to indicate a repeated occurrence, similar to English "whenever").

Thomas and Katrina have always used *wann* correctly, as has Frank from about age 4;6, but all three have, until recently, consistently used *wenn* for all other situations, including those where, as in the following example, *als* is required:

Thomas (5;1,21): Bert, hast du auch Schlangen gesehen, WENN du ein Junge warst? *(Bert, did you see snakes, too, WHEN you were a boy?)*

At present, Thomas (13;0) mostly uses *als* correctly, Frank (11;1) sometimes does, and Katrina (5;9) has still not started to use it. This failure to distinguish between *als* and *wenn* is most probably due to the influence of the similar sounding English *when*, although this may not be the full story. Firstly, it is often difficult for a child to deduce that *wenn* used in the past tense does not refer to a single action, but to one that is repeated. Secondly, just to make the matter more difficult, in German stories told in the present tense (as many stories for young children are) *als* is used to refer to a single event, as in the following example from the popular story *Jakob im Wald* (= Jacob in the Forest) by Ilse Christensen. (Reinbek bei Hamburg: Carlsen Verlag, 1976:25)

Es ist schon spät, ALS Jakob ins Bett geht. *(It's already late WHEN Jacob goes to bed.)*

Considering the fact that children pick up expressions from books and indeed get to know favourite stories practically by heart, it would not be surprising if the distinction between *wenn* and *als* became confused or that the two words came to be regarded by a child as synonymous and interchangeable. That it is *wenn* and not *als* which has then predominantly been used by the children *can* probably be attributed to its similarity to English "when". The rule for correct use is, after all, quite complex, particularly since the rule applying in normal conversational German differs from that encountered in storybooks. And for children living in a predominantly non-German-speaking environment storybooks represent a much larger percentage of their exposure to German than would be the case with the children in a German-speaking country.

The children show some awareness that semantic transfers are not always successful and often will utter them a little hesitantly while glancing at a parent for confirmation, or, as in the following example, explain in words they are sure of:

(I have just read Thomas (6;0,15) a chapter of an exciting adventure story and he is comparing it with a more sedate story being read to him by his mother, a story his mother has called "a bit tame after Daddy's". Thomas knows that German *zahm* is used like English *tame* to refer to animals which are not wild, but (justifiably) shows doubts about whether it can also be used in the sense of "dull".)

Thomas: Bert, Muttis Geschichte is ein bißchen ZAHM—ah, ist nicht so spannend. *(Bert, Mum's story is a bit TAME—ah, isn't as exciting.)*

If a semantic transfer is not possible because the particular term is not divisible into easily translatable parts, recourse may be had to what Ian Hancock (1977:64) calls *incoining*, that is, creating a new descriptive term from words (or parts of words) already existing in the language, e.g.:

Thomas (5;11,7) (watching children hurdling, a word he knows only in English): Das ist SPRINGLAUFEN, Bert. *(That's JUMP-RUNNING, Bert.)*

(Incoining is one of the means used by many languages to create new terminology when confronted with new phenomena, e.g. for "alcohol" the speakers of the Aboriginal Australian language Guugu Yimidhirr combined two existing words, *buurraay* [= water] and *gaga* [= poison] to incoin the term *buurraay gaga*, literally "poison water".)

Sometimes this procedure is followed even when a literal translation could easily be made of a word known in one language only, but it is suspected that the resultant loan translation would not be correct, e.g.:

Thomas (5;10,5) (to me when I come to break up a fraternal fight in the bath-tub): Bert, Frankie hat mich in der Hals getreten—da, in meine, ah voice—ah, SPRECHDOSE. *(Dad, Frankie kicked me in the neck—there, in my, ah, SPEAKING BOX.)*

"Voicebox" is the English model, and Thomas's word *Sprechdose* is what Uriel Weinreich (1953:51) calls a loan rendition, one element being translated literally *(Dose* = box), the other freely *(Sprech* = speak[ing]).

Lexical transference

Lexical transference is Michael Clyne's (1975:17) term for the transference in form and meaning of a word from one language to another, e.g.:

Frank (8;9,5) (buying ice-cream in Hamburg): How many *Kugels* (= scoops) are you going to get, Tom?

In the speech samples of Thomas, Frank and Katrina, lexical transfers have been counted as errors (except in cases where no equivalent exists in the other language); their speech in each language has thus been judged largely on its intelligibility to monolinguals (even though this is perhaps not fair.)

Speakers of all languages at times use words from other languages in this way, usually to fill a perceived or actual vocabulary gap. What begins as an impromptu use of a foreign word may then be accepted and adopted by other speakers and become part of the language as a whole as what is known as a *loanword* (its "foreignness" usually being removed in the process by "integrating" it, that is, by making it sound and function as if it were a native word of the language adopting it.) For example, when the British mariner and explorer, James Cook, landed in June 1770 at the mouth of the Endeavour River on the north-eastern coast of Australia, he and his companions saw for the first time a strange grey animal which had a long tail, resembled a greyhound, but which jumped instead of running (Haviland 1979:164). The Aboriginal inhabitants of the area (present-day Cooktown), who speak Guugu Yimidhirr, one of many Aboriginal Australian languages, referred to the animal as /gaɲurru/, which was recorded by Cook as "kangaroo" or "kanguru" (Dixon 1980:8). Thus the Guugu Yimidhirr word became the English word for this animal, "kangaroo". Subsequently, this word was adopted from English by most non-Australian languages, e.g. German *Känguruh,* Italian *canguro*, Indonesian *kangguru*, Afrikaans *kangoeroe*, etc.

A lexical transfer, as the term is used for the purpose of this study, differs from such a loanword in that it is not generally accepted as part of the other language: a person speaking English who uses the Guugu Yimidhirr word "kangaroo" is using a loanword, but if he uses the Guugu Yimidhirr word *dyaarbaa* (= snake) in his English, he is then using a lexical transfer, since *dyaarbaa* is not recognized as being part of English.

Lexical transfers are not frequent in the children's speech, mainly because I have never encouraged their use and, probably as a consequence of this, because the children themselves seem to want to avoid them if at all possible. Parents need to be aware that if they themselves regularly use lexical transfers from the dominant language of the community in their home language, their children will most probably unwittingly take them to be also part of the home language (e.g. see Michael Clyne, 1970:36), particularly if they are integrated into the sound and grammatical system of the home language. Einar Haugen (1972:10), the son of Norwegian immigrants in America, had personal experience with this:

...we never used any other word for a broom than the loanword *bromm*, and it was startling to me the first time I heard a visitor from Norway use the word *kost*.

The danger here is that an excessive number of lexical transfers may make one's speech difficult to understand for monolingual speakers of the language.

Lexical transfers occur in the following circumstances:

(a)   Because of a *vocabulary gap*. The children may have acquired a word for a particular concept in only one language, or have acquired a word in both languages but at the moment of speaking can recall only one and are forced to use it when speaking the other language. This is done consciously, the children usually indicating that they are using a lexical transfer by pausing slightly before uttering the word or by giving the word special emphasis, thus marking it off as an "intruder". This use of verbal quotation marks is also often a sign that linguistic assistance is being sought, e.g.:

> **Thomas** (5;4,23) (showing his mother his sore tongue): What's on my tongue?
> **Mother**: Show me. Is it a pimple?
> **Thomas**: It might be a GESCHWÜR *(ulcer)*. (He hesitated slightly before the word GESCHWÜR and gave a slightly embarrassed grin as he said it.)
> **Mother**: Oh, you mean an ulcer, do you?
> **Thomas**: Yeah, that's the word.

Linguistic assistance may also be explicitly requested, e.g.:

> **Thomas** (4;0,5): I'm just SCHRAUBing this on. (Pauses) What do you say for that, Mum?
> **Mother:** Screwing.
> **Thomas:** I'm just screwing this on — see?

Sometimes asistance may be sought with identifying a *suspected* lexical transfer, e.g.:

> **Frank** (4;6,9) (pointing at food being prepared by his mother for a party): Is that for Daddy's work people?
> **Mother**: Yes.
> **Frank**: I don't think they'll eat all of that. Then they'll PLATZ. (Pauses) Is that English?
> **Mother:** No, it's German. You say "burst" in English.
> **Frank**: Then they'll burst.

Occasionally, an attempt is made to "disguise" a lexical transfer by integrating it, making it sound and function like a word of the other language, e.g.:

> **Frank** (3;8,13): Daddy KITZLED me. (German *kitzeln* (= to tickle) has been adapted and used as if it were an English word.)

The children often make a definite effort, to avoid having to use a lexical transfer. Sometimes one is used somewhat reluctantly and then an explanatory comment added, e.g.:

> **Thomas** (4;0,7) (at beach): That's — ah — TANG *(seaweed)*, Mum — that's plants that grow in the water.

A lexical transfer may also be used and then immediately self-corrected, e.g.:

> **Frank** (3;11,8) (watching television, to his father): Warum wollen sie das Frau SHOOTEN [ʃuːtən] — (2 second pause) — schießen? *(Why do they want to SHOOT* [English] *— (2 second pause) — shoot* [German] *the woman?)*

One device employed by the children to avoid transfers is the use of circumlocution, e.g.:

> **Thomas** (5;3,4) (telling his mother about a great uncle who was blinded in one eye as a young man): Do you know when Tommy came out of the hospital he had a VER-, — ah, ah, ah, a piece of cloth over his eye?
> **Mother**: Oh, you mean a bandage?
> **Thomas**: Yes.
> (Thomas obviously has a mental block regarding the English word "bandage" and begins to use the German word *Verband,* but recognizes its inappropriateness and escapes from his dilemma by paraphrasing.)

Mimic gestures may even be resorted to in order to explain or avoid a lexical transfer, e.g.:

> **Frank** (4;9,20) (playing cops and robbers with his father): Mum, I hit Daddy BEWUSSTLOS *(unconscious)* — ah, ah, that's — (He whirls around, drops to the floor and closes his eyes. Then he says): But you're not dead.

(b)   A word for a particular concept is acquired in only one language, but the children assume that it is also the word in the other language, i.e. they are seemingly unaware that they are using a lexical transfer. This applies particularly if the word has a pronunciation which fits easily into the other language. This type of lexical transfer is more prevalent in the early years of speech, as seen in chapter 6, but also occurs spasmodically in later years. It is also the type of lexical transfer most likely to occur in speech to monolinguals, since the child is completely unaware that it belongs to only one of his languages, e.g.:

Thomas (4;4,2) (to his mother): Frank is two, ABER I'm four. (Thomas used ABER [= but] in both languages for about a month at this age, apparently oblivious of the fact that it was a German word only.)

However, such lexical transfers have caused few problems in the case of Thomas, Frank and Katrina since they are so few in number and it is rarely long before the children become aware of the situation, perhaps through a listener's failure to understand or by having it pointed out by their parents.

An interesting aspect of this type of lexical transfer from German has been that not only do the children not realize initially that they are not also English words, but occasionally monolingual English-speaking playmates have taken them to be English and used them, e.g.:

Playmate (age 6) (holding a stick upright in his hand): I've got a FACKEL [fakl] so I can see.

A *Fackel* is a torch, a burning piece of wood used as a light. However, in Australian English "torch" is also used to mean a small battery-powered electric lamp (American English "flashlight", German *Stablampe* or *Taschenlampe)*. Thomas and Frank consistently used "torch" to refer only to the electric lamp, but for the quite different object, namely the burning torch, used the German *Fackel*, the word they had first heard to describe this object and which was adopted by their friend. The children only slowly accepted that English "torch" could have both senses.

(c)   A lexical transfer thus may be used for what the child considers to be greater precision, that is, to make a distinction in one language which is normally not made in the other, as in the use of *Fackel* above. In fact, this can be a useful way of ensuring that a listener (at least a bilingual listener) understands which sense of a word is intended.

(d)   Michael Clyne (1967:71) gives as one of the main causes of the use of lexical transfers in the German of German-speaking immigrants in Australia the fact that they are confronted in their new country with many concepts which (i) they did not know of (ii) which did not exist in their homeland (e.g. "brick veneer home"), or (iii) which do not correspond exactly to what they understood by the nearest German equivalent (e.g. the Australian "drover", "rounding up" sheep on horseback, is seen as different from the German "shepherd" with a crook [*Schafhirt* or *Schäfer*] "tending" sheep on foot). This last type (iii) has not been a problem for my own children in Australia since their German has been acquired principally in an Australian context; for them *Schäfer* are simply people who work with sheep, whatever their appearance or wherever they may be. However, during their stay in Germany in 1984 the children did use a number of lexical transfers from German in their English (to their mother and each other) to refer to things which they saw as having no exact equivalent in Australia, e.g. *Imbißstube*, which could be translated into English as "snack bar" but which, because of its appearance and the types of food available, was seen as distinct from the nearest Australian equivalent. However, in conversations with monolingual English speakers such words were translated to the closest English term or explained: "That's a sort of 'snack bar'..."

Sometimes (type (i) above), a word does exist for a particular concept but is not known, so that a lexical transfer (or perhaps a semantic transfer — see previous section) is unavoidable; it may be replaced by the "native" term when it is discovered. (See the discussion under "Semantic Transference" on names for Australian fauna.) I myself had, for example, until 1984 referred in German to the drink made by mixing beer with lemonade either as *Shandy* or, to avoid this, *Bier mit Limonade* ; then in Hamburg I learnt that the drink is called *Alsterwasser* (and in Munich in 1986 that in the south it is called *Radler.*) Finding an adequate vocabulary does, it is true, require a certain amount of effort, but this can be a satisfying and rewarding pursuit. These sentiments are shared by Robert Lowie (1945:21), the Austrian-born American ethnographer, in his account of his and his sister's experiences growing up as bilinguals in the USA:

> ... in extending my English vocabulary I remained restive until I had learnt the proper German equivalent. This was a formidable undertaking, for, especially when travelling in the West and Canada as an ethnographer, I encountered many things that did not exist in Vienna as I had known it or among New York Germans, e.g., stern-wheelers and narrow-gauge railroads. It gave me a peculiar thrill to learn that they were rendered *Heckraddampfer* and *Schmalspurbahn*, and to the present day a never-failing source of pleasure has been to discover such terms as *Durchschlag* ("carbon copy"), *Kotflügel* ("fender"), and *umschalten* ("to shift gears").

However, sometimes an object or concept which exists in one language and therefore has a word to describe it, does not exist in the other, so that one has to use a lexical transfer (or perhaps, if the parts of the word are translatable, a loan translation). This may be necessary with regard to fauna and flora, food,sport, etc. Consider the following example:

> **Katrina** (5;9,23) (looking at a picture): Hm, ich mag LAMINGTONS, sie sind so lecker. *(Yum, I like LAMINGTONS, they're so nice!)*

Here Katrina really has no choice but to "borrow" the English word into her German to refer to the popular Australian small plain oblong cakes which are dipped in chocolate icing and then rolled in dessicated coconut. Something known to all Australians is unknown in the German-speaking countries; if they did ever become popular in Germany they might well be known there, too, as lamingtons (or some inventive person might create a German name for them). Both English and German have done this, for example, with the foods *spaghetti* and *pizza*, simply adopting the Italian words.

Similar difficulties have been encountered with sports such as Australian football which is only played in Australia; certain terms could be found in, and adapted from, related sports with an existing German terminology e.g. *Sprungtritt* from rugby for "drop kick", *Flachpaß* from soccer for "stab pass" and *Sprungball* from basketball for "ball-up"; but other terms e.g. "ruckman" have had to be taken over from English.

To sum up, then: a good policy for parents to follow would seem to be: avoid lexical transfers if you can (i.e. don't adopt a defeatist attitude like that expressed by Hofmann (1957:16) who regards the use of English words in German in an English-speaking environment as unavoidable, even for quite common concepts such as "car" and "library"), but at the same time be aware that they will at times be unavoidable. If you do this, your children's (and your own) speech will remain completely intelligible to monolingual speakers of the language!

The children's attitude to English loanwords used in German

Since the Second World War the influence of English on German has been great. Many words have been taken into German from English which are now more or less accepted as part of that language, e.g. *okay, Skateboard, Computer*, etc. An amusing side effect of Thomas, Frank and Katrina being encouraged not to use, if possible, English words when speaking German, has been their reluctance to use such English loanwords if what they regard as a genuine German word is available. Einar Haugen (1956:55) calls this phenomenon "negative interference" which occurs when bilinguals avoid acceptable native terms because they sound too much like certain foreign terms. In the case of Thomas, Frank and Katrina, these loanwords prove to be a problem only when they refer to a concept for which the children have first acquired a "native" German word, as can be seen in the following example:

> (Thomas (4;10,1) and I are reading about an airport in the KINDERDUDEN (Mannheim, 1970), a children's illustrated dictionary.)
> **Father** (reading): "Was has du denn da eigentlich in der Hand?" fragt der Vater ... ("What's that you've got in your hand?" asks his father...) "Na, mein TICKET natürlich! ..." antwortet Peter. ("Why, my TICKET of course! ..." Peter replies.)
> **Thomas** (looking at me increduously): Du hast "Ticket" gesagt. (You said "ticket"!)

The English word "ticket" is now frequently used in German, pronounced practically the same as in English, but virtually only to refer to an air ticket, for which concept Thomas had only ever heard *Flugkarte*. Other words of English origin used on the same page, such as *Cockpit*, did not provoke the same reaction since they were the only words he knew for these concepts in German. The children thus do not object to a word being used in German simply because it sounds and means much the same as an English word. After all, because of the fairly close relationship between these two Germanic languages, there are many familiar words which fall into this category, e.g. house/*Haus*, arm/*Arm*, ox/*Ochs*, beer/*Bier*, to name but a few. This fact is recognized by the children, e.g.:

> **Thomas** (6;2,0) (talking to his paternal grandfather): Did you know, beer (*Bier*) is a funny word because you use it in English and German.
> **Grandfather**: Yeah, English and German.

Even so, the children do seem to have a desire to keep the two languages as separate as possible, so that if there are two German words for a concept, one of which resembles the English, they show a definite preference for the one least like English, irrespective of the order of acquisition. For example, there are two words for "grapefruit" in German, *Grapefruit* and *Pampelmuse*, the first of which was the word used by the children and me in our German. However, when at age 7;6 Thomas discovered that there was also the word *Pampelmuse*, he commented, "Ich wußte nicht, daß es ein deutsches Wort gibt." (*I didn't know there was a German word.*) He was obviously happy to make this discovery and began to use *Pampelmuse* in his speech.

Basically the children have the same attitude today. Both Thomas and Frank, for example, were recently quite scornful of a Jerry Cotton story, *Du lebst zu lange, G-man.* (= YOU'VE LIVED TOO LONG, G-MAN!) (Stuttgart: Klett, 1980), which read to them and which to their mind teemed with English words (e.g. die Cops, der Highway, etc.), and they amused themselves by seeing who could produce the most outlandish German, e.g. :

> **Frank** (11;1,15): Die Cops driven ihre Patrol-Cars auf dem Highway.

In speech, the children's avoidance of what they regard as English words in favour of "native" German words (e.g. they never say *Sticker* like their friends in Germany, only *Aufkleber*) causes no communication problems. After all, they can understand such words when they hear them and are able to make themselves easily understood with their "more German" equivalents.

Phonological transference

Phonological transference is Michael Clyne's (1972:9) term to describe the transference of a phoneme or an allophone (or absence thereof) from one language to another. Put more simply, this means that a sound in one language is identified with and pronounced like the closest available sound in another language, e.g. a speaker of German, a language which does not have the /θ/ sound as in *"think"*, may identify this sound with German /t/ or /s/ and pronounce *"think"* as "tink" or "sink". In other words, phonological transference is what is perceptible in a person's speech as a foreign accent. Depending on the type and number of such sound transfers, as well as on the tolerance of listeners, communication with native speakers of the language may be hampered to varying degrees.

This type of problem is usually confined to persons who have become bilingual after the age of about 12. Children who acquire a language before this age, usually do so with no or very few traces of a foreign accent. Penfield & Roberts (1959) argue, as does Lenneberg (1967), that there is a physiological reason for this: the brain of the child has a plasticity which is lost after puberty; the brain of an adult is rigid and set. Scovel (1969), after considering the available evidence, also concludes that it is the nature of the human brain which is involved here:

> .... the onset of cerebral dominance, which seems to occur around the age of twelve, inhibits the ability of a person to master the sound patterns of a second language without an impinging foreign accent.

This may not, however, be the reason, since it has been argued in the meantime, first by Krashen (1973) and then again by Schnitzer (1978), that cerebral lateralization is complete well before puberty, perhaps around age 5, or even earlier. Schnitzer feels that the critical period of language development may be related to other maturational factors. Only future research will reveal the answer, but whatever it is, all researchers acknowledge that most people lose, after puberty, the capacity to acquire completely the sound system of another language. It should therefore follow that infant and child bilinguals will have much less difficulty than adults in acquiring a native or native-like accent in both their languages.

In the case of Thomas, Frank and Katrina there is, and has been, little phonological transference between their two languages. Most deviations from adult pronunciation in either language have been developmental rather than attributable to the influence of the other language, e.g. the difficulty with the consonant cluster /sk/, as in *skin*, which both boys pronounced as /s/ until they were almost 6 years of age, a difficulty shared with many of their peers. (Some others are mentioned below.) One problem, however, which the children have had with pronunciation in German may be attributable to the influence of English. At times the /l/ sound after vowels has tended to be velarized to some degree, resembling the "dark" *l* occurring after vowels in most forms of English. Consequently, the German word *bellt* (= barks) has sounded similar to Australian English *belt*, whereas most varieties of German require a "light" *l* after a vowel (the same sound which English has *before* a vowel, for example, as in "*l*ake".) After the children's six month stay in Germany in 1984 this problem largely disappeared, although it is still noticeable in Frank's speech.

Frank has also at times shown a tendency to pronounce English words which have been taken over into German and now belong also to that language (e.g. *Baby, Science-Fiction*) the same way as he does when speaking English. In some German words Frank also does not pronounce an initial /ts/ sound clearly, so that it sounds like /s/. He also often pronounces a short ü-sound long, so that a word like *füllen* (= fill) may sound like *fühlen* (= feel). From time to time, Frank's attention has been drawn to these features of his speech and at present (age 11) he is making a conscious effort to correct them.

When the children arrived in Germany for the first time in July 1984, adults were on the whole impressed by their pronunciation, although they could detect a slight foreign accent. Their peers were even more complimentary, just saying that their German accent sounded a little different from Hamburg German and like some other kind of German from somewhere in North Germany. Tapes of the children's speech as it was on arrival in Hamburg and as it was after four months were played to various native speakers in Hamburg and Aachen: there was general agreement that the slight foreign accent the children had at the start of their stay had become less perceptible.

The influence of the German sound system on the children's English has been minimal. From age 5;0 to 5;6 Thomas substituted the German voiceless *velar* fricative /x/ (the same as the *ch* in Scottish "loch") for the English voiceless *dental* fricative /θ/ (the *th* sound in "cloth") after the vowels *a* and *o*. So instead of saying [ba:] for "bath", he said [ba:x] (very similar to the German word *Bach* [= creek] which is pronounced [bax]).

Nowadays, virtually nothing in their English pronunciation reveals that they also speak German; only in a few isolated words is the influence of German suspected, e.g. Thomas's pronunciation of "episode" as "epizode" and Frank's pronunciation of "sumo" as "zumo" (in German *Episode* and *Sumo* the written "s" is pronounced as /z/). They also tend not to anglicise German trade names when speaking English, e.g. Volkswagen, but to retain the German pronunciation.

It should be noted here that just as children can understand what is said to them before they are able to produce similar utterances independently, they can also often clearly perceive, in hearing, differences between sounds which they do not yet make in their speech. To take one example: when Thomas was aged 4;5 it was noticed that he seldom distinguished between /t/, /k/ and /t ʃ/ when they occurred before a vowel in the initial position in a word, so that *talk, cork* and *chalk* were all pronounced by him as [kɔ:k] (the normal pronunciation of Australian English *cork).* A simple translation experiment, in which these words were interspersed among other words for translation, verified, however, that he clearly discriminated correctly between the words when listening:

> **Father:** Wie sagt man TALK auf deutsch? *(How do you say "talk" in German?)*
> **Thomas:** Sprechen. *(Talk.)* ...
> **Father:** Wie sagt man CORK? *(How do you say "cork"?)*
> **Thomas:** Ah, Korken. *(Ah, cork.)* ...
> **Father:** Und wie sagt man CHALK? *(And how do you say "chalk"?)*
> **Thomas:** Kreide. *(Chalk.)*

Adults should thus avoid imitating children's deviant pronunciation. Both Thomas and Frank, as well as other children mentioned in the literature (e.g. by Priestly, 1980) have reacted to such imitations with considerable annoyance and frustration and have, understandably, been reluctant to continue with the conversation.

Whilst children are often unaware that their own pronunciation deviates from the adult norm, they can sometimes detect that their pronunciation is not what it should be (although they may not be able to correct the defect). This can be seen in the following amusing incident which occurred at a stage when Thomas pronounced /s/ very much like / ʃ / (the *sh* of shoe):

> **Thomas** (3;7,26) (sitting on the branch of a tree while his mother watches): I sitting (pronounced with initial *sh* sound) in tree. (Then, realizing what he has actually said, as opposed to what he intended to say, he laughs and switches to German to explain his amusement to his mother): I sage kacken, Mum. *(I'm saying "shitting", Mum!)*

A possible danger to establishing bilingualism is for parents to be too critical of children's pronunciation in either language, particularly in the early stages. A child's failure to fulfil parental expectations regarding pronunciation may be attributed to the child's bilingualism and could be seen as a reason for discontinuing his or her bilingual upbringing. Research into children's language indicates that, whatever the language, certain sounds are mastered more easily and at an earlier age than others.

Menyuk, (1971:76) for instance, lists w, h, m, n, b, f, p, d, k, g, l, y as consonants generally mastered by four years of age, whilst t, z, v, s, ʃ(*sh*ip), ʒ(mea*s*ure), t ʃ(*ch*op), r, dʒ(*j*ob), ŋ (si*ng*), θ (*th*ink) and ð (*th*at) are given as sounds which are generally mastered *after* four years of age. The literature on child language (e.g. Priestly, 1980) contains many examples of the kinds of sound substitutions made by children before they master the correct sounds, e.g. /f/ for /θ/ (*f*ink for *th*ink), *t* for *k* (or vice versa) *t*um for *c*ome), *w* for *r* *(w*ed for *r*ed), etc. It is important that parents be aware that this is not abnormal and that most children will have mastered all the sounds of their language(s) by the age of six or shortly afterwards. In most cases, therefore, there is no need to become concerned about defects in young children's pronunciation or any reason to blame them on the children's bilingualism. The majority of the deviations in pronunciation will not be a result of bilingualism but will be the sort heard in the speech of monolingual children. Unfortunately, some parents seem to expect from bilingual children a level of phonological development ahead of that of many monolingual children of the same age. Bent Søndergaard (1981), for example, gives as one of the reasons he and his wife did not continue with raising their son bilingually in Danish and Finnish in Denmark the fact that "especially phonetically, the language development was remarkably late". However, if we look at the examples Søndergaard gives of this "late development" for his son at age 2;8 *(sic)* (e.g. *l* for *r, d* for *g, t* for *k*), it is clear that they are not really indicative of any significant retardation in the child's substitution of *t* for *k* (e.g. *toni* for *Conny*) is by no means unusual even in young monolingual children's speech, and is called by Priestly (1980) the "tum phenomenon" (from "tum" instead of "come"). Susan Beck (1979:91) reports on a monolingual English-speaking child who said *t* for *k* until he was nearly five. In the case of Thomas and Frank, both said a sound resembling *k* for both *k* and *t* in both English and German until just after they turned five. So probably the best advice for parents is to be patient and tolerant of children's efforts to master the sound system of the adult language. As in most things, some children, be they monolingual or bilingual, will simply reach this mastery more quickly than others.

To sum up, then: Thomas's, Frank's and Katrina's English is, at the time of writing, practically indistinguishable from that of their monolingual Australian English speaking peers in Sydney. The few differences detectable are not due to the influence of German but to the Tasmanian English heard within the family, which differs in some small details from mainland Australian English, e.g. they say [Iəl] for *eel* and [puəl] for *pool*, whereas their playmates say [əIəl] and [pəul]. The children's German contains, as has been seen, a few small deviations from normal German pronunciation, but these do not interfere with comprehension.

Communicative competence

To communicate effectively with speakers of a particular language, one needs not only to know the language but also to know how to function in the language in a culturally appropriate way. If one simply transfers the social conventions of one language into another, communication breakdown, to use Michael Clyne's (1977:130) terminology, or pragmatic failure, to use Jenny Thomas's term (1983), may take place, that is, what one says may have a different effect on the listener than was intended, e.g. a German-English bilingual of the writer's acquaintance leaves many a monolingual English-speaker a little bewildered by simply answering "Thank you" to their query "How are you?"; in German, "Danke" is a sufficient polite reply to the same question, whereas English requires an introductory "good" or "well". In some cases the result may not just be communication breakdown but communication conflict, e.g. when what is intended as a polite remark is interpreted as rudeness. In a case known to this writer, a German-speaking Australian teenager visiting Germany asked a middle-aged man at the counter in a post-office: "Hast du die neuen Briefmarken?" (*"Do you have the new stamps?"*) To her surprise and embarrassment, she was severely reprimanded for her impudence. The reason for this reaction (which is not evident from the innocuous English translation) is that for the English pronoun "you", German has an informal pronoun *du* and a formal pronoun *Sie*. School-age children in German-speaking countries address most adults who are not relatives with the formal *Sie* and until well into their teens receive the informal *du* back. To use *du* when *Sie* is called for is considered cheeky or insulting. But this unfortunate girl, accustomed as she was to speaking German at home in Australia only with her friends and family friends (and thus only using *du)* had forgotten that her question should have begun not with "Hast *du* ..." but with "Haben *Sie* ..."

This could have been a problem for Thomas and Frank when they first visited Germany at ages 10 and 8 respectively. (Katrina, at age 3, was still too young to be expected to use the formal *Sie.*) They had rarely heard *Sie,* except in stories and films, and had never actively used it themselves in Australia. Firstly, the formal *Sie* was obviously not needed when speaking to me. Secondly, partly because of the children's age and partly because of the situation in Australia, *Sie* had not been essential in communication with other German speakers living there; German-English bilinguals tend to use the informal *du* much more freely in Australia than in the German-speaking countries (perhaps as a mark of solidarity between fellow German-speakers, perhaps because of the greater degree of informality and much more widespread use of first names in Australia, and perhaps also because English, the dominant language of the society in which they live, has only one word, "you", for both formal and informal use). (Gertraut Stoffel (1983/84) has found much the same situation in a study of German speakers in New Zealand, a society very similar to that in Australia.) However, from their stories, Thomas and Frank did know what *Sie* was and roughly how it was used. To save them from possible embarrassing situations in Germany, in the three months before the family's departure from Australia, I got them to practise using *Sie* in role play. I assumed various roles, such as policeman, teacher, shopkeeper, etc., and the boys had to ask me questions. The use of *Sie* was also incorporated into their written exercises in German. This worked well, and from the very beginning of their stay in Germany they managed on most occasions to remember to use *Sie* when it was called for. Only Frank modified the system somewhat in that, whilst he addressed most adults appropriately with *Sie,* he addressed his best friend's parents exactly as the friend, Hendric, did i.e. with informal *du!* Fortunately, the parents were so easy-going and so taken by the fact that an Australian boy spoke German so well that they never mentioned this to him.

As already mentioned, communicative competence involves not only the language itself and how it is used, but includes behaviour which should appropriately accompany certain speech acts. To take but one example: it is extremely rare for children in Australia to shake adults' hands, but in Germany it is not unusual under certain circumstances. At age 3 in Hamburg, Katrina had to learn that the polite thing to do on greeting and taking leave of her kindergarten teacher was also to shake hands with her. This she had never had to do in Australia, since most German speakers in Australia quickly adopt the Australian system of virtually no handshaking with young children (even if they speak German). For young children in Germany not to shake the hand of their kindergarten teacher on arriving and departing would be considered impolite if it persisted; on the other hand, such behaviour in an Australian kindergarten would be found unusual and amusing.

It is difficult to separate a language from the culture(s) of the people who speak it. German books, magazines, films, etc., cannot but contain elements of German culture. Through these and discussions with their parents, Thomas, Frank and Katrina had become aware of differences in way of life, customs, beliefs, food etc. in Australia and the German-speaking countries (just as they had become aware of the differences between Australia and the other English-speaking countries from their reading, television, etc.). This awareness was to prove very useful on their arrival in Europe and it was added to considerably during their six months there.

Conclusions about the children's accuracy

Robert Politzer (1978) tested the reactions of 146 teenage native speakers of German to 60 test items, all of which contained an error of some sort. Using their responses, he drew up a list of what they considered to be the worst types of errors. These are, arranged in order from the most serious to the least serious error, as follows: (1) wrong vocabulary; (2) incorrect verb forms; (3) incorrect word order; (4) gender confusion; (5) faulty pronunciation; (6) wrong case. The three most serious categories of errors, as well as the fifth, do not feature significantly in errors made by Thomas, Frank and Katrina.

A parallel can be drawn between the linguistic situation and performance of Thomas, Frank and Katrina *vis-à-vis* Standard German and that of native German children who speak a German dialect at home. Reitmajer (1975) tested the speech and writing of 30 grade 4 children (approximate age 10 years) who at home spoke predominantly Bavarian dialect, a dialect differing in many ways from Standard German, the language of the school. These children made 11.8 errors per 100 words in speech and 16.3 errors per 100 words in writing. Of these errors, 61.9% in speech and 41.3% in writing were due to transference of features from the dialect to the standard language, e.g. lexical transfers from the dialect, such as *Schär* for Standard German *Maulwurf* (= mole). Reitmajer also analysed the speech of two other groups of children who were just about to start school (aged approximately 7 years). One group, which spoke both Standard German and the Bavarian dialect at home, made 8 errors per 100 words, whereas the group which spoke only dialect at home made 25 errors per 100 words. Since, according to a 1966 survey (Zehetner, 1977:19), 78% of the Bavarian population speaks dialect at home, mastering the standard language is not an insignificant problem for Bavarian schoolchildren, or for that matter for speakers of other dialects. Reitmajer's criteria for assessing errors in Standard German were somewhat stricter than those used to judge the speech of Thomas, Frank and Katrina, e.g. such widespread acceptable colloquial usage as the use of *raus* (= out) for *heraus* or *hinaus* was counted as an error. Even so, there is some similarity between the accuracy in Standard German of Thomas, Frank and Katrina and the bidialectal German children, a similarity which perhaps allows the three children's level of achievement to be seen in a more favourable light. In their case it is their dominance in another language, English, which affects their acquisition of German, whereas in the case of the German children it is their dominance in their dialect which affects their mastery of Standard German.

Measuring degree of bilingualism

Bilinguals are rarely equally proficient in every respect in their two languages: one language is dominant. Bilinguals usually perform better in one language than the other, although they are not necessarily more proficient in *one* particular language in all situations. For example, someone who is bilingual in German and English could have been trained as a mechanic in English and in this occupation may deal predominantly with English-speaking customers. As a result, his or her ability to discuss the functioning of a car engine in English might be superior to his or her ability to do the same in German. Yet, in some other contexts, his or her proficiency in German could be superior, for example, if he or she has a hobby which is associated primarily with the use of German.

The linguistic dominance of Thomas, Frank and Katrina was tested using the contextualized measure of degree of bilingualism employed by Martin Edelman (1969:175) to tap children's bilingual proficiency in several domains. Children are asked to name in 45 seconds, first in one language, then in the other, as many things as possible that can be found in the domains of family, school, church and neighbourhoood, the assumption being that they will produce more words in the language in which they are more proficient, or dominant. A ratio of language dominance is then calculated for each domain, using the formula:

$$\left(\frac{\text{Number of English words} - \text{Number of German words}}{\text{Larger of the two}} + 1 \right) \div 2$$

Results are given on a scale from 0 to 1, with 0.50 indicating "balance" between the two languages (i.e. that the same score was obtained in both languages, e.g. 16 words in German, 16 words in English). A result of zero would indicate *no* responses at all in English, while 1 would indicate that *all* responses were in English (i.e. none in German).

How Thomas, Frank and Katrina performed in this test at various ages can be seen in the following table:

TABLE 10

Domain	Score						
	Thomas 5;6	*Thomas 7;6*	*Thomas 12;6*	*Frank 4;0*	*Frank 5;7*	*Frank 10;7*	*Katrina 5;3*
Home	0.58	0.58	0.56	**0.44**	0.55	0.67	0.73
School	0.50*	0.67	0.50*	0.50*	0.55	0.55	**0.45**
Neighbourhood	0.56	0.56	0.50*	—	**0.47**	0.58	0.50*

The results indicate that overall the children are slightly more dominant in English: of the 20 scores in the table, 11 indicate dominance in English, 5 (asterisked) indicate balance between the two languages, and 3 (in bold print) indicate dominance in German. Some of the results are a little surprising, e.g. Katrina's score of 0.45 for the school domain; she was able to name 11 words in German and 10 in English, despite the fact that at that age she could talk more fluently about school in English.

Such word-naming tests can only be regarded as rough indicators of a child's language dominance. For the home domain, for example, Thomas was initially asked to mention in 45 seconds as many things as possible asssociated with the word *home* (or in German *Haus*). He named 19 items in English, 16 in German, which, computed as described above, gives a score of 0.58, indicating slight dominance in English. Martin Edelman, however, got the children he tested to react to the word *kitchen* as representative of the home domain. Yet in Thomas's case, when individual rooms were taken for the stimulus word, the results varied depending on which part of the house it was. For *kitchen,* for example, the result was 0.43, indicating dominance in German, whereas for *bedroom* it was 0.66, indicating dominance in English.

The results can also vary on a subsequent retesting a short time later. Even if monolinguals were tested on a particular domain one day and then retested a week later it is very unlikely that they would obtain exactly the same score on both occasions. It is, therefore, perhaps only considerable differences in performance between the two languages which can be considered significant (perhaps scores of 0.65 and over; 0.65 itself would, for instance, correspond to a score of 20 words in one language and 14 in the other).

Wendy's and my language dominance was also tested, with the following results:

TABLE 11

Domain	Score	
	Mother	Father
Home	0.75	0.42
Work	0.70	0.46
Neighbourhood	0.60	0.56

The results for Wendy, indicating a reasonably clear dominance in English, particularly in the domains of home and work, were as expected. Whilst she constantly hears German, and can speak it well, she has few opportunities to do so.

My own results were somewhat surprising, since they indicate dominance in German in the domains of home and work. I had been convinced that English was my dominant language and that I would perform better in it on all the word naming tasks. In view of the unexpectedness of the results, I had myself retested twice, but with no significant change in the results: in the home and work domains I still came out ahead in German. I was then tested with regard to various other settings, with the following results:

TABLE 12

Domain	Father's score
Zoo	0.42
Tools	0.45
Church	0.48
Supermarket	0.48
Linguistics	0.48
Fruitshop	0.50
Car	0.52
Family	0.52
Hospital	0.54
Kitchen	0.60

As can be seen, for zoo, tools, church, supermarket and linguistics I scored slightly better in German, for fruitshop I scored the same in both languages, and for cars, family and hospital I performed slightly better in English. These results are interesting, since I feel that English is my better language and I am more confident in using it, particularly at higher levels. However, the results are consistent with the nature of this particular task and the uses to which I put my two languages. Such a word naming task is something which I rarely have to do in English, whereas, as a teacher of German, I am frequently required to produce quickly lists of related vocabulary items for the benefit of students.

8 Biliteracy

A problem facing parents who wish to raise their children bilingually is the question of when, or if, the children should be introduced to reading and writing in the language not taught in the normal school system. "Just" speaking a minority language in the home may not be enough to assure its maintenance, and certainly not enough to develop it to a level approaching that of the majority language which children begin to read and write as soon as they start school. Once children can read, they are exposed to a wider range of language, to a greater richness of language than individual parents can possibly produce. This is particularly important for children whose main input in a minority language comes from their parents, or perhaps from only one parent. Moreover, it is psychologically important for children to be aware that their parents' language is also, like the majority language, a fully-fledged medium of communication, with its own literature, its own writing conventions, etc. Children tend to regard a language which they can speak but not read as not being equal to the language of the school which can be used for all functions.

However, there are many bilingual children who are growing up in communities where, sadly, no provision is made in the school system for one of their languages, who may speak that language well but be unable to read or write it. Smolicz & Harris (1977:98), for example, in their study of language use and maintenance among Australian students of various ethnic backgrounds, discovered that:

> The ethnic children's use of their native tongue in reading and writing was even more restricted than their ethnic speech patterns (...) Two thirds or more of the students... admitted they had very little or no competency in reading and writing their ethnic language.

Of 70 children of Polish-Polish parents, only 7% regularly wrote letters in Polish and only 1% regularly read books in Polish. Yet 83% of these same children spoke either only Polish or Polish and English to their parents, while *all* of them spoke Polish or Polish and English to their grandparents. Illiteracy in one of a bilingual's languages represents a considerable loss to the individual and to the community as a whole. Literacy in the home language greatly extends its use and makes possible its reinforcement and enrichment.

In their *Handbook of Bilingual Education*, Saville & Troike (1971:26) rec-ommend that a bilingual child should begin reading in his or her dominant language and that the transfer to a second language should not be made until initial reading skills have been well established, usually during grade two at school. There is considerable support for this recommendation in the literature (e.g. in Rosier & Farella's (1976) report on their research with Navajo-English bilingual children and in Kielhöfer & Jonekeit's (1983:59) assumptions.) However, there is evidence to suggest otherwise, e.g. from Percilia Santos's (1984) research (cited in Robert Lado 1987) into the reading achievement of low-income Spanish speaking 3 - 5 year old children in an early bilingual reading program in Washington. These children's performance on standardized reading tests was average or above average in Spanish *and English* compared to the norm groups at the end of kindergarten. The children were thus more proficient in reading two languages than monolingual children reading one. In addition, in their language development 94% of the children who were evaluated in their dominant language were found to be above their chronologi-cal age, and 63% of the children tested in their second language scored above their chronological age. Since these children belong to a group normally found to be below the US national norms in English, it may well be that their higher speech development was caused by their early reading experience.

But what can be done if, as is often the case, the normal school system makes no provision for such children? Some minority language groups have established Saturday schools and the like to teach literacy in their languages, and this may be a possibility for some families, although it will depend on the language involved and where a family lives whether anything like this is available. Another possible solution to this problem is for parents to teach their children to read (and write) at home. Indeed, some writers (e.g. Robert Lado, (1977), Chester Christian (1977) and Theodore Andersson (1981)) consider it advisable that minority language children become literate in their home language *before* entering school, which means, in most cases, that some sort of home literacy programme would have to be attempted by the parents. Readers, particularly those who live in countries where, by tradition, children are not taught to read until about seven years of age, and then only at school, may baulk at the idea of *personally* teaching their children to read at a *much younger* age *at home.* However, parents should not underestimate either their young children's ability to learn to read or their own ability to teach them to do so.

Research indicates that even very young children can learn to read, and many parents have already successfully taught their young children to read. Chester Christian (1977), for instance, reports that he taught his two children in the U.S.A. to read in their home language, Spanish; later when they began school they quickly learned to read English as well. Evidence is even emerging that early reading has a favourable effect on the development of a native language pronunciation in bi-lingual children of preschool age (Ana Montero, 1985, cited in Robert Lado, 1987).

Many parents who have taught their children to read have used the system suggested by Glen Doman (1964) in his book *How to Teach Your Baby to Read.* This book is well worth reading by parents wondering about the mechanics of teaching a young child to read. It is perhaps best read in conjunction with Felicity Hughes's (1971) book *Reading and Writing before School,* since she examines and suggests useful refinements and alternatives to the quite rigid procedures recommended by Glen Doman. She also has a useful chapter on teaching children to *write* in which she shows that preschool children's desire to be shown how to write words can be satisfied in a constructive and rewarding way. Although these two books deal specifically with reading in English, the techniques mentioned are, with a little imagination, easily transferable to other languages.

It should be pointed out, incidentally, that parents do *not* have to be linguists or teachers or have special training to be able to teach their children to read. Traditionally, this job has been left to schools, but that is more a matter of convenience than a necessity. In his helpful book *A Guide to Family Reading in Two Languages: The Preschool Years,* Theodore Andersson (1981) in fact, emphasizes that reading is learnt rather than taught, and that the best "teacher" often is a person who is intimately associated with the child and provides the environmental stimulation for learning. I have reported elsewhere (Saunders, 1984:3), for example, how a Turkish father who left school after fifth grade and who, as an immigrant in Australia, worked in a factory, taught his two daughters to read and write Turkish at home in the evenings after they had finished their English homework from school. Indeed, the present writer's mother, who left school after seventh grade, successfully taught him to read and write (English) at age six because at that time the family were the sole inhabitants of a small town 70 kilometres from the nearest school.

Derrick Sharp (1973:53), in his book *Language in Bilingual Communities,* also advises that children begin reading in their dominant language in order to avoid mental confusion. However, he does add that those children who have what he calls "genuine bilingual proficiency" should not be held back by this consideration. The present writer's view, based on his own research, is that as long as children are presented with written words and constructions with which they are *already familiar and whose meaning they know* from speaking or listening, there will be no distress or confusion, even if it happens to be the children's weaker language.

Al and Kay Past (1976, 1978) show that a functionally bilingual child has little difficulty in learning to read two languages simultaneously. They found that there was practically no confusion caused by learning to read two languages at the same time, far less, in fact, than there was in learning to speak the two. Their findings are supported by my own observations of Thomas, Frank and Katrina. Thomas first became interested in the alphabet at age 4;0, mainly through watching the television programme *Sesame Street*, and began asking about German equivalents of the letters. At age 5;3 he started school and began learning to read formally (in English). At the same time I introduced him to reading in German. The fact that the same letters may represent different sounds in each language rarely troubled him. Indeed, this knowledge stood him in good stead as he progressed with English reading and encountered such words as *cent* where *c* was no longer pronounced as in *cat*, etc. There was no perceptible adverse effect on his English reading. He read well for his age and has consistently been among the best readers in his class at school. In his school report which he received at the end of grade one (age 7;1), his teacher wrote the following comments:

> Thomas's reading comprehension is excellent ... In spelling his general word knowledge is very good ... He has a very good general knowledge and an excellent vocabulary.

At that time, his exposure to English reading was considerably greater than that to German, the latter being confined to half a dozen sentences which he read to me each evening. Nevertheless, it seems that the skill of reading, practised constantly in English at school, transferred readily to his other language, since his ability to read German was roughly equal to his reading ability in English. German does also have an advantage over English in that its writing system has a more regular correspondence between letters and sounds. This advantage is shared with some other languages such as Finnish, Malay, Pitjantjatjara and Spanish. Gaarder (1967) reports that, because of this, children in Spanish-speaking countries master reading and writing much more quickly than their counterparts in English-speaking countries.

Both Thomas and Frank began writing occasional simple words in German and English before commencing school. After starting school, their German writing was continued at home, in almost daily doses. This is a practice which has been kept up until the present day with both boys, and also with their sister (although in her case learning to read and write occurred *before* she started school — this will be discussed below). The children have writing exercise books, which I have prepared for them and in which about 4–5 times a week they write several sentences. Naturally, the nature and complexity of the reading and writing tasks required changes as the children grow older. Initially, their writing exercises usually involved answering questions and/or selecting and writing out the correct sentence to describe a picture. Other exercises included simple crossword puzzles and short dictations. As their proficiency has developed, more complicated exercises have been able to be interspersed with those just mentioned, e.g. exercises which practise grammatical features with which they have difficulty (gender, case, etc.), free writing exercises (e.g. writing about an outing or an interesting film, summarizing an article or book they have read), and even occasional translations between their two languages, usually to contrast certain constructions in the two languages and thus consolidate German expressions which differ from their English counterparts but which in the children's speech have shown the influence of English e.g. Where is he going? (In English one can say "*Where* is he?" and "*Where* is he going?", and all three children have at times tried to use *wo* in the same way in German, whereas if *where to* is meant, German requires *wohin*, not just *wo*; thus "Where is he going?" is *Wohin* geht er? or *Wo* geht er *hin*?, not just *Wo* geht er?))

A facsimile of a page from Katrina's exercise book when she was aged 5; 5 is shown in Figure 2; it is shown in its uncorrected form, and an English translation has been added for readers who do not know German.

It has been found that by making the writing tasks reasonably relevant and interesting or amusing, and by restricting them in length so that they can be completed in about 5–15 minutes, the children's interest has been sustained and progress made.

As far as spelling is concerned, the children write German which at times is nearly as accurate as their English, although the gap between the two would probably be wider if English had a more consistent spelling system. Very few of the spelling errors which the children make in either language could be attributed to interference between the two languages. Right from the start they became aware of the differences between the two writing systems (e.g. that a sound could be written one way in one language and another way in another, such as English *sh* (e.g. fi*sh* and German *sch* (e.g. Fi*sch*) and accepted these differences just as they had long ago accepted that each language had different names for things. This rarely caused any confusion.

There is even evidence that children will not be confused by learning to read in two *different scripts* at the same time. Bonnie Kupinsky's (1983) study of two kindergarten classes in an English/Hebrew bilingual school in Detroit in the United States of America is encouraging in this regard. Hebrew, like Arabic, a Semitic language, also has a different script from English and is also written from right to left. In the Detroit school, instruction is given in Hebrew in the morning and in English in the afternoon. At the end of the nine-month programme, the children's ability to read was similar in Hebrew and English, although, understandably, somewhat better in English, their dominant language and that of the general non-school environment. The report concludes with the words:

> This study has demonstrated the success of beginning a bilingual reading programme in kindergarten. The children acquired reading skills in both their dominant and second language... Even at kindergarten level, children are capable of learning to read two languages taught concurrently. The results suggest that reading instruction in two languages may be introduced at early ages.

FIGURE 2   *Sample page from Katrina's writing exercise book (age 5;5).*
(Mistakes not corrected. English translation added for German and Malay.)

Beantworte folgende Fragen: *(Answer the following questions:)*

Wo sind wir gestern hingefahren? *(Where did we go yesterday?)*

.....Zu...dem..Strant.........✓...........(To the beach)

Was hast Du dort gemacht? *(What did you do there?)*

...Ich.haber..gesschwommen.....✓....(I went for a swim)

Wie war das Wetter? *(What was the weather like?)*

.......sehr..Sonnich.........✓.....................(Very sunny)

Warum ist Frank heute nicht zur Schule gegangen? *(Why didn't Frank go to school today?)*

....Wei.l.er..Krank.Ist...........✓............(Because he's sick.)

Was ist das Gegenteil von **seicht**? *(What's the opposite of* shallow?)

...............tief..........✓...........................(Deep)

Was bedeutet *flüstern*? *(What does* whisper *mean?)*

..........leise..sprechen.....✓.....................(To speak quietly)

Bahasa Malaysia untuk Katrina *(Malay for Katrina)*

Siapa nama boneka Katrina? *(What's your doll's name?)*

............Susanne......✓.....................(Susanne)

Siapa nama anjing nenek? *(What's Grandma's dog's name?)*

...............Jock........✓.............................(Jock)

Mobil kakek putih atau biru? *(Is Granddad's car white or blue?)*

.........biru.........✓...............................(Blue)

Mal einen Elefanten, der Blätter frißt *(Draw an elephant which is eating leaves.)*

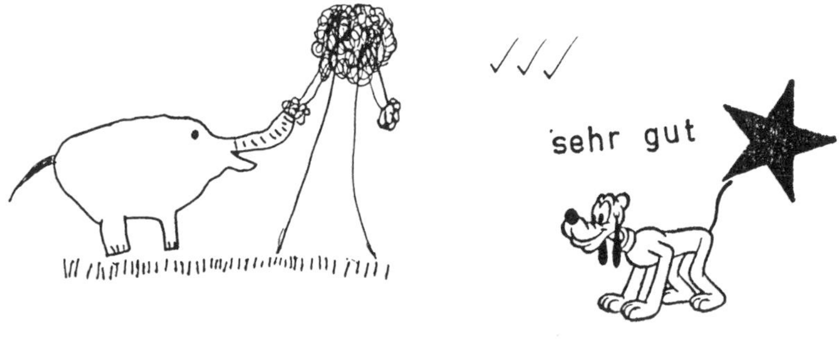

✓✓✓

sehr gut

This evidence, as well as the evidence from the experiences of my own children described in this chapter, indicates that there is little justification for the concern expressed by writers such as Bernd Kielhöfer & Sylvie Jonekeit (1983:59) that learning to read and write in two languages simultaneously will cause confusion between the two writing systems.

As mentioned at the beginning of this section, Katrina became literate at an earlier age than her brothers and, unlike them, did not learn to read both languages at the same time, but rather learned to read (and write) first in German. Since at the time of writing, she (aged 5;9) can read both languages as well, if not better, than her two brothers at age 7, it is worthwhile looking briefly at how this came about.

At age 2;2 Katrina began to show great interest in letters of the alphabet and also words. At first I wrote the names of family members on filing cards. She learned these very quickly and kept requesting new words. I wrote one German word on each card and within two months she could (at age 2;4) easily identify 69 different words. (Interestingly, she could also identify these words whatever size and in whichever colour they were written, which showed that it may not be necessary to adhere to Glen Doman's (1964) rather rigid recommendations about this.) However, Katrina then began to tire of this game and her reading lapsed for well over a year. Then, one evening, at age 4;0, 24, while her brothers were doing their homework, she insisted that she wanted to do some homework, too. I wrote out twelve of the German words and, to my surprise, she still recognized seven of them.

The old word cards were then brought back into service, and added to, as Katrina's enthusiasm grew. A picture was now added to one side of each card to illustrate the word on the other side. A standard game was for me to place six cards on the table with the word side visible. I would then say a word and Katrina would select what she thought was the correct word card and turn it over to verify her choice by looking at the picture on the other side. When she chose correctly (as she usually did) there was much praise and admiration expressed, which kept her level of enthusiasm high. Then one day this game took a somewhat novel twist. Katrina already knew about twenty Malay words, so one evening, just to tease her, I said some of the words in Malay instead of German. She was most amused by this and soon insisted that the reading game be played this way. So I would say a word in Malay and she would select the correct written German word. At first she was not aware that the written word, e.g. Hund (*dog*), was only the German way of writing it — she thought this was the written symbol for the animal in *any* language, thus also for Malay *anjing* and English *dog*.

I then made a little reading book using the words from the cards in sentences directly relevant to her own experience and with a picture cut out of a magazine or a drawing to illustrate the sentence e.g. Katrina mag Blumen (*Katrina likes flowers*). She would read these sentences aloud with me.

It was not long before Katrina started experimenting by herself with copying letters and words on to scraps of paper. I decided to use her interest and obvious enthusiasm to teach her to write (at age 4;7). At first, a few times a week while her brothers were doing their homework, she did little writing exercises which required her to write single word answers to half a dozen short questions, such as Mag Opa Bier? (*Does Granddad like beer?*). The whole family praised her every effort, so she was highly motivated to progress. Until this time she had been reading by recognizing words as units, but she now began to realize the significance of the letter combinations and was able to sound out words she had not previously learnt and also to do the same when attempting to write unfamiliar words.

In the early stages of Katrina's writing, I did not worry too much about how she formed the letters. At first they were rather shaky, sometimes back-to-front, and varied greatly in size. However, gradually, without any pressure from me, her letters became less shaky and more uniform in size. Learning to handle a pencil takes time and requires considerable manual dexterity, and it would not be wise to place much emphasis on symmetrical handwriting in the early stages, as this could prove frustrating for the young writer (and perhaps beyond his or her capabilities) and take away much of the pleasure of producing something in writing.

Katrina began school at age 5;0 in the preparatory class already able to read German quite well. I had made no attempt to teach her to read in English, although she had already asked her mother about written English words and had learnt to write some. The teaching of English reading in Katrina's first year at school proceeded at snail pace, most of the year being taken up with children learning the alphabet and then, towards the end of the year, a few sentences. (The assumption is that children need this first year to get ready for "proper" reading when they go into first grade.)

On the other hand, at home she was by age 5;2 already reading children's storybooks in German. By age 5;7 she was reading such books very fluently. Wendy and I had refrained from teaching her to read English, having decided to leave this to the school. But Katrina could not wait and took matters into her own hands, "teaching" herself to read English by transferring the reading skills she had already acquired in German, quickly figuring out the different relationships between letters and sounds. Within a short time her English reading caught up with her German, and by age 5;8, to the amazement of her brothers, she was able to read English comic books, both silently and aloud, very fluently and with understanding, only stumbling over, but not being deterred by words whose meaning she did not know, e.g. *audition;* she would read on, being satisfied if she could get the gist of a sentence despite the presence of a difficult word. By age 5;10 she was reading up to 50 pages a day in English, the *Famous Five* books by Enid Blyton being her favourite reading matter. (Some idea of the level of language in these books can be gained from the fact that some of them are used, in German translation, in German schools in grades 5 and 6.)

As other parents who have taught their children to read have discovered, the achievements much admired within the family may meet with disapproval and criticism outside the home, from teachers and/or other parents who believe that teaching reading is something which should be done by schools and only at the time decided on by the educational authorities. Another argument is that, whilst children may well be able to learn to read at home before this stipulated time, this will only cause them to be bored at school. The first argument underestimates many children's ability to learn and assumes that *all* children are ready to do the same things at the same time and that only schools can teach them; this is clearly false. The second argument did not prove to be so in the case of Katrina. She enjoyed the preparatory grade at school for its social aspects — having friends, singing songs, playing games, drawing, etc. The fact that the reading she had to do at school was ridiculously easy for her, did not seem to worry her unduly, although she was frustrated by the fact that, because she was not supposed to be able to read "officially", she was allowed to borrow only *picture* books from the school library! But at home her ability to read became a most enjoyable pastime for her, giving her hours of pleasure, as she read anything that took her interest in either English *or German*. One could even argue that *holding back* children's desire to learn to read at their own pace and ignoring their curiosity about reading will cause them frustration and boredom.

When I realized that Katrina was using her reading skills in German to read English, I, as a joke (when she was aged 5;3,26), wrote her writing exercise in her exercise book not in German, but in Malay, using words from the approximately one hundred words she already knew, e.g.: "Siapa nama ibu Katrina?" *(What's Katrina's mother's name?)*. She was amused at being fooled, but quickly realized that she *could* read — and answer — the questions. The fact that the Malay writing system was a little different from the German and English systems scarcely bothered her. As long as the words were within her vocabulary she quickly decoded them and wrote her answers. Since then, one or two uncomplicated Malay sentences have usually been included (at Katrina's request) at the end of her German "homework".

A question which arises with regard to children's writing is whether all mistakes should be corrected. In the case of Thomas, Frank and Katrina, the amount of correction of their written work was, in the early stages, kept to a minimum. Emphasis was placed not so much on correct spelling or grammar as on intelligibility, i.e. what could not readily be understood was corrected. It was felt that it was more important that they should first gain confidence in writing the language. Gradually the amount of correction has increased, but never to the extent that it might discourage them from wanting to write German. Parents are best guided by their children's reactions with regard to the amount of correction which is advisable, and these reactions may vary from child to child, from day to day, due to tiredness, etc. If correction is undertaken in moderation and sympathetically, the children's interest will most probably be maintained and their writing will gradually move towards the adult norms of spelling. When I have to be away from home, I am so pleased to receive a letter in German from the children and interested in *what* they have to say that it is of no concern if the letter contains an occasional spelling or grammatical error!

One problem faced by parents wishing to bring up their children literate in a language which is not the dominant language of the community and which is not used in the school system, is procuring suitable printed material to carry out this teaching themselves. Personally, I have usually found it to be cheaper and, more importantly, more relevant for me to prepare short writing exercises in German myself than to try to use or adapt materials produced specifically for German schools. This procedure also enables the children to have some say in what sort of exercises should be included. Of course, the preparation of such writing exercises does require a little imagination and time, in this case about 15 to 30 minutes (depending on my inspiration!) four or five times a week. But, in view of the results which can be achieved, this is time well spent.

In the initial stages of the children's reading it was again found to be simpler to use home-made reading materials. These contained plenty of pictures of interest to the particular child, either cut from magazines or hand-drawn, and had simple captions describing the pictures. Humorous and incongruous pictures were very popular. Often the children would volunteer to draw a picture and suggest a caption for me to write in (as was the case with the picture below drawn by Frank at age 5;7). From these home-made readers the children graduated to reading simple German storybooks which had much less text than pictures. From these they could then move on to more complicated books.

Frank 1980

Die Maus frißt das Auto

Storybooks may not be easy to obtain in languages other than the dominant language of the community. However, many Australian libraries do now have available some material in languages other than English, or can procure it for borrowers through interloan, although whether this proves adequate or satisfactory for a particular family depends largely on what language is required and where the library is located.

Fortunately, however, it is possible to buy reasonably cheap paperback children's books, either through a foreign language bookshop or by establishing contact with a bookshop or publisher in the country where the language is spoken (or by arranging for friends or relatives in the country to post suitable material); the occasional arrival of a parcel of books, comics or magazines from abroad can do a lot to maintain or renew interest and enthusiasm. Such books are a worthwhile investment and do not strain the purse-strings too much. In the case of my three children, my expenditure on German books over a year would amount to about the equivalent of the price of two or three loaves of bread per week. Moreover, the books get well used. They may be used initially as storybooks which I read aloud, first to the boys and then, as she reaches that particular level of linguistic sophistication, also to Katrina. Later, the books are used by the children as reading books.

Even though our oldest child is at the time of writing thirteen years old, almost every evening I still read to the children in German and Wendy does the same in English, continuing an activity which began before the children could talk. This is a time of the day enjoyed by both parents and children. Jim Trelease (1984), author of *The Read-Aloud Handbook*, regards reading aloud to children as an ideal way of instilling in them a love of books and a desire to read. He believes this reading aloud can even begin when a child is still a young baby. To people who say, "But they're too young to understand!", he replied in a radio interview in the ABC (Australian Broadcasting Corporation) programme "Offspring" (7 August 1986) that parents still *talk* to children at that age and that "a child old enough to talk to is old enough to read to!"

With regard to reading aloud, there is also strong research evidence (Tizard *et al.*, 1982) that children whose parents listen to them read aloud make greater progress in reading than those who do not engage in this sort of literacy sharing with their parents. Even more encouraging for parents is the finding that children who read aloud to their parents achieve a greater improvement in reading than children who receive small-group tuition in reading from a highly competent specialist teacher. An interesting aspect of this research is that the improvement in children's reading occurs even when the parents hearing them read are illiterate and understand little of the language they are listening to! This should be encouraging for parents who are worried that they cannot help their children's reading in a particular language because they themselves are not very proficient at it.

One of the problems over the years in my own family, particularly as the two boys have grown older, has been trying to encourage them to read independently in German. At the time of writing (December 1986), for instance, both boys read much more in English and can read more quickly in English (about 1.5 times faster than in German), most probably because the amount of reading material available in English far exceeds that available in German and they have much more practice reading English. However, it has been found that if interesting material is available in German, they do read it. From about age 9, for example, Frank has had a large collection of German comics which he regularly reads with much enjoyment.

The efforts to make children literate in their home language as well as in the majority language can help them to realize that their home language is a living language which extends far beyond their own immediate family and which can be, and is, used for all the functions which the majority language is. In the case of Thomas, Frank and Katrina there has been, moreover, the realization that knowing German can be a definite advantage, since many attractive and interesting stories (such as many of the comics in Frank's collection) are just not available in English.Theodor Elwert (1959:318) stresses the importance which his mother's acquainting him with literature in English had in his acquisition of a good standard of English in a non-English-speaking environment. He emphasizes the value of being literate in the home language, saying that there are limits to the knowledge of a language which can be acquired from a parent by oral means alone.

The children's written German is mainly used to write notes or letters to me and to correspond from time to time with friends in Germany. Most of their own independent creative writing (stories etc.) is done in English, no doubt because this sort of activity is largely associated with school in English. Occasionally, however, the children do seemingly have a desire to express themselves in writing in German. Thomas, for instance, writes quite a lot of science fiction stories as a hobby, virtually always in English. But sometimes he produces a German version of sections of his English story, more or less just to see how he would manage this task in German. The following is a typical (uncorrected) example, written when he was aged 12;11:

English

Darren was falling down, down. A swift current of wind parted him from his bowler hat. He tried to keep calm, but his fear was uncontrollable. His screams were as high-pitched as his male larynx would allow. Darren was descending faster and faster until he caught sight of many long tentacle-like vines hanging from the bottom of the mountains. Gathering his wits about him he grabbed one of the vines and hung on tight. At least he hadn't been destroyed below.

German

Darren fiel hinunter, hinunter. Eine schnelle Luftströmung trennte ihn von seinem Hut. Er versuchte ruhig zu bleiben aber seine Angst war zu groß. Er konnte nichts dafür. Die Frequenz von seine Schreie war so hoch wie seine männliche Kehle es schaffen konnte. Schneller und schneller fiel Darren hinab bis er viele lange wie Krakenbeine aussehende Lianen bemerkte. Sie wuchsen aus dem Unterteil des Berges. Darren begann wieder vernünftig zu denken und packte eine Liane. Die Hauptsache war das er nicht zerstört worden war.

Translation of German version:

Darren was falling down, down. A swift current of air parted him from his hat. He tried to keep calm, but his fear was too great. He couldn't help it. The frequency of his screams was as high as his male throat could manage. Darren was falling down faster and faster until he noticed many long vines resembling octopus tentacles. They were growing from the bottom of the mountain. Darren began to think sensibly again and grabbed a vine. The important thing was that he had not been destroyed.

There are a few errors in the German version and it is a little less idiomatic than the English version (which has only one mistake, a spelling mistake), but it does show that Thomas can express his ideas well in an easily understandable German.

9 How the children view bilingualism

The children's attitude to their two languages

In view of the analysis of the children's English and German described in chapter 7 and elsewhere, it is interesting to examine the children's own attitude to their bilingualism to see whether they show a preference for one or the other language, and whether they consider themselves more competent in one than the other.

It is true, as has been seen in chapter 6, that two of the children independently went through an approximately 5-month period (Thomas age 3;5 to 3;10 and Frank 2;7 to 3;0) during which they showed some reluctance to speak German to me. This reluctance was particularly noticeable when the children were extremely tired or upset, as in the following example:

> (Thomas (3;9,25), who is feeling tired and irritable, is building a toy railway.)
> **Father:** Das ist ein schönes Gleis. Und wieviele Tunnel [tun∂l] hast du?
> *(That's a nice track. And how many tunnels have you got?)*
> **Thomas** (obviously agitated): Ah, ah, ah *tunnels!* [tʌn∂lz] I want to talk English!
> **Father** (appeasingly): Okay, wenn du willst. *(All right, if you want to.)*
> (Thomas then explains in English, I still comment in German.)

It does not seem that this reluctance to speak German was the result of the boys' finding German more difficult than English, but rather an attempt by them to rationalize their linguistic situation, a situation in which they were expected to communicate in English with everyone except one person, their father, who, they knew, could in any case both understand and speak English too. After all, if pressed, they could express themselves perfectly adequately in German. The boys' resistance to German was overcome in a relatively short time, and from that time on they were quite willing to speak the language to me.

However, in situations where the children have a choice of which language they may use (usually when addressing both parents simultaneously — see chapter 3 for the stategies involved here), they do seem to have a preference for English, their more widely used language. This is particularly noticeable when the children have just come from an intensive all-English situation, such as school, when there seems to be a desire not to break the continuity of the day spent in English, some effort being involved in changing over to German. The children may, therefore, chat predominantly to their mother in English (knowing that I am listening and will understand anyway), unless they consider a matter concerns me especially, in which case they will switch to German. If only I am present in such circumstances, the children, of course, have to use German; they do not have the "escape route" of using English to their mother. However, at times it seems that the children may then be less talkative in German than they would be in English, especially when speaking about routine matters; more stimulus or incentive seems to be needed to cause the same level of talkativeness in German, e.g. when what is to be communicated is of particular interest, is exciting, etc.

It is interesting that when, after a day speaking only English (e.g. at school), the children have to speak German, it takes them a while to distance themselves from this English influence, this being reflected in both quantity and the *quality* of their German. Einar Haugen (1972:10), born in the USA of Norwegian immigrant parents, recalls similar problems during his childhood:

> My earliest recollections are from the problems I encountered in keeping apart the Norwegian I spoke at home with my parents and the English I spoke on the street with my playmates... Thanks to my parents' adamant insistence on my speaking their native language at home, the threshold of the home became the cue to my code switch... I know that in coming in from a lively time among my playmates I committed many a violation of Norwegian idiom.

My subjective observations about the quality of the children's German after a period of intensive contact with only English have been tested by taping the children's speech before and after such situations. To a large extent, these recordings confirm the subjective impressions. For example, when Thomas was aged 5;10,5 his speech was taped at home before school and then again immediately after school when I met him at the school gate and took him home. Although his speed of delivery was roughly the same on both occasions, namely 88.9 words per minute before and 89.9 words per minute after school, his fluency was much better before school, his speech containing only 9.4 filled pauses and 3.5 repeats with every 100 words, compared with 15.0 and 4.5 respectively after school. His German was also not as accurate after school, containing 5.5 errors per 100 words, as compared with 4.0 per 100 words before school.

It could be argued that the performance after school might simply not be as good because of the child's natural tiredness after spending 6.5 hours in the classroom and playground. However, examinations of the children's *English* before and after school reveal no significant differences in performance.

Despite the fact that the children do not speak German as accurately as they do English, this seldom troubles them in family communication, although in the case of Thomas and Frank there was, after about age 10, an increasing awareness of shortcomings in their grammatical accuracy and an evident desire on their part to bring their German closer to the adult norm. However, they do speak German confidently, and their confidence is not without justification, since they can communicate easily and effectively in the language. Moreover, this confidence has been bolstered over the years by frequent encouragement from Wendy and me and by their and others' recognition of their ability to express themselves in German.

Katrina still, at age 5;10, just like her brothers at that age, does not show all that much concern for grammatical accuracy in German. However, she is some-what less confident about expressing herself in German than they were at the same age, mainly because her *active* German vocabulary is not as extensive as theirs was and has not kept pace with her English. Since she remains determined to speak only German to me, this means that she has difficulty in talking about more complex matters, having to search for words or to seek help with vocabulary. She receives encouragement for her efforts from the rest of the family, parents and brothers, and has been told that she should feel completely free to ask them for linguistic assistance, a factor which is probably psychologically very important for her.

Over the years the children have at various times given their views on their ability in their two languages and the respective difficulties of English and German. At age 3;5, for example, an age when he was not particularly willing to speak German, Thomas obviously did not regard the language as difficult. On being told by an uncle that he could not understand a German storybook Thomas had handed to him, Thomas looked a bit nonplussed and then earnestly made a comment which would hardly convince learners of either language:

Thomas: But, Graeme, German's just like English, just a bit different.

In the years before they started school, and during the early years of school, Thomas and Frank usually expressed the view that it was just as easy to speak German as it was English, that is, it did not require great effort. For them, speaking German was simply a fact of life. When they began school and began to read and write (at school in English and at home in German), their confidence in their ability in German did not wane. They both initially expressed the opinion that reading and writing German was easier than English, an opinion no doubt due to the much closer correspondence between German spelling and sounds than in English; the comparative complexity of the English spelling system, for example, makes previously unseen words much more difficult for a beginner to decipher than German words seen for the first time.

Lest an impression be conveyed that the boys had total confidence in their ability in German, it should be pointed out that on occasions they did express doubts — and still do sometimes. When this happens, then Wendy and I consider it important that the children receive assurance and encourgement. Whilst some of the mistakes in the children's speech might be lamented, the children should not be deterred from using the language to communicate because of any doubts about their ability to speak it accurately. This does not mean that grammatical accuracy must be discarded as a goal, but it should never take precedence over having the children using the language spontaneously and naturally for everyday communication. In the following example, Thomas (6;1,25) has obviously been worrying about the correct form of various utterances and has asked me several questions about them. After some thought, he asks:

> **Thomas:** Bert, spreche ich sehr gut Deutsch? *(Dad, do I speak very good German?)*
> **Father:** Ja. Warum fragst du denn? *(Yes. Why do you ask?)*
> **Thomas:** Weil, weil, ich habe ein paar kleine Fehler gemacht. *(Because, because, I made a few little mistakes.)*
> **Father:** Ein paar kleine Fehler. Das macht doch nichts. Wir machen ja alle Fehler. *(A few little mistakes? That doesn't matter. We all make mistakes.)*
> **Thomas:** Oh. Gibt es niemand in die Welt, das keine Fehler macht? *(Oh. Isn't there anybody in the world who doesn't make mistakes?)*
> **Father:** Nein, niemand. Ich mache auch manchmal Fehler, wenn ich Deutsch spreche, und auch wenn ich Englisch spreche. *(No, nobody. I make mistakes too sometimes when I'm speaking German, and also when I'm speaking English.)*

From about age 4, Katrina has expressed the view that English is the language she speaks best. She has also said she knows more words in English, can say things more easily, and can read more complicated books and read them faster in English. She recognizes that this is due to the amount of contact with each language:

> **Katrina** (5;9,1): Mein Englisch ist besser, weil ich es mehr spreche. *(My English is better because I speak it more.)*

Surprisingly, though, English is not always the language Katrina considers she can understand best. At age 5;9, for instance, she observed that she could understand German videos of *Sesamstraße* better than its American counterpart *Sesame Street* ; this is probably largely because the German version is presented at a more sedate pace than the American version and the characters also tend to speak more clearly.

Despite her accurate self-assessment of her overall clear superiority in English, however, Katrina obviously identifies German closely with me and considers it an integral part of her relationship with me. The following remark, taken from a conversation with Frank, sums up her feelings fairly accurately:

Frank (9;9,6): Katrina, what if you spoke English to Daddy?
Katrina (4;4,24) (smilingly sheepishly): No, that doesn't work.

Her attitude to her two languages is also made clear in the following remarks made when her mother asked whether Katrina wanted her to read a German storybook in English or German:

Katrina (4;4,3): In English. English is a tops language!
Mother: Is it? Do you like German, too?
Katrina (definitely): Yes, but I like English best.
Mother: Do you like talking German to your dad?
Katrina (definitely): Yes.

The children's reading, and even more so, writing exercises the children do for me, have brought home to them that some features of their speech do not conform to the grammar of Standard German (see chapter 8 for further details on biliteracy). This has worried them to a certain extent, although not too greatly. Signs of linguistic insecurity have always been countered with parental expressions of re-assurance. At the same time I attempt to make the children aware of the more glaring grammatical deviations from Standard German in their speech and writing and to help them overcome them; if this is not overdone, the children do not mind and, little by little, their grammatical awareness is heightened and begins to be put into practice. The basic correction techniques used are very similar to those employed by Alvino Fantini (1985:84) and his wife with their children: (i) instruction and/or clarification about a specific grammatical point or vocabulary item, (ii) a correc-tion, followed by a request for the child to repeat the correction, (iii) a request for the children to repeat their own statement (or part of it), in the hope that they will self-correct; (iv) the adult repeats what the child had just said, providing the corrected form, but without calling overt attention to the matter. It is important that the corrections made by the parent or expected from the children are within the children's capabilities and comprehension at a particular age.

The extent to which such correction can be carried out depends a lot on the personality of the child, the mood he or she is in, whether what he or she is saying is urgent or not, etc. A bit of humour helps, too. In my family, for instance, I sometimes deliberately misunderstand some of the children's mistakes, e.g. when

Frank (11;0,2) asked "Gehst du auf dem Zug?", a literal translation of the English "Are you GOING ON the train ?" instead of "Fährst du mit dem Zug?" as required in German (literally "Are you travelling with the train?"), I replied, "Nein, das wäre doch viel zu gefährlich!" (*No, that would be far too dangerous!*). Frank instantly realized what was going on, grinned, gave me a playful punch, and corrected his sentence. Another method of correction which is used and which amuses the children (but which will probably shock some more serious parents) is the *Herzinfarktmethode* (Heart Attack Method). When the children commit some gross violation of German grammar, I clutch my chest and gasp, "Oh, mein Herz!" *(Oh, my heart!)* They may save me from this dreadful fate by correcting the error (and they have become very adept at detecting and correcting the faults in sentences) — I then recover quickly from the shock. This is seen by the children as a game, merely an extension of the general banter and teasing which occurs regularly between us. Sometimes the children even amuse themselves by deliberately provoking this game ("Let's give Dad a heart attack.") by producing the most atrocious German sentences they can think of. Again, I use this method of correction in moderation (when the children are in the right mood) and usually only in the case of quite glaring deviations from the norm which I know the children are aware of and can correct; these deviations thus obviously vary from child to child and with the age and level of linguistic development of each particular child.

A typical problem for bilingual children is that not only will the language spoken basically only in the home usually be spoken with less grammatical accuracy than the dominant language of the community, but the children's vocabulary, particularly their active vocabulary, in the home language will not keep pace with their more widely used language. This has been mentioned in a number of places in this book; it is a problem the children are well aware of, e.g.:

> **Frank** (7;8,17) (to his mother): I can say anything in English, I know all the words. In German I can nearly say everything, but sometimes I don't know some words.

At age 13 and 11 respectively, Thomas and Frank still agreed with this accurate self-assessment by Frank; Katrina (nearly 6) agreed with the first part, but was not so sure of her ability in expressing herself in German — this, too, is an accurate self-evaluation. Again, Wendy and I have explained that it is natural to sometimes not know or not be able to recall how to say something in one of their two languages, since no-one can hope to have a completely equal knowledge of two languages. As mentioned elsewhere, they are encouraged always to seek help from us rather than refrain from saying something because they do not know or have forgotten a word or expression. This they do, although they are obviously embarrassed at times if it is a common word which slips their mind. It should not be forgotten, however, and this has been pointed out to them, too, that monolinguals are not immune from having trouble calling a word to mind, not knowing correct terminology in certain areas, etc.

From time to time, particularly before their first visit to Germany in 1984, the children have had doubts about their ability to comprehend spoken German when they have been confronted with an unfamiliar variety of the language, particularly if spoken rapidly and/or indistinctly. This can no doubt be attributed to the fact that in Australia they have really only one constant source of German input, and an adult one at that. On one occasion, for example, Thomas (6;11,19) and Frank (5;0,27) watched a German film, *Die Vorstadtkrokodile* (The Suburban Crocodiles) (based on the novel of the same name by Max von der Grün) on the Special Broadcasting Service, Australia's multilingual television station. The picture and sound quality was marred by poor reception and this did not facilitate comprehension, but what really startled the boys was the very rapid speech of the child characters which they followed with great difficulty. On the other hand, adults in the film, whose diction was clearer and slower, were understood relatively easily.

Different accents of German also caused — and to a certain extent still cause — the children some consternation, again simply because they have little contact with anything but the type of "standard" North German accent normally used on German radio and television, in commercially available recorded stories, and by me. In English, however, they are used to hearing a wide variety of both native and non-native accents of English, both in everyday life and in radio and television programmes. When faced with a pronounced South German accent, for example, particularly if used in rapid speech, the children may be baffled. While watching the film *Anschi und Michael,* which is set in Bavaria, Thomas (7;6,1) made the following somewhat exasperated comment:

> **Thomas:** Bert, ich kann diesen blöden Jungen Michael nicht verstehen. Er spricht so schnell und komisch. Aber ich kann seine Mutter verstehen, und seine Freundin auch. Und die Eltern von seiner Freundin. Warum spricht Michael anders? *(Dad, I can't understand this stupid boy Michael. He speaks so fast and funny. But I can understand his mother, and his girl-friend, too. And his girl-friend's parents. Why does Michael speak differently?)*

The boy Michael referred to, a toolmaking apprentice, spoke rapidly with a distinct Bavarian accent, occasionally even switching into Bavarian dialect, whilst the other characters mentioned spoke more distinctly and with an accent closer to Standard German. Even a short utterance, produced rapidly and with an unfamiliar pronunciation and intonation, might not be understood, e.g. *Die hoaßt nit Claudia!* instead of standard *Die heißt nicht Claudia!* (Her name's not Claudia!) In this case, I attempted to dispel Thomas's concern by drawing parallels with similar instances in English-language films when the children had initial comprehension difficulties with various accents and dialects (e.g. Yorkshire English in the BBC television serial *The Secret Garden:* "Thou mon talk like that to Master Colin. Thou'll make him laugh and there's nowt as good for ill folk as laughin' is."; compare Australian English: "You should talk like that to Colin. You'll make him laugh and there's nothing as good for sick people as laughing is."), and by explaining that some practice and perseverance were needed before different kinds of German and English could be understood easily. This explanation was accepted readily enough, with Thomas recalling accent variations he had encountered previously in English and then going on to enjoy the film, being helped by me when the Bavarian German proved too much for him. Nevertheless, the experience did make an impression on him, as evidenced by his remarks towards the end of the film:

> **Thomas:** Bert, gibt es ein Norddeutschland-Deutsch? *(Dad, is there a North Germany German?)*
>
> **Father:** Ja, Ernie. *(Yes.)*
>
> **Thomas:** Ist das wie unser Deutsch? *(Is that like our German?)*
>
> **Father:** Ja. *(Yes.)*
>
> **Thomas:** Werden wir nach Norddeutschland gehen, wenn wir nach Deutschland gehen? *(Will we go to North Germany when we go to Germany?)*
>
> **Father** (realizing the significance of the question and laughing): Ich glaube ja. Warum denn? *(I think so. Why?)*
>
> **Thomas** (smiling): Damit wir die Leute verstehen können! *(So that we can understand the people!)*

Fortunately, the majority of German films the children saw before they ever went to Germany were in more or less Standard German and, despite the fact that the dialogue in many of them, being aimed primarily at an adult audience, was quite complex, they understood them quite well, almost as well as adult English films. This success in understanding did much to strengthen their confidence in their competence in German.

When a decision was finally made that the family would spend 6 months in Hamburg, the children obviously began wondering whether the sort of German they would encounter would cause them difficulties, as shown in the following some-what chauvinistic comments by Frank:

> **Frank** (7;8,17): Sprechen die Kinder in Hamburg das beste Deutsch, das wir sprechen? *(Do the children in Hamburg speak the best German which we speak?)*
>
> **Father** (amused): Ja, sehr ähnlich. Aber die anderen Arten von Deutsch

sind doch auch gut. *(Yes, very similar. But the other kinds of German are good, too.)*

Frank: Aber unser Deutsch ist das beste Deutsch. *(But our German is the best German.)*

Bilingual children, who may feel relatively secure in both their home language and the dominant language of the community in which they live, may have doubts and become linguistically somewhat insecure if they visit a country where their home language is the official language, particularly if they have to go to school during their stay. For now their variety of the language, which may have until then been perfectly adequate within their family, comes into direct contact with the language as used by monolingual native speakers in all aspects of their life. They can no longer insert a word from their other language if they have vocabulary difficulties, as it will usually not be understood. They are in a different position from people learning the language as a second language: because of their native or native-like accent and fluency much more may be expected of them. Understanding parents can help to smooth the way for their children if they are placed in such a situation. The time children take to adjust to their new linguistic situation will, of course, depend on this parental support, but also on other factors: personality, sensitivity of the child, the child's initial degree of proficiency in the language, the attitude of the "natives" to their child's variety of the language, etc. How Thomas, Frank and Katrina fared in this respect is described in chapter 10.

A closely related question which concerns some parents who wish to pass on their language to their children in a foreign environment and who normally speak a dialect, is whether they should use their dialect with their children or whether they should speak the standard language. In the linguistic homeland this would normally not be a great problem, since the children would be exposed to the standard language in many domains in everyday life, e.g. the mass media, school, and would grow up with a knowledge of both the dialect and the standard language. But in a foreign environment the children will largely acquire the variety of the language which is spoken in the home by their parents. There is no clear-cut answer to the question, and in such cases parents will need to make a family language planning decision. If they are not comfortable or not proficient in the standard language, then it is perhaps advisable that they speak their dialect, in which they feel at ease and competent, with their children. This would be especially advisable if the main contacts which the children will have with their parents' country will be with speakers of that dialect. The parents could give the children some exposure to the standard language through books, records, tapes, videos, etc. On the other hand, dialect speaking parents who also feel at home in the standard language, could decide for a number of reasons that it would be an advantage for their children if they were spoken to in the standard language, e.g. giving them a wider range of communication, easier access to the written language, to the education system, etc.

As mentioned in chapter 8, Thomas, Frank and Katrina are literate in both English and German. However, the two really avid readers among the children, Thomas and Katrina, show a marked preference for reading English, since they read it much more quickly and easily than they do German. They usually choose to read English in their leisure time, although they will read German if the material is very interesting. At age 12;8,29 Thomas compared his reading ability in his two languages, saying that he could read about 100 pages in an evening in English, but if he had to read similar material in German he thought he could read only 60–65 pages in the same time. But he felt that despite his slower reading speed in German his reading comprehension in that language was at least 90% as good as in English. This would seem to be a very accurate assessment of his reading ability in his two languages.

Frank (11;2) does not read as much or as quickly in either English or German. However, he does spread his reading fairly equally between his two languages. He has a large collection of reading material in both languages, mainly comics, which he reads regularly and with much enjoyment. His reading speed is similar in both languages. While he does meet more unfamiliar words in German, this does not discourage him; in fact, he studies German dialogues carefully, showing an interest not only in what is said, but *how* it is said.

When asked whether they thought being bilingual was an advantage or a disadvantage, the children agreed that it was mostly an advantage, mentioning that there were more people they could communicate with, more films to see, more books to read. Thomas (13;0) also mentioned that it was easier to learn other languages because one was not as surprised or confused by differences in the language being studied, as one was already aware that different languages operated in different ways. Mentioned as disadvantages were: sometimes being frustrated at not being able to say something as precisely in German as they could in English, and, in the case of Thomas, being teased on a few occasions by a small minority of what he aptly called *Ignoranten* (= ignoramuses), being called "a Nazi" and the like, in grades 6 and 7 in Australia, simply because he spoke German with his father, and also in grade 5 in Germany because his German was slightly different (see chapter 10). However, overall the children's impression of their bilingualism is a positive one, and it is not regarded as a burden. As they have grown older and come into contact with people who use their bilingualism in their jobs (e.g. flight attendants, pilots, interpreters, translators, etc.), the children have begun to realize that having two languages has professional possiblities as well. For example, at age 11;0,8, Frank, on learning, to his amazement, that people actually got paid for watching films and writing subtitles for them, decided that he could combine his love of movies and his English and German and become a subtitler! Such was his enthusiasm for this idea that he asked me to give him regular translation practice.

When Thomas was aged 13;5,7 and Frank 11;6,11, they were asked to assess their own proficiency in their two languages in the four skills of listening comprehension, speaking, reading and writing. They were asked to give themselves a mark out of 100, with 100 representing perfect mastery, and 0 indicating zero proficiency. They considered the matter very carefully and then awarded themselves the following marks:

TABLE 13 *Self-assessment*

	Frank		Thomas	
	English	*German*	*English*	*German*
Listening comprehension	100	95	96	89
Speaking	100	95	92	78
Reading	100	100	95	82
Writing	100	90	89	76

The results reflect in part the different attitudes of the two boys. Frank, more confident and less self-conscious about making mistakes, has taken his ability in English to be perfect (even though he does admit that there are English words which he does not understand and English words which he cannot spell correctly, etc.). Thomas, however, is more cautious, more self-critical, and perhaps more realistic, in judging his linguistic ability; he, for example, revealed that he compared his own English with that of adults when making his assessment, whereas Frank compared his English with that of his peers.

The children have always been encouraged at home to regard their bilingualism as something positive and advantageous, and their attitude and behaviour more or less reflect this. They have pride in their ability to speak German in addition to English. There is, after all, a certain amount of prestige attached to a skill which is outside the scope of most of their friends and acquaintances.

The children and language and languages

It is most probable that children's bilingualism will arouse their interest not only in their own two languages (e.g. why and when, where and to whom each is to be used), but also in other languages, who speaks them and where, and so on. This has been the case with Thomas, Frank and Katrina, although much more markedly with Thomas.

At age 3;6, after some contact with people other than his father who spoke German, Thomas began to show great curiosity about exactly who could and who could not speak the language. This curiosity continued unabated for several months. It seemed from his interminable questions that each individual person had to be classified as knowing German or not, e.g.:

> **Father:** Der Techniker an der Universität hat mein Radio repariert. *(The technician at the university fixed my wireless.)*
> **Thomas** (3;8,3): Hast du Deutsch gesprochen? *(Did you speak German?)*
> **Father:** Nein, Englisch. *(No, English.)*
> **Thomas:** Kann der Techniker kein Deutsch? *(Doesn't the technician know any German?)*

When Thomas was aged 3;7, I showed him a Malay primary school reading book and, for fun, read him some of it in Malay. His initial reaction was one of amazement, which quickly turned to curiosity. He wanted to know how to say various things in Malay and quickly learnt a number of greetings and other words which he delighted in using. The realization that there were other languages besides German and English led him to ask about and to request to be taught how to say various things in them. This obviously fascinated him, and his confidence after mastering a few words was boundless, as evidenced by the following amusing/embarrassing incident when I was enrolling him in a German-language kindergarten (see also the section "Ethnic schools and playgroups" in chapter 11):

> **Teacher** (to Thomas): Sprichst du zu Hause Deutsch? *(Do you speak German at home?)*
> **Thomas** (3;8,0): Ja, und Englisch und (Fran)zösisch und Malaiisch. *(Yes, and English and French and Malay.)*
> **Teacher:** (taken aback, addressing his father with concern): Glauben Sie nicht, daß das ein bißchen zuviel ist? *(Don't you think that's a bit too much?)*

In another incident, he (5;0,2) was praised at his English-language kindergarten for singing the Christmas song "Jingle Bells" so fluently and with so much expression in Spanish. The whole song was, however, unbeknown to his teachers, in his own *invented* Spanish!

At age 4;6 Thomas invented an imaginary friend to whom he gave the name Kinnetkopf and who spoke an imaginary language called Gedisch. If Kinnetkopf wanted to communicate with other members of the family, or they with him, Thomas had to act as interpreter, since only he and Kinnetkopf spoke Gedisch.

Thomas's realization that quite a bit of Dutch and Afrikaans, read to him from magazines for fun, was intelligible to someone knowing German and English (e.g.

Afrikaans *perd* = German *Pferd* (horse), Afrikaans *siek* = English *sick,* thus "My perd is siek" = "My horse is sick"), started him on a new track of enquiry: which languages are similar, related, and why? For example:

Thomas (5;1,0): Mum, is *Estnisch* (= Estonian) related to Hungarian?
Mother: Oh, I don't know, Thomas. You'll have to ask Daddy about that.
Thomas (somewhat accusingly): Aren't you interested in languages?
Mother (amused): Yes, I'm interested, I just don't know.

In games, Thomas frequently requested that I speak other languages to him, particularly languages such as Dutch, much of which he could understand if spoken slowly and clearly and if vocabulary was used which was similar to the German or English words, as in the following game where Thomas is a doctor, I am a Dutch patient:

Father (groaning): Ooh! Goeden middag, dokter. *(DUTCH: Ooh! Good afternoon, doctor.)*
Thomas (6;0,4): Guten Tag. Was ist los? *(GERMAN; Good day. What's the matter?)*
Father: Ooh! Ik ben ziek! *(DUTCH; Ooh! I'm sick.)*
Thomas (listens with his stethoscope and then reaches for his scalpel): Ja, du bist sehr krank. *(GERMAN: Yes, you're very sick.)*
Father (in mock fear): Wat is dat? Een mes? Wat doet u met het mes? *(DUTCH: What's that? A knife? What are you going to do with the knife?)*
Thomas: Ich muß operieren ... *(GERMAN: I have to operate ...)*

Not long after he began to read and write (see chapter 8), Thomas became aware that some languages did not use the same writing system as English and German. Consequently, Chinese, Japanese, Arabic, Hindi, etc., became objects of fascination. He often amused himself by imitating these scripts and then reading out, in pseudo-Arabic etc., what he had written.

Thomas's enthusiasm for languages was increased even further during his first ever journey outside Australia in mid-1984. He revelled in visiting countries where languages other than English or German were spoken and meeting people who spoke these languages. A brief stay with a Welsh-speaking family in Wales, for instance, inspired him to buy the book *Teach Yourself Welsh* and work through a few chapters; he responded similarly after a visit to an English/Danish/Finnish family in Denmark and a week's stay with a family with English/Finnish bilingual children in England, learning various common Danish and Finnish phrases. During a visit to Malaysia on the return journey to Australia he purchased a Malay phrase book and a short guide to writing Chinese characters. During his stay in Hamburg he even set about writing a grammar for his own invented language, which he modestly called Saundish: he wrote over twenty pages of grammatical description before his enthusiasm for the project waned, e.g. "oäu" was the word for "dog" which formed its plural regularly as "soäu". After his return to Australia at the end of 1984, the intensity of Thomas's interest in languages lessened, although it by no means disappeared. This was probably due in part to the low priority unfortunately given to other languages in the community and in the school system to which he returned; for instance, out of 201 pupils in seventh grade at his high school, only 17 elected to do a foreign language in eighth grade!

Frank and Katrina have also shown interest in other languages, although a less intense interest than Thomas. Both have learned some phrases from various languages, particularly Malay/Indonesian; as mentioned in chapter 8, Katrina has even learned to read and write simple Malay sentences. They occasionally use such phrases, mainly for fun with me within the family. One interesting exception to this occurred when Frank was aged 3;10,3. Some time before, he had learnt the Chinese expression "Ni hao ma?" *(How are you?)* from an English story called *Moy Moy* by Leo Politi (New York: Charles Scribner's Sons, 1960). On this occasion he was in a building waiting with the rest of his family for the lift to reach their floor. When the lift eventually did arrive, it was packed with people. The first person Frank saw was a Chinese woman, and to our great surprise he immediately and quite spontaneously exclaimed, "Ni hao ma?". Before the startled woman could respond in any way to indicate whether she had understood Frank's version of the Chinese greeting, the doors snapped shut and the lift moved on.

The advent of a multilingual television service in Australia (see chapter 11), as well as contact with various bilingual children who speak languages other than English or German at home has maintained the children's interest in other languages. The fact that both their parents are interested in languages as well and have been willing to discuss them with the children has no doubt also contributed to their continuing interest.

Bilingualism and an interest in other languages seem to have given the children an appreciation of the fact that no particular language is superior to any other. One incident can clearly illustrate this awareness. I was reading to Thomas (7;11,9) from a German translation of an adventure novel by a Russian author, called *Dort, weit hinter dem Fluß* (= There, Far Beyond the River). The particular chapter being read was called "Die Forellensprache" (= The Trout Language), and in it the central character, a young boy called Mischa who speaks only Russian, is told by his uncle that trout have their own language which is a perfectly adequate means of communication; the boy reacts as follows:

Mischa: Es gibt doch nur eine wirklich reiche Sprache, nur eine wahre und eine freie! Unsere russische Sprache! Alle anderen Sprachen sind schlelchter und ärger, überhaupt blödsinnig! *(But there's only one really rich language, only one true and free language! Our Russian language! All other languages are worse and inferior, altogether stupid!)*

At this point Thomas interjected in disbelief.

Thomas: Nein — das ist nicht wahr, Bert. Es gibt viele andere Sprachen, die das haben: Englisch, Spanisch, Polnisch, Portugiesisch, und Tschechisch und Dänisch, und, ah — alle! *(No — that's not true, Dad. There are lots of other languages which have that* [i.e. these qualities]: *English, Spanish, Polish, Portuguese, and Czech and Danish, and, ah – all of them!)*

This, in fact, turned out to be exactly the point of this particular chapter, as the uncle then proceeds, by comparing Russian and Uzbek (a Turkic language of central Asia), to convincingly cure his nephew of his linguistic chauvinism. The uncle's final remarks met with Thomas's obvious approval:

Uncle: Alle Sprachen sind groß und jede Sprache ist groß auf ihre Art... *(All languages are great and every language is great in its own way.)*
Thomas: Ja. *(Yes.)*

Thomas is the only one of the children to have actually pondered the mechanisms of bilingualism. At age 7;10,19 he speculated on how the two languages might be kept separate in the brain, and came up with his own original explanation. His speculation was prompted by what he perceived as his mother's use of an English /r/ instead of a rolled /r/ when reading out a German word. He attempted to explain how the two sounds of the two languages could be kept separate:

Thomas: (quite earnestly): It's easy, Mum. I'll explain it to you. Ah, in your brain there's two visions (= divisions) — one's for German and one's for English, and you use one 'vision when you want to speak German and the other one if you want to speak English. So you wouldn't say "rabbit" (pronouncing it with a rolled r) in English and you wouldn't say "rouse" (pronounced with an English r and diphthong), you'd say *raus* (= out). You have to use the right 'vision.
Mother (amused): That's all right for you, but what about your poor old mum?

His explanation, despite its simplicity, is not *so* very different from some of the theories put forward by linguists and psychologists to explain how bilinguals keep their languages separate (see chapter 1).

10 Two varieties of German meet: a family language and a national language

On 1 July 1984 the three children, then aged 10;7,21 (Thomas), 8;8,29 (Frank) and 3;4,18 (Katrina), left Australia for the first time to spend nearly 6 months in Hamburg in the Federal Republic of Germany. This was to be their first experience of an environment where German, until then basically a family language, would be a language which they would constantly hear all around them and which they would need to use to communicate with virtually everyone apart from their mother and among themselves. In other words, for half a year the roles of their two languages would be reversed. German would now need to assume functions which had so far been basically the preserve of English, e.g. communication with playmates, at school, etc. This would be their very first contact with people who spoke only German, so that recourse to an English word or expression in moments of linguistic difficulty would not be possible as it was in Australia. For the first time the children would also clearly realize that I was not German and that my and their German would probably not be considered "native" by speakers in Germany. I was thus a little apprehensive as we boarded our Lufthansa jet in Sydney, as I felt that if the children's experiences in Germany turned out to be negative, this could have an adverse effect on their existing favourable attitude towards the German language.

However, certain precautions had been taken to minimize any culture or linguistic shock. In the few months preceding the family's departure from Australia, I tried to prepare the children linguistically and culturally for their stay in Germany. Although they already spoke German, they did so within an Australian context, within a somewhat less formal life style than that in Germany. All adult Australian German-speakers with whom the children had had contact had, for example, been addressed by first name (not unusual in Australian English) and by *du,* the informal pronoun for "you", and not the formal pronoun *Sie* (see the section "Communicative Competence" in chapter 7 for more about this). It was explained to the children that to do so in Germany could make them sound rude and cause them problems. They were given practice in using *Sie,* the formal word for "you", which they had never used personally but which they had heard in stories, films, etc. The use of the informal, plural words for "you", *ihr* (as subject), *euch* (as object), was also practised. The simple question "Are you coming?", for example, can have three different forms in German, depending on who is being asked. A simplified explanation of their function is as follows:

(a) Kommen Sie? (formal, to one or more persons)
(b) Kommst du? (informal, to one person)
(c) Kommt ihr? (informal, to more than one person)

The children actively used only (b). (c) was, in any case, usually not necessary in the family, as a question addressed to me plus other family members would either be in German to me (thus requiring only (b)) and English to the others, or just in English to include both the other family members and me. Sometimes they used the *du* form when the *ihr* form was obviously required. The differences between *du* and *ihr* were thus also discussed and practised, as it was felt this would prevent confusion when the children came into contact with children in Hamburg. A few other features of the children's German which it was felt would not be understood or would be misunderstood were also pointed out and acceptable alternatives practised. Differences in social conventions were also pointed out, e.g. in Australia children are not expected to shake hands with adults, whereas children in Germany often are.

Another preparation was introducing Frank to running writing (*Schreibschrift*). In Australian schools, children print until about half way through grade 3, whilst in German schools running writing begins in grade 1. Frank would therefore have had virtually no experience with handwriting before he left Australia and even then the style of handwriting he would need in Hamburg would be different. Therefore, to make his transition to the German school easier, Wendy and I taught him to write using the German handwriting style. (This was to cause him some problems later on his return to school in Australia in grade 4, since his by then very fluent and neat German handwriting was not considered acceptable and he had to change back to the Australian system!)

My worries began to dissipate as Lufthansa Flight 691 began its 30 hour, 20,000 kilometre flight, and Thomas and Frank ordered drinks, meals etc. from the flight attendants in German. When we finally alighted, somewhat jet-lagged, in Hamburg, the children's excitement and wonder that everyone spoke German was evident. The boys obviously found this a strange but thrilling experience and revelled in being able to use their "father tongue" to buy ice-creams, etc. They volunteered to do various bits of shopping, to ask for information etc., seemingly just to try out their German in these novel situations. They were definitely encouraged in this by the friendly reactions from the people of Hamburg. The Hamburgers are much maligned by other Germans as "cool Northerners", a description the Hamburgers themselves surprisingly seem to acknowledge and apologize for, but which the family found to be quite inaccurate, since they encountered virtually nothing but friendliness and helpfulness during their stay. Admittedly, being Australian does have certain advantages in Germany, since Australia's great distance from Europe, its vast spaces, a standard of living similar to Germany's, and having a prestigious international language, English, as its official language, mean that for many Germans it has a certain air of fascination, of the exotic. Australians, especially if they speak German, tend therefore on the whole to be viewed much more favourably than many other nationalities, e.g. than the so-called "guestworkers".

Even in those first days there was over 95% mutual intelligibility between Hamburg German and the children's German. Most people were surprised to meet Australian children who could speak German so fluently and showered them with compliments. The children understood most of what they heard but, accustomed to their father's not very rapid speech (in any language!), they initially had difficulty if someone spoke fast — as most children their age seemed to do! However, their ears quickly adjusted to more rapid forms of German. The children were pleasantly surprised — and relieved — to find that the variety of German spoken in Hamburg was very close to the variety they were used to, as close, say, as Australian and New Zealand English. The differences interested, but did not trouble them. Among the differences they observed was the pronunciation of written 'g' after certain vowels as /ç/ (the 'ch' sound in German *ich*) rather than as /k/ as in the father's German (and in Standard German), e.g. in a word such as *Weg*; the use of words with a slightly different or added sense, e.g. *Wurzel*, which in Standard German means "root", also means "carrot" in Hamburg (although the children's word, *Möhre*, is universally understood); the use of different syntax in certain constructions, e.g. *"Da weiß ich nichts von."* (I don't know anything *about that.*), as opposed to the "Standard" *"Davon weiß ich nichts."*; the use of some words mainly used only in the north of Germany, e.g. *Bax*, a "slap", Standard *Ohrfeige;* and so on. However, these differences were relatively minor in comparison with what would have been if the family had spent six months in South Germany. This was brought home to the children when they first visited Stuttgart after having lived in Hamburg for 4 months and had considerable difficulty understanding the Swabian accent, intonation and vocabulary. One example: they were quite perplexed when, buying a can of juice, they were asked if they needed a *Röhrle* (= "straw"); their word is *Trinkhalm,* which is also the "Standard" word.

In the first week of August 1984, the beginning of the new school year in Hamburg, Thomas (10;8) began grade 5 in a *Gesamtschule* (comprehensive high school), and Frank (8;10) started grade 3 at a *Grundschule* (primary school). They had little difficulty in communicating with their fellow pupils, although they did receive some verbal and physical abuse from a small minority of children because they were "different"; after several torrid fist fights this unwanted attention largely ceased. These interactions, both peaceful and otherwise, were, linguistically, obviously very significant, since they introduced them to children's German, something which previously they had known practically only from dialogues in books, films and on tapes.

However, communicating in German in an informal way with one's peers is not the same as being taught formally through the language and having to come to grips with all school subjects in German, something which until then they had experienced virtually only in English. There were some small technical difficulties, such as different mathematical symbols being used. For example, what in Australia had been written as 2 x 3 = 6 became 2. 3 = 6 in Germany. Other difficulties disappeared once the new terminology for already known processes had been learned, e.g. how 3^2 was said in German.

Other problems were, however, not so easy to solve. Thomas, for instance, had been in Australia among the top 5% in his grade (100 pupils) in English expression and composition writing; writing stories was one of his favourite school activities. Now, suddenly, he had to carry out this activity in German, and he became acutely aware that he did not have the same stylistic control of German as he did of English; his essays in German, he felt, lacked the richness and breadth of vocabulary he was able to display in English, and he also lost marks for grammatical and spelling mistakes which would not have been present in an equivalent piece of work in English. This was rather demoralizing for him. I tried to console him by:

(a) pointing out that to get a 3 (an average mark) for an essay in a German school in his weaker language was a considerable achievement;

(b) pointing out that it is not unusual for bilinguals to be more competent in the language they use more and have more exposure to, and that I myself could also write complex English more easily and with greater stylistic flexibility than German;

(c) offering him linguistic assistance when he was searching for the most apt way to put his thoughts into words, searching for appropriate adjectives, verbs etc.

(d) reminding him that he would still be among the top pupils in English when he returned to Australia.

These measures were effective to a certain extent, although the time was too short for him to become as competent in written German as in English; I estimate that probably about two years in a German school would be required for this to come about. At times, particularly during the first few weeks at the German school,

Thomas did find the unusual experience of *having to speak* German all the time somewhat demanding, as the following excerpts from a conversation with his mother after only 8 days at school reveal:

> **Thomas** (10;9,6): It makes you tired when you have to use German all the time. It makes you tired in your mind because it's not as easy to think of what to say as it is in English ... It's hard to say complicated things.

And in a conversation with me on the same day he made the following assessment of his German (which was probably reasonably accurate as far as speaking was concerned):

> **Thomas**: Jetzt kann ich Deutsch sehr gut, Bert. Ah, Bert, sagen wir mal, mein Englisch ist hundert Prozent. *(Now I can speak German very well, Dad. Ah, Dad, let's say my English is one hundred percent.)*
> **Father**: Ja. *(Yes.)*
> **Thomas**: Bert, ich glaube jetzt, daß mein Deutsch, ah, achtzig Prozent sein würde. *(Dad, I think now my German would be eighty percent.)*

Again, Wendy and I pointed out and praised his ability and performance in the two languages, saying that to speak German 80% (his own evaluation) as well as English was a significant achievement and that his proficiency and German would surely improve further during the coming months. And it did, both in accuracy (see chapter 7 for details), fluency, and breadth of active vocabulary — many words and expressions which he already knew but had never used, now appeared in his speech, as did some completely new vocabulary. His ability to follow fast, complex German on television improved noticeably within the first few months in Hamburg.

But apart from the actual subject German, in which, as mentioned above, Thomas understandably performed less well than in the subject English in Australia, he did not feel that his German disadvantaged him in other subjects, and this seemed to be the case, e.g. in the report he received from the school when he left in December 1984 he received a 2 (the second best mark) not only in mathematics, music and art, subjects where performance is probably less dependent on language, but also in politics, where ability to express ideas in German is important. In the comments included in his report, the following reference was made to his German:

> In allen Fächern hat er sich sprachlich erstaunlich gut zurechtgefunden. *(Linguistically, Thomas has coped amazingly well in all subjects.)*

Thomas's time at school in Hamburg was also an interesting experience culturally. He was plunged straight into secondary school which begins in grade 5 in Germany but not until grade 7 in Australia. He was the only non-German in his class. School hours (8 a.m.–1.30 p.m., with no lunch break) were different from

Australia (9 a.m.–3 p.m. including a lunch break). Discipline, which in Australia is quite mild, was even milder in Hamburg, so that the noise level in most classes was very high, which Thomas found irritating, as it often made it difficult to hear what the teacher was saying. However, the real culture shock came when he realized that his fellow pupils, and even teachers, had little knowledge about Australia or anywhere outside Europe. Even the term "südliche Halbkugel" ("southern hemisphere") seemed to be not well known, let alone what this implied. To his evident disgust, for instance, Thomas was laughed at when he happened to mention what he had done in his *summer* holidays *at Christmas!* For his German peers summer was from June–August and Christmas was in winter, and that was that. Some could not believe that the seasons were reversed in the Southern Hemisphere and those who could, or already knew this, believed Australians would still have to have Christmas in *winter* (i.e. in June and not in December! (A German children's fortnightly magazine *Erzähl mir was* (= Tell me a story) (Heft 4,1986) which I bought the children contains an amusing story called "Weihnachten im Sommer" (= "Christmas in Summer"), in which an obviously Northern Hemisphere Father Christmas, tired of delivering presents in winter, decides to do so in summer, with disastrous results, because families are away on their summer holidays, children are still awake because of the heat etc, etc. Thomas, Frank and Katrina found this story somewhat naive, as *their* Father Christmas *always* came in summer in Australia and they thought it odd that the authors of the story apparently believed they were writing about a totally impossible event.)

This is probably a common enough experience for anyone from the Southern Hemisphere who visits the Northern Hemisphere, but can still come as a surprise — virtually all Australian school children, for example, would know that Europe, the U.S.A., Canada, etc., have winter when Australia has summer, and vice versa, and probably not unnaturally expect their Northern Hemisphere counterparts to know this too.

In Germany, children begin learning English in Grade 5, the very grade in which Thomas found himself in Hamburg in 1984. This was to cause certain problems, the sort of problems faced by many children in various countries who are expected to sit in classes with complete beginners and be "taught" a language they already speak at home and in which they may even be more competent than their teacher. This is a situation likely to lead to boredom for the child and perhaps to conflict with the teacher and antagonism from the other children. If a child has not yet learned to read and write the language at home or elsewhere, the degree of boredom would be less as the child could feel some sense of accomplishment in adding literacy skills in the language he or she can speak. And in higher grades, where the work is more advanced and demanding, the child would have the opportunity to consolidate his or her grammatical knowledge of the language, extend his or her vocabulary etc. But the initial years of instruction in the language are a problem.

In countries where pupils can *choose* to take a particular language, no difficulty arises. This is the case in most Australian schools. When Thomas started high school in grade 7 in Australia, he, Wendy and I decided he would choose languages other than German and would pick up German later, in grade 11. However, in Germany this was not so easy, since English is a *compulsory* subject for most pupils (as it is also in many other countries). I approached the school principal with the request that Thomas be permitted to do English with a higher grade, say grade 7 or 8, where the other children would already have been learning English for a few years. I felt that this would give him reasonable practice in written English and also be useful to the German English-learners to have a native speaker to practise their English on. However, this was not to be. According to the school principal this suggestion was "socially inadvisable" and also "organizationally impossible". Although the first reason is debatable and the second unbelievable in a school of 800 children who *all* had 5–6 periods of English per week, the principal would not budge.

Apparently, this is not an unusual attitude encountered by parents of English-speaking children in Europe. (Tove Skutnabb-Kangas & Robert Phillipson (1985), for example, tell of similar experiences in Denmark where an intransigent Ministry of Education has insisted that their three children, who speak English at home, must attend English lessons at school, even if they are obviously entirely unsuitable for them, because English is a compulsory subject *for everyone.*) If my family had been intending to stay longer than 6 months in Germany, this matter would obviously have had to be pursued with the Education Department, as treating native speakers of English as if they know no English is clearly educational nonsense. It would seem that parents need to be quite persistent in this regard and be prepared to fight for some acceptable solution for their children. Of course, I realize that other language groups, e.g. Turks in Germany, could well ask "Why are you complaining? At least your child can study his family language at school — ours can't!" This is, in many cases, regrettably true and should not be so, but it is not an argument against the points mentioned above. (Recently in Germany there have been determined efforts made to improve this situation. A comprehensive *Memorandum zum Mutterspra-chlichen Unterricht* (= Memorandum on Mother Tongue Teaching), produced by a study group consisting of associations of immigrant workers, embassy represen-tatives, churches catering for foreign workers, and a number of German linguists (see BAGIV 1985), has made a number of strong and carefully argued recommen-dations regarding equitable education opportunities for minority children in Ger-many, which include the systematic fostering and developing of children's home languages in the school system; it is to be sincerely hoped that these recommenda-tions are put into practice.)

So what became of Thomas in his beginners' English class? He did find it boring, learning "I am a boy. Are you a girl?" and the like, but he did take an interest in how English was taught and which children in the class mastered the English sounds best, and so on. However, the fact that he could already speak English and could speak it to the teacher was openly resented by many of the children, so that he became somewhat reluctant to contribute to the English lessons. However, on one occasion his proficiency in English was appreciated by the other children: their regular English teacher was away and they were taken by a relief teacher who entered the classroom and spoke only English to the children and said she knew no German. There was great consternation and frustration as the children's meagre knowledge of English was totally inadequate for understanding or responding to what the teacher was saying. Consequently Thomas was called on to act as interpreter for the whole period between the children and the teacher. But, looking at the situation overall, the five months which Thomas spent in the beginners' class could have been much more profitably spent.

Another problem with being an English speaker is that, as far as the German-speaking world is concerned, people who speak English are "Engländer" (= English); sometimes it is acknowledged that Americans also speak English, although, curiously, many Germans refer to American English as 'Amerikanisch' (American) as if it were a different language. (American books translated into German, for instance, almost always have the words "Aus dem Amerikanischen" *(Translated from the American)* inside the front cover.) Because he could speak English, the German children referred to Thomas as an "Engländer", which raised his ire on more than one occasion — Australians (like the Irish, Welsh, Canadians, etc.) do not take kindly to being called English. His protestations — "Ich bin doch kein Engländer — ich bin nie in England gewesen!" *(But I'm not English — I've never been to England!*), whilst important to him, seemed initially to his class mates and teachers, to be unnecessary hair-splitting. I approached his teachers who were also somewhat puzzled that Australians wished to be known as "Australier" and not "Engländer", although they did understand when asked if they, as Germans, could be called Austrians, since both Germans and Austrians spoke German. Thomas was then invited by his class teacher to give a talk on Australia to "set the record straight", as it were. He went off to school that day armed with pictures and maps and spoke for an hour in German on the history and geography of Australia, a performance which gave him much satisfaction and importantly, at least in his mind, established his identity as an "Australier". Linguistically, it was also a boost for his morale, as his teacher praised him for explaining everything so well in such good German.

Many of Frank's experiences were similar to those of Thomas. However, his school experiences were somewhat different. Being only in grade 3 at a primary school, he did not have the problem of learning English as a beginner, since no

English was taught at all. Moreover, unlike Thomas, he was not the only bilingual in the class, there being also a few children who spoke Turkish at home and whose German, like Frank's, was not their stronger language. Psychologically this was probably quite important, i.e. to realize that he was not the only one who was a little different. In fact, of the two boys who became his best friends, one, Murat, spoke Turkish at home and the other, Hendric, although he spoke only German, had an Indonesian father.

Frank's teacher was also bilingual, having once been married to an Englishman. This caused Frank some anguish in his first week of school when his teacher, probably assuming, because of Frank's initial shyness and reticence, that his German was not as good as his parents had said, spoke to him continually in English. Frank found this most disconcerting, as he wished to be addressed just like the other children in the class and because he had been looking forward to the challenge of using and improving his German in a German school. He resolved the problem by always answering his teacher in German. She soon realized that his German was adequate and from then on nearly always spoke to him only in German.

As seen elsewhere (chapter 7), Frank's German on arrival in Germany, contained quite a few deviations from the norms of Standard German. However, he spoke his variety fluently and with confidence and, when he found that it was nearly always easily understood, he continued to speak that way for some time, whereas Thomas was more conscious of the differences between his German and that of Hamburg and made efforts to converge towards the local variety. This occurred more gradually and seemingly less consciously in Frank's speech. The interesting thing here was that when this convergence towards the local variety of German did occur, features other than vocabulary and grammatical adjustments, such as intonation, pronunciation etc., were still not used by the boys when speaking German to their father — with me they basically spoke my German. For example, tag questions (a statement followed by a "tag", e.g. didn't she?, which turns it into a question seeking confirmation) are in Hamburg often formed by attaching *ne?* I, however, use *nicht* (= not?) or *nicht wahr*? (= not true?). It was observed that the boys freely used *ne?* with other people in Hamburg but only *nicht* with me — on some occasions they even corrected themselves when talking to me (this was even more interesting, since tag questions were a very late acquisition in the children's German — they occurred very rarely in their speech before their stay in Hamburg.) These observations fit with research on linguistic convergence, e.g. David McKirnan and Else Hamayan (1984:22): "There is evidence that interlocutors attempt to converge to the speech style they expect the other speaker to value ..." A similar observation can be made about the children's English — in Sydney English tag questions are often formed with *eh?*, a form not found in the Tasmanian English of their parents. Whilst the children will say to their friends "It's a hot day, eh?", the same question to their mother is invariably "It's a hot day, isn't it?"

One interesting matter which emerged from conversations with the children about whether they wished they could modify their German to such an extent that they would be indistinguishable from their German-speaking friends in Hamburg, was that they thought it would be good if their German were *nearly*, but *not exactly* the same. They did not want to be taken for Germans, but wanted to remain slightly different: Thomas: "Wir sind Deutsch sprechende Australier, nicht Deutsche." *(We're German-speaking Australians, not Germans.)* They compared this with when they visited England for a week — they were English-speakers, but not English. At the same time they obviously regarded themselves, as German-speakers, as being very close to their fellow German-speakers in Hamburg: when they were first referred to as *Ausländer* (= foreigners), they quickly retorted: "Wir sind nicht Ausländer, wir sind Australier!" *(We're not foreigners, we're Australians!)*

Even before the children's arrival in Germany they were aware that I was not a native speaker of the language, although this did not worry them (see chapter 6). Seeing me interacting with native speakers of German in Hamburg did not shake their faith in me as a reliable source of German. There was, however, a certain amount of psychological pressure on me to speak my very best German in the presence of native speakers who, I suspected, were perhaps subjecting my speech to particularly close scrutiny once they realized that this was the language I always spoke to my children. Only rarely was my German usage challenged by native speakers, e.g. on one occasion, when I said to Katrina at a duck pond "Die Enten quaken ja laut!" *(The ducks are quacking loudly!)*, I was corrected by a native speaker who insisted that the verb to refer to ducks' quacking was not *quaken*, but *schnattern* (which I used for the sound made by geese!) (Later questioning of other native speakers revealed that about a third of them also used *quaken* in this way.) Whilst this incident did not trouble the children, it did demonstrate to me the vulnerability and powerlessness of the non-native speaker in such discussions, even when one is reasonably sure that one may be right! The children readily accepted that I asked native speakers various questions about German usage and style. Thomas and Frank were rather amused (and impressed) that non-university educated friends of mine were doubtful at first about being able to help me linguistically, because the friends considered my knowledge of German grammar and spelling better than theirs. The fact that the children did see me seeking linguistic opinions was probably psychologically important in helping them to cope with any feelings of linguistic insecurity they might have had about their weaker language, as it showed that there is nothing wrong with asking for help when one is not sure about something.

Frank enjoyed school in Hamburg and, apart from a few schoolyard fights, had no problems. He had expected he would find the subject German difficult, but the work he was required to do (written comprehensions, dictations, compositions, etc.) was little different from the written work he had been doing for me in Australia.

He did have some problems with mathematics until he mastered the terminology needed to complete various tasks. (On his return to Australia he had the same problem in reverse — he had learnt new mathematical procedures through German and had to learn the appropriate English terminology.) He also admitted that in maths classes he often calculated in his head in English and wrote the result down in German — he said this was because he was used to doing this in English and because German numbers were said "the other way round from the way they're written" (24 is twenty-four in English but "vierundzwanzig", i.e "four-and-twenty", in German).

A noticeable improvement in Frank's German did occur during his stay in Hamburg. This is reflected not only in the grammatical accuracy analysis (see chapter 7) but also in the expansion of his active and receptive vocabulary, and the increase in his comprehension of rapid and complex German. Certain registers were added, others expanded, e.g. swearing! On arrival in Germany the children knew only half a dozen common German swear words and obscenities – which they saw as a deficiency in their German compared with their English. This deficiency was certainly rectified in the rough and tumble of the schoolyard, so that by the end of their stay their proficiency in this sphere exceeded my own. Some parents would probably frown on this, but it is important for children to be able to be familiar with this aspect of their peers' speech. As Edith Harding & Philip Riley (1986:142) write:

> ... without wishing to seem to recommend the habit, it has to be admitted that the ability to swear *convincingly* in a language is a mark of solidarity with and acceptance by the other speakers of that language.

I did not discourage Thomas's and Frank's acquisition of, or even their use of, these terms, as I realized from their facility with similar English expressions that they knew *when* and *where* their use would be inappropriate.

Certain grammatical features were also added to Frank's German, e.g. the subjunctive which rarely occurred in his speech in Australia but which is required in German in, for instance, conditional sentences with *if*. For example, German requires a different form of the verb for 'had' in the following sentences:

(i) I had enough money for an ice-cream. — Ich *hatte* genug Geld für ein Eis.
(ii) If I had enough money,... — Wenn ich genug Geld *hätte, ...*

Not only did Frank add the subjunctive in conditional sentences, but he added a form of the conditional sentences without the *wenn* (= if) being included, which is possible in German (and to a limited extent in English) but which I myself virtually never use, e.g.

Hätte ich genug Geld, ...
Had I enough money ...

This is now Frank's usual way of forming a conditional sentence.

As has been stated, other children on the whole accepted the German of Frank and Thomas without question; only rarely did other children attempt any correction — on one occasion, for example, Frank, (9;1) at the fish market in Hamburg with his friend Hendric, forgot that the German word *Knochen* corresponds to the English word 'bone' in all cases except when referring to a fish bone, in which case the word *Gräte* must be used:

> **Frank:** ... Wir müssen auf die Knochen aufpassen. *(We'll have to watch out for the bones* (Knochen).)
> **Hendric** (laughing): (Knochen)?! Du Arsch, das ist doch kein Wal! *(Bones* (Knochen)?! *You dickhead, it's not a whale!)*
> (Whales, being mammals and not fish, do have *Knochen* and not *Gräten.)*

Grammatical correction by other children seems to have been minimal and occurred mainly when Thomas or Frank had to work on some joint written task at, or for, school with another child, e.g. shortly before Thomas's departure from

Hamburg he and his friend Matthias had to prepare together a written report on dinosaurs. They shared the task of preparation, with Matthias being the editor and providing guidance on grammatical and stylistic points.

Adults, too, were in general appreciative of the quality of the children's German and the ease with which they could communicate in it. However, there was a small minority of people who were not so appreciative. These were the perfectionists, people with unrealistic expectations. Surprisingly, some of these were linguists or language teachers. They expected the children to be indistinguishable from monolingual German children after only a few months in Germany and focussed on the children's faults rather than their achievements, concentrated on *how* they spoke rather than on what they had to say (but, fortunately, not in their presence!). They were also the people who expressed doubts about the advisability of my speaking German to my children, since it was not my native language and because I spoke it with a faint accent. I attempted to counter their arguments by pointing out that the level of German the children had *already* attained would be matched by German children's English only after many years of study at school, perhaps never; although their German was deficient from the monolingual German point of view, it was a language they had always used, and probably always would use, daily for everyday communication; and how many Germans spoke English without at least some tinge of a German accent? Some seemed convinced, some obviously were not. Whilst such people can dampen one's spirits, they are, fortunately, the clear minority. Their attitude is also very like that of one group of people who as immigrants do not pass on their language to their children because their children are not acquiring the language "perfectly", i.e. like monolingual children in their homeland. Their view is "better not at all than imperfectly". This book stresses quite a different attitude, namely that it is better to have a reasonable command of a second language than no command of it at all.

Frank's linguistic achievements at school in Hamburg are perhaps best summed up by quoting some relevant parts of the school report he received when he left in December 1984:

Frank kam mit guten deutschen Sprachkenntnissen in die Klasse und überwand so die Anfangsschwierigkeiten rasch ...
Im Rechtschreiben unterliefen ihm nur noch bei schwierigen Wörtern Fehler. Frank liest auch ungeübte Texte fließend und deutlich ...
Seine Aufsätze schreibt er sprachgewandt und bereichert sie mit netten Ideen ...
(*Frank joined the class with a good command of German and thus quickly overcame any initial difficulties ...*
In spelling, he made errors only with difficult words. Frank reads even previously unseen texts fluently and clearly ...

He writes his compositions articulately and enriches them with nice ideas ...)

Katrina was aged only 3:4,18 when she arrived in Hamburg. At first she found it rather bewildering to be in a new home and in a new environment where *everyone* spoke German, not just her father. During the first three weeks she seemed a little resentful of me and if her mother spoke German to someone for more than a few sentences, Katrina would object by interrupting loudly in English and sometimes even placing her hand over her mother's mouth! Katrina still continued to speak German to me during this time, (but only if no-one else was present), and she would not say a single word to anyone else in German.

After three weeks Katrina no longer attempted to interrupt if her mother spoke German to someone and she began to speak German again to me in the company of other people. However, the stay in Hamburg coincided with a time when Katrina was already going through a stage where she was often overcome by shyness and would not speak to adults. The sudden transition to a German-speaking environment seemed to make her even more shy and during her whole stay in Germany she could not be persuaded to speak to any adults (apart from her parents) in German — or English! This proved to be somewhat awkward at times, as people then thought she did not understand German. But, fortunately, most adults simply accepted her shyness as being nothing unusual for a three year old.

However, with other *children* Katrina showed no signs of shyness right from the start and happily talked to them in German. From August till December 1984 she attended a kindergarten one afternoon a week, at first apprehensively, but, as time went on, with enjoyment. There, too, she did not speak to the teacher but only with the other children.

Katrina had much less contact with German children than did her brothers (2 hours of kindergarten per week, plus another few hours of casual contact), and English remained the language she heard and used most (with her mother and brothers). Nevertheless, by spending 6 months in Germany, she did have an advantage which her brothers had not had at that age: she was able to see that there was a whole country where German was used by practically everyone (just as English was in Australia) and that it was not merely a language spoken in her family and by a few others.

All in all, the stay in Hamburg demonstrated the significant beneficial effects on the maintenance and, importantly, also on the development, of a home language, which can be derived from an extended period of exposure to the language in a country or region where the language is the normal means of everyday communication.

11 Other aids to the development of bilingualism

So far in this study various ways used by the family to foster bilingualism in the home have been mentioned, some in detail, some in passing, e.g. co-operation between the parents to provide vocabulary for new experiences for the children by allowing them to hear it from their mother in English and from their father in German. In the following section a number of aids are discussed which parents can ultilize to develop their children's bilingualism.

Books and magazines

The value of books and storytelling in language nurture and maintenance has already been touched on in the section on biliteracy in chapter 8 and in the section on storytelling by the parents in chapter 4, but a few additional points are worth mentioning here. From an early age, the three children have had stories read aloud to them almost daily in German by me, and in English by their mother. This has had a definite beneficial effect on the children's German and English vocabulary. Any vocabulary acquired from material read to them has been more easily detectable in their German, particularly in the period before they had ever been to Germany, since, apart from me, their only other regular source of German was stories (including recorded stories — see next section). Such vocabulary extension has occurred, with the children actively using words and expressions heard in stories but perhaps not even used by their parents, e.g.:

> **Thomas** (5;10,13): Oh, jetzt *besinne* ich mich. *(Oh, now I remember.)*
> (My expression would be "Jetzt *erinnere* ich mich.")

It is not only the children's vocabulary which benefits. Stories have also exposed the children to and in some cases made them aware of different styles and levels of formality in German speech, differences which would be absent from the informal German spoken with me (see the section "Communicative Competence" in chapter 7).

Books are also useful for acquainting children with the poetic uses of language, particularly in the language they basically use only in the home and not at school. This may encourage them to experiment with such forms of language themselves. For example, at age 6;2,30 Thomas was reading aloud from *Safran* (12/1972:32), a German children's magazine, short rhymes such as the following:

Der Wal, der Wal
rutscht auf dem Bauch ins Tal.
(The whale, the whale
Slides on his belly into the vale.)

He found these rhymes amusing and then spontaneously produced one of his own:

Der Bert, der Bert
Er sprang auf ein Pferd.
(Bert, Bert, of course
He jumped on a horse.)

Although by no means a poetic masterpiece, it does rhyme and shows his awareness of the literary past tense *sprang* for "jumped" which had been acquired only from stories; in his own speech he would say *ist gesprungen* for "jumped", as in fact do most German speakers in everyday conversation.

Another good way of supplying children with regular reading material could be by subscribing to magazines suitable to their age and interests in the linguistic homeland. A teenager interested, for example, in pop music could be given a subscription to a pop magazine. An alternative to a subscription would be to get relatives or friends to send on magazines they have finished with.

To assist children with any problems they may encounter in their reading (and writing), parents should consider the purchase of a good dictionary, preferably a monolingual dictionary which explains words of the language in that language. However, for older children interested in the relationship between their two languages, a good bilingual dictionary (e.g. German-English, English-German) is also a useful aid, since it allows them to compare the two languages and to find equivalents for words which they know or can recall in only one of their languages but which they would like to use in the other; this can give them a sense of linguistic independence, as it gives them an alternative course of action to asking their parents what something means, how to say something, how something is spelt, etc.

There are also some storybooks available which are useful for raising children's esteem for their bilingualism because the usefulness of knowing more than one language plays an important part in the plot. A typical example, enjoyed by my children in the pre-school stage, is *Even for a Mouse* by Lisl Weil (1976).

Little Ollie the mouse shows little interest in learning a foreign language. But one day she is captured by Mr Cat and is about to become mouse stew, when she desperately recalls her foreign language lessons and shouts, "BOW WOW WOW!", scaring the cat who drops her, enabling her to escape. The moral of the story is expressed in her mother's words: "A foreign language is most helpful in life." To which Little Ollie now replies "Oh, yes. Even for a mouse!"

Books which make use of children's two languages are also popular. One such book, *I like you – und du?* by Emer O'Sullivan & Dietmar Rössler (1983), was very much enjoyed by Thomas at age 12. As suggested by the title itself, the text of the book is written in both German and English. The main characters are Paddy, an Irish boy, and a German girl, Karin, and in the story Paddy speaks English to Karin and she speaks German to him.

Records, audio and video cassettes

Records and cassettes of songs and stories are a useful aid for fostering a minority language. They help children who may be used to hearing a language in one particular variety from a small number of speakers to become acquainted with different accents and varieties of the language. They have proved beneficial for this purpose in the case of Thomas, Frank and Katrina (see the second half of chapter 6).

At the first playing of new recordings I usually listen with the children and explain any difficulties they may have with the vocabulary or accent used. Stories which are especially interesting or exciting are listened to frequently and, just as in the case of written stories, words and expressions heard on the recordings make their way into the children's speech.

If commercial recordings are not easily available or are too expensive, parents can easily make their own, for example by reading or simply telling favourite stories onto tape. Relatives, friends or acquaintances who speak the language, if possible with a variety of accents, speaking speeds, etc., can be asked to assist in the making of such tapes. With practice and a bit of ingenuity with sound effects and the like, quite professional-sounding recordings can be produced. Over the years a number of such recordings have been made for Thomas, Frank and Katrina and have proved popular. They are not seen by me, or the children, as normally being a substitute for actually reading and telling stories to the children in person, but rather as a supplement to this, or for use when I have to be absent for some reason.

Video cassettes are also very useful, especially if there is no regular opportunity to see films in the minority language on television or at the cinema. Although video recorders are not exactly cheap, they are becoming increasingly common in households throughout the world. They can be a valuable piece of equipment for maintaining and extending the language of children (and their parents). Video cassettes could be purchased from a country where the particular language is spoken, or arrangements could be made with someone there to send video cassettes — perhaps video cassettes could even be exchanged with someone in a similar situation in the other country. Thus, an Australian family wishing to maintain German in Australia could receive German video cassettes from a family in Germany interested in English and send English-language video cassettes in return. Such exchanges are very useful in enabling a family to keep in touch with television programs of various sorts being shown in the other country; one can not only be entertained, of course, but also informed about current affairs, attitudes etc. in the other country if documentary programs and school programs are included in the exchange. Another source of video cassettes which may be available in some countries, depending on the language involved, is to hire videos from a video shop which stocks cassettes in other languages.

Technically, there are a few problems to be considered. Basically most private owners of a video recorder will have either a VHS or a Beta machine. A VHS video cassette is bigger than a Beta cassette and therefore cannot be played in a Beta video recorder. Nor can a Beta cassette be played in a VHS recorder. If arranging an exchange of videos one therefore first needs to find someone who has a video recorder of the same format. A further problem which needs to be taken into account is the television system by which the recording was made on the video *and* the television system to be used to play back the video cassette. What works for the Australian family mentioned above as an example would not, for instance, work for a family in the U.S.A. – a video cassette recorded in Germany would not work in a U.S. video recorder, nor would a video cassette sent from the U.S.A. work in a video recorder made for Germany.

The reason is that there are different television standards or systems used in various countries.There are basically three television standards used in the world: PAL, NTSC and SECAM. The countries using each system are as follows:

(i) PAL

Afghanistan, Albania, Algeria, Australia, Austria, Azores, Bahrain, Bangla-desh, Belgium, Brunei, China (People's Republic), Cyprus, Denmark, Eng-land, Faroe Islands, Finland, Germany (Federal Republic), Ghana, Gibraltar, Greenland, Hong Kong, Iceland, India, Indonesia, Ireland, Israel, Italy, Jordan, Kenya, Korea (north), Kuwait, Laos, Liberia, Luxemburg (also SECAM), Madeira, Malaysia, Maldives, Monaco (also SECAM), Mozam-bique, Namibia, Netherlands, New Zealand, Nigeria, Norway, Oman, Paki-stan, Paraguay, Portugal, Qatar, Saudi Arabia (also SECAM), Scotland,

Seychelles, Sierra Leone, Singapore, South Africa, Spain (including Canary Islands), Sri Lanka, Sudan, Swaziland, Sweden, Switzerland, Tanzania, Thailand, Turkey, Uganda, United Arab Emirates, Uruguay, Wales, Yemen Arab Republic, Yugoslavia, Zambia, Zanzibar.

(ii) SECAM

Albania, Benin, Bulgaria, Burkina, Congo, Cyprus, Czechoslovakia, Djibouti, Egypt, Faso (formerly Upper Volta), France, Gabon, German Democratic Republic, Greece, Guadeloupe, Guiana (French), Hungary, Iran, Iraq, Ivory Coast, Lebanon, Libya, Luxemburg (also PAL), Madagascar, Martinique, Mauritania, Mauritius, Monaco (also PAL), Mongolia, Morocco, New Caledonia, Niger, Poland, Puerto Rico, Reunion, Romania, Saudi Arabia (also PAL), Senegal, Syria, Togo, Tunisia, USSR, Zaire, Zimbabwe.

(iii) NTSC

Antigua and Barbuda, Bahamas, Barbados, Belau, Bermuda, Bolivia, Burma, Canada, Chile, Colombia, Costa Rica, Cuba, Diego Garcia, Dominican Republic, Ecuador, El Salvador, Guatemala, Guam, Haiti, Hawaii, Honduras, Jamaica,Japan, Korea (South), Mexico, Micronesia, Montserrrat, Netherlands Antilles, Nicaragua, Panama, Peru, Philippines, Surinam, Taiwan, Trinidad and Tobago, USA, Venezuela, Vietnam, Virgin Islands, Yemen (People's Democratic Republic).

Provided one obtains video cassettes from a country using the same standard, there will be no problem. In addition, the PAL and SECAM systems are what is called *monochrome* compatible, which means that video cassettes *can* be exchanged between the two systems, *but* one will only see a black and white picture, not colour. The NTSC system is, however, unfortunately *not* compatible with either the PAL or SECAM systems. (The only exception is Brazil which has a unique system called PAL-M which is *monochrome* compatible with the normal PAL system and also with SECAM.) People living in a country using the NTSC system (USA etc.) and who wish to obtain video cassettes from a PAL or SECAM country (or vice versa) therefore face a big problem. They would need both a video recorder and a television set specially made to take the different television standards; this sort of TV set has a knob which enables one to switch to NTSC, PAL or SECAM as desired. However, the big drawback here is that such a set is expensive. Another possibility, also very expensive, would be to bring back a television set and video recorder from the country where one wishes to obtain video cassettes, or have them transferred from one system to the other by a video shop — again not exactly a cheap exercise. So people in the USA (NTSC) wishing to have French-language video cassettes, for example, would be advised to look to Canada or Haiti (both NTSC), not France (SECAM) or Belgium (PAL). In some cases there is no way out but to contemplate the somewhat expensive procedures just mentioned, e.g. Japanese-language video cassettes can, as far as this writer is aware, be obtained only from Japan (NTSC), so that families living in PAL or SECAM countries would really have no alternative. In such cases, sharing the cost among a number of families could be a possibility.

Using tapes, whether audio or video, can also be a useful means of maintaining close contact with relatives and friends in the country where the language is spoken. For young children particularly they are much more meaningful than letters, since for a short time it is as if the person speaking were actually there in person. Telephone calls between countries can also fulfil this function, with the added advantage of enabling a two-way conversation.

A parent who has to be absent from home for a period of time can also use tape recordings to good effect, sending them in addition to letters, postcards or making telephone calls to the children. When Thomas was aged 3;6,4 and Frank 1;7,2, for instance, I went overseas for a month. I took a small cassette recorder with me and each week while I was away I sent home one or two cassettes on which I talked to the children about my trip. In addition, I left at home stories read on to tape which were played to the children at bedtime. Preparing such tapes does, of course, require a bit of time and effort, but it is time and effort well spent. That particular overseas trip, for example, occurred at a time when Thomas was somewhat reluctant to speak German: two weeks before my departure Thomas was speaking only 59% German to me. As a temporary language maintenance measure the tapes proved helpful: two weeks after my return the amount of German Thomas was speaking to me had increased to 69% (see chapter 6).

Radio and television

Until fairly recently, Australians who wished to be informed or entertained via the electronic media in a language other than English had to rely on overseas shortwave broadcasts. However, due to fluctuating reception conditions, and because virtually no shortwave broadcaster caters in any way for children, these transmissions have been of limited use in language maintenance as far as children are concerned.

These shortwave broadcasts can, however, be very helpful for parents. I have found a good quality shortwave receiver to be an invaluable aid in maintaining and extending my own German. Despite the vagaries of atmospheric conditions, German-language transmissions can usually be picked up in Australia reasonably clearly from a variety of stations, the main ones being the Deutsche Welle (Federal Republic of Germany), Radio Berlin International (German Democratic Republic), Swiss Radio International, and Radio Austria. Other shortwave stations, such as

Radio Japan, Radio Sweden and the BBC, to name but a few, also broadcast German-language programs which, although intended for listeners in Europe, can be received in Australia and elsewhere from time to time. But wherever you happen to live and whatever country you wish to pick up, to ensure that the best quality shortwave reception is obtained with your radio it is advisable to erect some sort of *outdoor* aerial, however simple, e.g. even a length of wire attached to the branch of a nearby tree will provide much better reception than just using the radio's whip aerial.

Some families may be fortunate enough to live in a country (e.g. Belgium) which has cable television that gives them access to programs from other countries (e.g. from Britain). It is also possible in some countries to receive, via a small dish antenna mounted on one's roof and appropriate equipment, satellite television transmissions from other countries, e.g. USSR television programs could be received in Britain or Israel. Whilst the cost of obtaining and setting up the necessary equipment could well prove prohibitive for many families at the present time, it is likely that this will become a much more common form of televison reception in the not too distant future.

In Australia itself, radio and television transmissions in languages other than English were severely limited by law until the end of 1973; they could not exceed 2.5% of a station's total broadcast time and had to be accompanied by an English translation. However, since then there has been a growing awareness and recognition of the multilingual nature of Australian society. After experiments with broadcasting in non-English languages from 1975, the government established the Special Broadcasting Service (SBS) in 1978. Its two radio stations in Sydney and Melbourne now broadcast in over forty languages. The SBS is also linked to some public broadcasting stations in other towns throughout Australia. That this has been a boon for immigrants is probably illustrated no more spectacularly than by the case of a Turkish-speaking lorry driver reported in *The Sydney Morning Herald* (7 June 1982):

> Driving down Parramatta Road in his vehicle, the Turk suddenly happened upon 2EA (Sydney's multilingual radio station), while tuning his truck radio. Halting the lorry, he leaped to the roadway dancing and singing with joy. 'That's my language, that's my music!', he rejoiced as a huge traffic jam built up.

In 1979 and 1980 experimental television programs in languages other than English were broadcast for three hours per week. In late 1980 the SBS began operating a multilingual television station in both Sydney and Melbourne; by 1986 this service had been extended to all state capitals. SBS television now transmits daily for approximately eight hours in many languages, including some news and documentary programs in English. All programs not in English are provided with English subtitles.

Unfortunately, few of the SBS radio programs in languages other than English cater very much for young children. (Of the seven hours of German broadcast each week in Sydney, for example, only fifteen minutes is for children.) However, SBS television does devote a reasonable amount of its time to children's programs. These have proved very useful in fostering the linguistic and cultural awareness of Thomas, Frank and Katrina. The programs which are in German are, as already mentioned in chapter 9, valuable for exposing them to different varieties of German, especially the German of children, and, particularly in the period before they had ever been to Germany, for making them aware that in other parts of the world German is used just as English is in Australia, i.e. at school, with playmates, etc. Subtitles can be a little distracting once children can read fluently, although this problem is easily solved by sticking a narrow strip of paper along the bottom of the television screen. On the other hand, some children may find it linguistically interesting to compare the subtitles with the sound track, as Thomas occasionally does.

SBS's children's television programs in languages other than German have also proved to be valuable. Firstly, Thomas, Frank and Katrina have gained an increased appreciation of the fact that there are many other Australian children like themselves who at home speak a language other than English, a realization which can only help maintain their positive attitude to their own bilingual situation. Secondly, before the children could read rapidly, I at times used such films to provide them with additional exposure to German by translating the English subtitles into German. This worked very well, although it could become somewhat exhausting for me if a film contained very rapid dialogue!

Only one fifth of the children's weekly televison watching (total 7–9 hours) is on the multilingual channel. The rest is in English. However, it has been found that even English-language programs can be utilized to foster German if they are viewed with the children. A difficult plot and/or difficult vocabulary can be explained by me in German. Whilst such explanations were required more when the children were younger, as they grow older they can still be encouraged to discuss what has happened or might happen in a program. Such explanations and discussions have proved to be an effective way not only of helping to keep the children's German vocabulary apace of their English vocabulary, e.g. when the word "monotremes" occurred in a nature program which Thomas was watching at age 7;6, it was not only explained:

Father: Das sind australische Tiere, die Säugetiere sind, die aber auch Eier legen — wie das Schnabeltier und der Ameisenigel. *(They're Australian* *animals which are mammals but which also lay eggs — like the platypus and the echidna.)*

but the German term was also given:

Father: Auf deutsch heißen *monotremes* Kloakentiere. *(In German monotremes are called "Kloakentiere".)*

Some English-language programs have also been useful for conferring esteem on bilingualism; some of the principal characters have been bilingual and this has been portrayed as an ability which is a definite advantage and to be admired, e.g. even at age 13 Thomas was impressed with the ability of Dr Who, the hero of his favourite television science fiction series, to switch from English to Hokkien and German to extricate himself from difficult situations.

Another possibility with regard to radio and television, at least as far as certain languages are concerned, is programs specially prepared and broadcast for people studying these languages as foreign languages. Various programs of this type are broadcast in Australia for students of German, and some of these have proved usable with Thomas, Frank and Katrina. From age 4;7 to 5;0, for example, Frank looked forward to watching *Kontakte* (which is entirely in German) each Friday on television just as much as he did to watching *Playschool* (in English). The language used in *Kontakte* is simple and clear, much of the dialogue is humorous, and a good view is given of life in Germany. Radio plays produced by the BBC for Higher School Certificate students have also been used with the children after about age 6. The language in these is more complex than in *Kontakte,* but has presented few difficulties to the children, and, most importantly, the stories have proved popular because they are interesting and exciting.

Games

Games played with the children are a very useful and enjoyable means of reinforcing and extending their language, particularly in German. From a very early age the children quickly acquired the German vocabulary needed to play particular games with me, e.g. it was much more effective to say *"Hüh!"* (giddy-up) to a horse (= their father) who obviously seemed to understand no English. These games may be invented by the children or be based on a story heard (in either language), a television program, a game played at school, etc. The playing with me of a game already played frequently with playmates in English offers an ideal opportunity to create a vocabulary of similar sophistication in German. A simple game of *Räuber und Gendarm* (cops and robbers), for instance, imparts a wide range of German vocabulary connected with crime and law enforcement, e.g. "Untersuch die Waffe auf Fingerabdrücke." *(Examine the weapon for fingerprints.)* The frequent repetition of such phrases quickly establishes them as part of the children's active vocabulary and helps restore the balance between English and German. In addition, such games offer an opportunity to iron out some grammatical problems relatively unobtrusively.

Even reading and writing can be incorporated painlessly into games, e.g. with a treasure hunt at the beach in which the treasure can only be found by following a series of clues written with a stick in the sand.

As the children get older, various types of board games in the language can also be played with pleasure. For instance, when Thomas was 12 years old and keen on the English game *Trivial Pursuit,* I capitalized on this interest by buying a German-language version of the same game; the game is both fun and an excellent way of extending the children's vocabulary. Similar games which rely strongly on actually using the language can be purchased to suit most age levels. *Scrabble* and similar games are a way of practising spelling so that it seems more like play than work!

Older children's interests, such as various sports (e.g. table tennis), hobbies (e.g. stamp collecting), etc. can also provide parents with the opportunity to enjoy themselves with their children and at the same time increase the children's contact with and use of the parents' language.

The most important thing, of course, about games and similar activities is that they are an enjoyable and reasonably effortless way of increasing and consolidating the children's range of language.

Outings

In families where only one parent speaks the minority language to the children, it can prove very useful for that parent occasionally to arrange some sort of interesting outing alone with the children, an outing on which the language can be used exclusively. I have found that outings like this (e.g. a walk in the bush, going fishing) ensure that the children get a lot of speaking practice, and some improvement in the ease with which they express themselves is usually noticeable after quite a short time.

Shops, restaurants, etc.

Depending on the language in question, it may be possible to locate shops, banks, restaurants, etc., where someone knows that language and is prepared to speak it to customers. The children can then see that the language does have certain possibilities outside the home. At age 8, for instance, Thomas still found it an exciting experience to be able to carry out some simple transaction in German, for example buying a book from the German-speaking staff of a Sydney bookshop. The beneficial effect of such an experience was evident from the enthusiasm with which he later told friends about what he had done. Even if a language not known to the children can be heard, for example, in a restaurant, this too can be a useful experience for promoting interest and pride in bilingualism.

Ethnic schools and playgroups

In countries of immigration, various groups of interested and concerned immigrants establish "ethnic" schools to give their children instruction in the language and culture of their former homeland. These usually hold classes outside normal school hours, either in the late afternoon or at the weekend. For younger children, playgroups may be organized at other times.

It is estimated, for example, that in Australia today there are approximately 1,000 ethnic schools attended by about 100,000 children (Kringas & Lewins, 1981:1). Ethnic playgroups and schools can provide parents with valuable support in preserving and fostering a language. The children — and the parents — then realize that there are others in the same position as they are, and that it is feasible to retain a linguistic (and cultural) system different from that of the community at large, whilst still being able to function adequately in that community. Such schools are particularly useful in making children literate in the language of the home, as many parents are unsure about how to teach their children to read and write or are apprehensive about tackling this on their own (see also chapter 8 for discussion of biliteracy).

However, such schools do have their problems. Firstly, they usually take place *in addition* to the children's normal school hours. If held in the late afternoon, the children are not only tired after a full day at normal school but may regard it as an imposition when their monolingual peers are free to play or watch television. This applies probably even more so to classes held at the weekend. Secondly, many parents shift most of the responsibility of language maintenance on to the ethnic school. They rarely, if ever, speak the language to their children at home or encourage the children to speak it to them, and then expect the ethnic school to teach it to them in, say, three hours every Saturday morning. For such children the ethnic school is virtually a foreign language school. Unfortunately, this attitude is even held by some of those running ethnic schools. For example, at a migrant studies seminar held in Melbourne in 1979, the coordinator of a number of Saturday schools for a particular language, when asked if the children who attended the classes also used the language at home, remarked, "No, very little — we think it's a bit much to demand that children use the language at home."

Ethnic schools can be successful if considered as an *aid* to, not a substitute for, someone in the home regularly and consistently using the language for communication with the children. Without the support of the home, such schools can, in the limited time available, impart but a smattering of the language.

A solution to the problems caused by the ethnic schools being conducted outside normal school hours would, of course, be for the teaching of the home language, or even for some teaching *in* the home language, to be incorporated into the normal school curriculum. However, this is only possible with the co-operation of the school authorities and normally only if a particular minority language group constitutes a significant proportion of the school population. But when children's bilingualism is acknowledged and provision made for it in the normal school, studies show that the results can be very pleasing. Not only does the minority language receive in this way a certain amount of status — it is now part of the normal school curriculum just as arithmetic is — but the scholastic progress of the children can actually be improved. Wallace Lambert (1978), for example, reports on an experiment conducted in the northern regions of Maine in the USA, where French is spoken by 85% of families. Several schools were permitted to teach about one third of their elementary curriculum in French, and the progress of the children in these schools was compared to that of other bilingual children of comparable intelligence and socioeconomic background who received instruction only in English. After five years the children who had received part of their instruction in French clearly outperformed those children in the all-English schools in *English* language achievement tests and on academic content such as mathematics, learned partly through French. Moreover, they were biliterate, having learned to read and write both English and French, whilst the children in the all-English schools had become literate only in English.

Similar evidence is emerging in the Australian context. For example, Graham McGill (1980) reports that at Milingimbi in the Northern Territory, Aboriginal children taught at school in *both* English *and* Gupapuyngu (one of the more than one hundred Aboriginal languages still spoken in Australia) have been found to perform significantly better than children in an English-only program on such measures as *English* reading, *English* written composition, oral *English* and arithmetic.

In the case of my own children, there is no language except English taught at the primary school which Thomas attended for six years and which Katrina and Frank are still attending at the time of writing. Only Thomas has had any experience with an ethnic school. Between the ages of 3;8 and 4;1 he attended the kindergarten section of a German Saturday school in Melbourne for 2.5 hours on Saturday mornings. It was beneficial in that it brought him into contact with other German speakers. However, it was not, unfortunately, as successful as it could have been, because many of the children attending spoke little or no German at home, so that the teacher often used English to communicate with them. Trying to cater for children of disparate linguistic competence is a problem faced by many ethnic schools.

Parents may also provide their children with reading and writing instruction in the minority language themselves at home, either instead of or in addition to using an ethnic school. Details of how this has been attempted with Thomas, Frank and Katrina are given in the section on biliteracy in chapter 8.

Since age 2;6 Katrina has attended a small German-language playgroup which was formed by a small group of interested parents and which meets for one afternoon a month in a suburb of Sydney. This has been beneficial for all children who attend. In the early stages some of the children were inclined to switch to English if a parent was not in the immediate vicinity, as they were accustomed to speaking German only to adults, not to children. However, the playgroup soon came to be regarded as a place where German was spoken to *everyone,* and the children now play happily together in German. In fact, these children now also speak German to each other even when they meet on other occasions. The parents need to do very little organization — each family brings a selection of toys and games and a supply of cakes, juice and coffee for the very popular *Kaffee und Kuchen* (afternoon tea)! In this case, a church kindly allows the playgroup the use of a small hall and grounds. It should be pointed out that not only the children benefit from such playgroups, but also the parents, since it is a good opportunity to chat with fellow speakers of the language, discuss problems, exchange books, magazines, etc.

In her book *Raising Children Bilingually: The Pre-School Years,* Lenore Arnberg (1985:125), based on her study of minority language playgroups for preschool children, gives a number of helpful suggestions for parents setting up a playgroup, including the following: It is important (i) to have someone who is responsible for being the leader and for keeping the group going, arranging with parents some sort of schedule to be followed; (ii) to use mainly activities which require the children to speak as much as possible; (iii) to structure the children's time so that they are not left too much on their own (many children then start speaking to each other in the majority language); (iv) to try, depending on the size of the group, to divide the children into relevant age groups and/or according to proficiency in the minority language.

An interesting development regarding the playgroup was that although it was originally intended primarily for preschool children, Thomas and Frank also showed an interest and still wish to attend. Sometimes they chat with the adults, or they may just read by themselves. However, their presence has also proved useful as far as the younger children who have no older siblings are concerned: they see that it is not unusual for even older children also to use German with their father and others in an Australian environment.

Correspondence schools

It may be possible for some parents to arrange for their children to receive school lessons by correspondence from a country where the particular language is spoken. The availability of such a service will vary from language to language, and it may be provided free or at minimal cost by the education authorities of the particular country, or it may have to be obtained privately and paid for accordingly. Children can do one or more subjects in the particular language at home under the supervision of a parent who receives advice and support from the correspondence school on what is to be done. Work is sent to the school regularly for checking. Such a system is very useful for parents who may be apprehensive about teaching their own children in their language. However, care needs to be taken that the level of linguistic difficulty of correspondence lessons is appropriate for children who may be dominant in, and already be doing their schooling in, the language of the country in which they are living, and that children are not expected to do an excessive amount of work by correspondence in addition to their normal school work. Angela Magness (1987) reports on the success of one such correspondence school, the World-Wide Education Service (44–50 Osnaburgh Street, London NW1 3NN), a non-profit making educational charity in Britain, which has children all over the world taking single subjects or a complete school curriculum in English. Once more it is worth pointing out that parents do not need to be highly educated to help children with correspondence lessons – there are many ordinary parents who, with the support of the correspondence school, cope very well in their role as "home teachers". My own mother, for instance, who left school at the end of grade 7, despite initial apprehensiveness, successfully taught me via correspondence lessons in my first year of schooling.

Holiday and weekend camps, clubs

Some immigrant groups organize camps, either at weekends or during school holidays, for children at which a variety of activities is carried out exclusively in the language, e.g. the Latvian community in Australia holds an annual summer camp for this purpose. Similarly, some immigrant groups run clubs for their young people at which the immigrant language is used. Such activities could even be organized on quite a small scale, e.g. a few families going away together on a weekend camping trip.

Visits to and from the linguistic homeland

An ideal aid in establishing and maintaining bilingualism in the home would be for the family to make regular trips to a country or region where the language is spoken, or to be visited fairly regularly by relatives and/or friends from that country. Of course, the feasibility of this will depend on geographical, political and financial considerations. For example, someone making a trip from London to Helsinki, Moscow or Ankara has less distance to cover (and consequently less to outlay in fares) than someone travelling from Sydney on one side of Australia to Perth on the other side of the country, not to mention someone departing from Sydney to Europe. Immigrants who are refugees (e.g. Vietnamese) often do not have ready access to their former homeland. Some languages do not even have a homeland where the language is spoken by a monolingual populace, e.g. Yiddish, Esperanto.

However, if such visits to the homeland can be managed, the benefits are many. Both the children and their parents are for a time totally immersed in the language, the children come into contact with the language of children of their own age (something usually lacking in a foreign environment) and see the language being used as a completely viable means of communication in all spheres of life. It is an opportunity for their language to be revitalized. (The beneficial linguistic effects of six months spent in Germany by my family are described in chapter 10.)

Similar, but not so striking, benefits can result from visits by grandparents, etc., to the new country, as their presence increases the amount and variety of language used in the home, particularly in mixed marriages. Some immigrant families, of course, have this benefit on a permanent basis, in that the grandparents are also immigrants and live with or near the family; their presence means that the home language is heard and *used* much more by their grandchildren. Smolicz & Harris's (1977) interviews with 70 children of Polish parents in Australia showed, for example, that 94% of them spoke only Polish to their grandparents, whereas only 57% spoke only Polish to their parents.

Correspondence

One way of getting children interested in reading and writing the language is for them to be encouraged to regularly exchange letters in it with friends and/or relatives, particularly with children of similar age and interests in a country where the language is the majority language. Another possibility would be to obtain a penfriend who speaks the language by writing to a magazine with a "Penfriends Wanted" section, or by contacting an organization which puts prospective correspondents in touch with each other. (Since their 1984 stay in Hamburg both Thomas and Frank have been corresponding with friends there; this not only serves the important function of maintaining social contact between friends, but is linguistically useful, too, enabling them to keep in touch with the language of their age group — the latest "in" words, etc.)

Live-in assistance, babysitters, etc.

Some of the bilingual families mentioned in the literature referred to in this book (e.g. Fantini, Hoffmann, Ronjat, Taeschner) have been fortunate in being able to have in their homes maids, au-pair girls, etc., who are speakers of the minority language and who play a role in caring for the children and, of course, speaking to them in their native language. Such arrangements would obviously be a considerable help in giving the children added input in the language, but unfortunately most families would not be able to afford them. However, it may be worth considering some sort of part-time assistance, e.g. if it is necessary to have a babysitter for the children at certain times, it could be possible to find someone who speaks the language.

A magazine for bilingual families

Since 1984 there has existed a quarterly magazine for parents of bilingual children. Edited by the writer of this book, the *Bilingual Family Newsletter* serves as a support for parents. Written in non-technical English, it contains summaries of research into various aspects of bilingualism, reviews of books dealing with bilingualism, reports from readers covering a wide range of bilingual family situations, a contacts section for readers wishing to make contact with other bilingual families, a bilingual humour section, and a question and answer section where the editor and an advisory board suggest answers to readers' queries and problems. So far the response from readers suggests that the magazine has proved to be a valuable source of information and encouragement for parents bringing up their children bilingually. A sample copy of the *Bilingual Family Newsletter* and details of how to subscribe can be obtained simply by writing to the publishers: Multilingual Matters Ltd, Bank House, 8a Hill Road, Clevedon, Avon BS21 7HH, England.

Books on bilingualism for parents

Parents who are particularly interested in the various aspects of bilingualism can receive new insights and inspiration from reading easily accessible and informative books on the subject. Of the works listed in the bibliography at the back of this book, the following are especially recommended for both their content and for their clear explanations and discussions: Harding & Riley (1986), Arnberg (1987), Grosjean (1982), Jonekeit & Kielhöfer (1983), Fantini (1982, 1985), Skutnabb-Kangas (1984).

Language maintenance for parents

In many ways the quality of language acquired by children mainly or only from their parents in a foreign environment will obviously depend very much on the quality of language they hear from their parents. It therefore follows that if parents wish to pass on what they regard as a good standard of the particular language, they should offer their children a good model. This requires some effort and vigilance on the part of the parents to keep their own language active, fresh and up-to-date. Many of the points already mentioned in this section are also useful here: reading of newspapers, magazines and books, writing letters, listening to records, cassettes and radio broadcasts, watching films in the language, etc. All of these can help parents not only to maintain their language but also to extend it by introducing them to new vocabulary and idioms which have come into being in the linguistic homeland and which may not even yet be found in dictionaries, e.g. on the occasion of the first flight by the American space shuttle Columbia, I learned immediately from a shortwave news broadcast beamed towards Australasia by the Deutsche Welle *(Voice of Germany)* in Cologne that this new concept was expressed in German as *(Welt)raumfähre* (literally "space ferry"), and I was thus able to use the correct specific term when discussing the event with the children.

Nevertheless, a good quality dictionary is virtually indispensable for checking and finding information. Brand new vocabulary (such as "space shuttle" just mentioned) can be written in for later reference.

Opportunities can also be sought to speak the language as frequently as possible with other speakers of the language; in countries with immigrants, many ethnic groups have formed various clubs and organizations (cultural, social, sporting, religious, etc.) which could be joined or whose functions could be attended.

There is much truth in what Einar Haugen (1953:6) says:

Once acquired, an extra language is like swimming or dancing or bicycling, in not being easily forgotten in disuse. But for successful and skilful performance, it requires, like these, constant practice and effort.

12 Conclusions

Considering the disproportionate amount of exposure which Thomas, Frank and Katrina have had to their two languages, the results attained in this attempt at creating bilingualism would seem to be very satisfactory. The children, it is true, are more fluent and accurate in English, but have approximately equal vocabularies in German and English. In the home they function more or less equally well in English and German. Outside, they can be indistinguishable from their monolingual English-speaking peers, and they can also communicate effectively and easily with German-speakers.

Moreover, their German has been acquired at no expense to their English, the official language of their country. Knowing German has not impeded the children's speech development in English, nor has being able to speak, read and write in German had any harmful effect on their educational progress in an English-speaking school. In this regard, it is worth recalling that there is much evidence to suggest that bilingualism can enhance children's intellectual capacity in various ways.

Family harmony has not been disturbed by the use of two languages in the home. Indeed, in some ways family relationships may well have benefited from this home bilingualism, for example, the relationship between the children and their father — my endeavours to ensure that they are exposed to as much German as possible mean that I spend as much time as possible talking to and playing with them.

Virtually no formal *teaching* of German has been required (except in reading and writing); instead, the children have been given the opportunity to *acquire* the language (just as monolingual children acquire their one native language) by being consistently spoken to in German and by being encouraged to use the language themselves as a natural means of communication. Once using a language like this becomes the established routine in a family, much of the battle is already won. Nevertheless, as has been seen, some effort and perseverance have been required to establish and maintain German in the home in a predominantly English-speaking environment. But the effort required is by no means daunting and is more than compensated for by the rewards. The important thing is not to give up at the first

257

hint of difficulties. If parents are patient, determined and persistent, it is very likely that they will succeed in raising their children as bilinguals.

It is hoped that the results achieved in this one Australian family, as well as the evidence from other studies referred to throughout this book, will help remove some of the mystery and doubts about bilingualism in the family, and that as a consequence other parents who speak languages other than the dominant language of their community will be encouraged to pass on their languages to their children. This can only mean enrichment for the community, the parents, and the children.

Bibliography

ANASTASI, A. & CORDOVA, F. 1953, Some effects of bilingualism upon the intelligence test performance of Puerto Rican children in New York. *Journal of Educational Psychology*, 44, 1–19.

ANDERSSON, THEODORE 1981, *A Guide to Family Reading in Two Languages: The Preschool Years*. Rosslyn, Virginia: National Clearinghouse for Bilingual Education.

ANDREWS, ILSE 1980, Look at bilinguals. *International Review of Applied Linguistics*, XVIII/4, 273–88.

ANSFIELD, ELIZABETH 1964, *A comparison of the cognitive functioning of monolinguals and bilinguals*. Ph.D. thesis, McGill University.

ARNBERG, LENORE 1987, *Raising Children Bilingually: The Pre-School Years*. Clevedon: Multilingual Matters.

BAETENS BEARDSMORE, HUGO 1982, *Bilingualism: Basic Principles*. Clevedon: Tieto Ltd.

BAGIV (BUNDESARBEITSGEMEINSCHAFT DER IMMIGRANTENVERBÄNDE IN DER BUNDESREPUBLIK DEUTSCHLAND UND BERLIN WEST) (ed.) 1985, *Muttersprachlicher Unterricht in der Bundesrepublik Deutschland. Sprach- und bildungspolitische Argumente für eine zweisprachige Erziehung von Kindern sprachlicher Minderheiten*. Hamburg: Rissen.

BAIN, BRUCE 1974, Verbal regulation of cognitive processes: A replication of Luria's procedures with bilingual and unilingual infants. *Child Development*, 47, 543–46.

BALKAN, L. 1970, *Les effets du bilinguisme français-anglais sur les aptitudes intellectuelles*. Bruxelles: Aimav.

BECK, M. S. 1979, *Baby Talk. How Your Child Learns to Talk*. New York: New American Library.

BEEN-ZEEV, SANDRA 1977a, The influence of bilingualism on cognitive strategy and cognitive development, *Child Development*, 48, 1009–18.

— 1977b, Mechanisms by which childhood bilingualism affects understanding of language and cognitive structures. In P. HORNBY, (ed.), *Bilingualism. Psychological, Social and Educational Implications*. New York: Academic Press, 29–55.

BERGAN, J. & PARRA, E. 1979, Variations in IQ tesing and instruction and the letter learning and achievement of Anglo and bilingual Mexican-American children. *Journal of Educational Psychology*, 71(6), 819–26.

BERTHOZ-PROUX, M. 1976, L'enfant de travailleur migrant à l'école français. *Langue Française*, 29, 116–26.

BETTONI, CAMILLA 1981, *Italian in North Queensland*. Townsville: James Cook University.

BLOOMFIELD, LEONARD 1933, *Language*. New York: Holt.

BÖDIGER, ANNE 1985, Reader's letter. *Bilingual Family Newsletter*, Vol. 2, No. 1, 6.

259

BRANDT, THOMAS 1957, Letter to the editor. *The American-German Review*, Jan., 39–40.

BRENNAN, ANNE 1987, Teaching a trilingual child to read. *Bilingual Family Newsletter*, 4(3).

BUBENIK, VIT 1978, The acquisition of Czech in the English environment. In PARADIS, MICHEL, (ed.), *Aspects of Bilingualism*, pp. 3–12, Columbia: Hornbeam Press.

BURLING, ROBBINS 1959, Language development of a Garo and English speaking child. *Word*, 15, 45–68.

BUTZKAMM, WOLFGANG 1982, Zur Vermittlung von Weil-Sätzen: Problemskizze anhand einer Unterrichtsanalyse. *Deutsch lernen*, 7(4), 71–81.

BYRAM, MICHAEL 1981, Reader's response. *Journal of Multilingual and Multicultural Development*, 2(3), 213.

CARRINGER, D. 1974, Creative thinking abilities of a Mexican youth. The relationship of bilingualism. *Journal of Cross-Cultural Psychology*, 5(4), 492–505.

CARSTENSEN, BRODER 1965, *Englische Einflüsse auf die deutsche Sprache seit 1945.* Heidelberg: Carl Winter Universitätsverlag.

CHRISTIAN, CHESTER 1977, Minority language skills before age three. In MACKEY, WILLIAM & ANDERSSON, THEODORE (eds), *Bilingualism in Early Childhood*, pp. 94–108. Rowley: Newbury House.

CLYNE, MICHAEL 1967, *Transference and Triggering. Observations on the Language Assimilation of Postwar German-Speaking Migrants in Australia.* The Hague: Nijhoff.

— 1968, The maintenance of bilingualism. *The Australian Journal of Education*, 12, 125–30.

— 1970, Some aspects of the bilingualism and language maintenance of Australian-born children of German-speaking parents. *ITL*, 9, 35–47.

— 1972a, *Perspectives on Language Contact.* Melbourne: The Hawthorn Press.

— 1972b, Some (German-English) language contact phenomena at the discourse level. In FIRCHOW, E *et al.* (eds), *Studies for Einar Haugen*, pp. 132–44. The Hague: Mouton.

— 1973, Thirty years later: some observations on "Refugee German" in Melbourne. In SCHOLLER, H. & REIDY, J., (eds), *Lexicography and Dialect Geography, Festgabe Für Hans Kurath*, pp. 96–106. Wiesbaden: Franz Steiner Verlag.

— 1974, Language contact and language ecology in Australia. In RADO, MARTA, (ed.), *Bilingual Education. Papers Presented at the Third Language Teaching Conference held at La Trobe University, pp. 51–76.* Bundoora: La Trobe University.

— 1977a, Bilingualism of the elderly. *Talanya*, 4, 45–56.

— 1977b, Language contact and inter-cultural communication breakadown and conflict. In MOLONY, CAROL, ZOBL, HELMUT & STÖLTING, WILFRIED, (eds), *Deutsch im Kontakt mit anderen Sprachen/German in Contact with other Languages*, pp. 129–146. Kronberg/Ts: Scriptor Verlag.

— 1979, Community Languages in Australia – what the 1976 Census will (and will not) tell us. Paper presented at the A.G.M. of the Society of Linguistics and Education, Melbourne.

— 1980, Community Language and language policy: A demographic perspective. Paper presented at Applied Linguistics Association of Australia Conference, Melbourne. (Also published in GARNER, MARK 1981, 13–36.)

— 1981, *Deutsch als Muttersprache in Australien: Zur Ökologie einer Einwan-derersprache.* Wiesbaden: Franz Steiner Verlag.

— 1982, *Multilingual Australia, Resources, Needs, Policies.* Melbourne: River Seine Publications.

— 1985, Bilingual language acquisition and language separation. *Journal of Intercultural Studies,* 6(1), 41–48.

CORSETTI, RENATO & TAESCHNER, TRAUTE 1986, Early language differentiation in a trilingual child, ms.

CUMMINS, JIM 1976, The influence of bilingualism on cognitive growth: A synthesis of research findings and explanatory hypotheses. *Working Papers on Bilingualism,* 9, 1–43.

— 1978, Bilingualism and the development of metalinguistic awareness. *Journal of Cross-Cultural Psychology,* 9(2), 131–49.

— 1984a, *Bilingualism and Special Education: Issues in Assessment and Pedagogy.* Clevedon: Multilingual Matters.

— 1984b, Wanted: a theoretical framework for relating language proficiency to academic achievement among bilingual students. In RIVERA, CHARLENE (ed.), *Language Proficiency and Academic Achievement,* 2–19. Clevedon: Multilingual Matters Ltd.

DAY, ELAINE & SHAPSON, STAN 1987, Assessment of oral communicative skills in early French immersion programmes. *Journal of Multilingual and Multicultural Development,* 8(3), 237–60.

DE HOUWER, ANNICK 1984a, Repairs and the use of the monitor in early second lan-gauge acquisition. In KRENN, HERWIG, NIEMEYER, JÜRGEN, EBERHARDT, ULRICH (eds), *Sprache und Gesellschaft. Akten des 18. Linguistischen Kolloquiums Linz 1983,* pp. 130–42. Tübingen: Max Niemeyer Verlag.

— The development of the verb phrase in a bilingual child. In SINGLETON, DAVID M. & LITTLE, DAVID G. (eds), *Language learning in formal and informal contexts. Proceedings of a joint seminar of the Irish and British Associations for Applied Linguistics held at Trinity College, Dublin, 11–13 September 1984,* pp. 41–53. Dublin: Irish Association for Applied Linguistics.

DE JONG, EVELINE, 1986. *The Bilingual Experience. A Book for Parents.* Cambridge: Cambridge University Press.

DIEBOLD, A. 1961, Incipient bilingualism. *Language,* 37, 97–112.

DIMITRIJEVIC, N. 1965, A bilingual child. *English Language Teaching,* 20, 23–28.

DIXON, R. M. W. 1980, *The Languages of Australia.* Cambridge: Cambridge University Press.

DODSON, CARL 1984, Living with two Languages. *Bilingual Family Newsletter,* 1(1), 2–3.

DOMAN, GLENN 1975, *Teach your Baby to Read.* London: Pan Books.

DÖPKE, SUSANNE 1986, Discourse strategies in bilingual families. *Journal of Multilingual and Multicultural Development,* 7 (6), 493–507.

DORIAN, NANCY 1981,*Language Death. The Life Cycle of a Scottish Gaelic Dialect.* Philadelphia: University of Pennsylvania Press.

DOYLE, ANNA-BETH, CHAMPAGNE, M. & SEGALOWITZ, NORMAN 1978, Some issues on the assessment of linguistic consequences of early bilingualism. In PARADIS, MICHEL, (ed.), *Aspects of Bilingualism,* pp. 13–20. Columbia: Hornbeam Press.

EDELMAN, MARTIN 1969, The contextualization of school children's bilingualism. *Modern Language Journal,* 53, 179–82.

ELLIOTT, LAWRENCE 1977, The French Correction. *Reader's Digest*, 9, 533–56.

ELWERT, W. THEODOR 1959, *Das Zweisprachige Individuum: Ein Selbstzeugnis*. Mainz: Verlag der Akademie der Wissenschaften und literatur.

FACEY, ANDREA 1986, Bilingualism with a difference. *Bilingual Family Newsletter*, 3(3), 5–6.

FANTINI, ALVINO 1976, *Language Acquisition of a Bilingual Child: A Sociolinguistic Perspective (To Age 5)*, Vermont: The Experiment Press.

— 1978a, Bilingual behaviour and social cues: Case studies of two bilingual children. In PARADIS, MICHEL (ed.), *Aspects of Bilingualism*, pp. 283–301. Columbia: Hornbeam Press.

— 1978b, Emerging styles in child speech: Case study of a bilingual child. *The Bilingual Review*, No. 3, 169–89.

— 1982, *La adquisición del lenguaje en un niño bilingüe*. Barcelona: Editorial Herder.

— 1985, *Language Acquisition of a Bilingual Child: A Sociolinguistic Perspective to Age 10*. Clevedon: Multilingual Matters.

— 1986, Developing bilingualism: two world views? *Bilingual Family Newsletter*, 3(3), 1–3.

FELDMAN, C. & SHEN, M. 1971, Some language-related cognitive advantages of bilingual five-year-olds. *The Journal of Genetic Psychology*, 118, 235–244.

FISHMAN, JOSHUA 1965, Bilingualism, intelligence and language learning. *The Modern Language Journal*, 44, 227–36.

FRIEDLANDER, B., 1971, Listening, language and the auditory environment. In HELLMUTH, J., (ed.), *Exceptional Infant (Vol. 2)*. New York: Bruner/Mazel.

— JACOBS, B., DAVIS, B. & WETSTONE, H. 1972, Time-sampling analysis of infants' natural language environments in the home. *Child Development*, 43, 730–40.

FTHENAKIS, WASSILIOS, SONNER, ADELHEID, THRUL, ROSEMARIE & WALBINER, WALTRAUD 1985, *Bilingual-bikulturelle Entwicklung des Kindes. Ein Handbuch für Psychologen, Pädogogen und Linguisten*. München: Hueber.

GAARDER, A. BRUCE 1967. *Bilingual Education*. A prepared statement presented to the special Subcommittee on Bililngual Education of the Committee on Labor and Public Welfare, United States Senate. Washington, D.C.: United States Government Printing Office. (Quoted in LLOYD, G., *Studies of Infant School Children 3 — Deprivation and the Bilingual Child*. Oxford: Blackwell, 1977, p. 106.)

GARNER, MARK (ed.), 1981, *Community Languages. Their role in education*. Melbourne: River Seine Publications.

GENESEE, FRED, TUCKER, G. RICHARD & LAMBERT, WALLACE 1975, Communication skills of bilingual children. *Child Development*, 46, 1010–14.

GRIMM, HANNELORE 1975, On the child's acquisition of semantic structure underlying the worldfield of prepositions. *Language and Speech*, 18, 97–119.

GROSJEAN, FRANÇOIS 1982, *Life with Two Languages. An Introduction to Bilingualism*. Cambridge: Harvard University Press.

— 1985, The bilingual as a competent but specific speaker–hearer. *Journal of Multilingual and Multicultural Development*, 6(6), 467–77.

GROVER, MIKE & MARJUKKA 1982, Readers' Response. *Journal of Multilingual and Multicultural Development*, 3, 61–2.

GRZIMEK, BERNHARD 1971, *Mit Grzimek durch Australien*. Gütersloh: Bertelsmann.

HAAS, MARI 1953, Results of the conference of anthropologists and linguists. *International Journal of American Linguistics*, 19, 42–3.
HARDING, EDITH & RILEY, PHILIP 1986, *The Bilingual Family. A Handbook for Parents*. Cambridge: Cambridge University Press.
HANCOCK, IAN 1977, Lexical expansion within a closed system. In BLOUNT, BEN & SANCHES, M., *Sociocultural Dimensions of Language Change*, pp. 161–71. New York: Academic Press.
HARRISON, G. J. & PIETTE, A. 1980, Young bilingual children's language selection. *Journal of Multilingual and Multicultural Development*, 1(3), 217–30.
HASSELMO, NILS 1970, Code-switching and modes of speaking. In GILBERT, GLEN, (ed.), *Texas Studies in Bilingualism*, pp. 179–209. Berlin: de Gruyter.
— 1972, Code-switching as ordered selection. In FIRCHOW, E. *et al.* (eds), *Studies for Einar Haugen*, pp. 261–280. The Hague: Mouton.
HAUGEN, EINAR 1953, *The Norwegian Language in America: A Study in Bilingual Behaviour*. 2nd printing, revised 1969. Bloomington: Indiana University Press.
— 1956, *Bilingualism in the Americas*. Alabama: University of Alabama Press.
— 1972, Bilingualism as a social and personal problem. In FILOPOVIC, R., (ed.), *Active Methods and Modern Aids in the Teaching of Foreign Languages*, pp. 1–14. London: OUP.
— 1973, Bilingualism, language contact, and immigrant languages in the United States: A research report 1956–1970. *Current trends in Linguistics*, 10, 505–92.
HAVILAND, JOHN 1979, How to talk to your brother-in-law in Guugu Yimidhirr. In SHOPEN, TIM, (ed.), *Languages and their Speakers*, pp. 161–239. Cambridge, Mass: Winthrop.
HEARST, SUSAN 1981, *Ethnic Communities and their Aged*. Richmond: Clearing House on Migration Issues.
HESSE, SILKE 1980, Reflections of an Australian bilingual. *Journal of Intercultural Studies*, 1(3), 53–5.
HOFFMANN, CHARLOTTE 1985, Language acquisition in two trilingual children. *Journal of Multilingual and Multicultural Development*, 6(6), 449–66.
HOFFMEISTER, WALTER 1977, *Sprachwechsel in Ost-Lothringen*. Wiesbaden: Franz Steiner Verlag.
HOFMANN, MARGRET 1957, Can the mother tongue be retained for children of German immigrants? *The American-German Review*, Aug.–Sept., 15–17.
HOPE, LAURA LEE 1955, *The Bobbsey Twins at Snow Lodge*. Manchester: World Distributors.
HORGAN, D. 1978, The Development of the full passive. *Journal of Child Language*, 5, 65–80.
HUERTA, ANA 1977, The acquisition of bilingualism: A code-switching approach. *Sociolinguistic Working Paper No. 39*, 1–33.
HUGHES, FELICITY 1971, *Reading and Writing Before School*. London: Cape.
IANCO-WORRALL, ANITA 1972, Bilingualism and cognitive development. *Child Development*, 43, 1390–400.
IMEDADZE, NATELA V. 1967, On the psychological nature of child speech formation under conditions of exposure to two languages. *International Journal of Psychology*, 2, 129–32.
ISAACS, EVA 1967, *Greek Children in Sydney*. Canberra: ANU Press.
JESPERSEN, OTTO 1922, *Language. Its Nature, Development and Origin*. London: George Allen & Unwin Ltd.

JOHNSON, WENDELL, 1967a, Stuttering. In WENDELL JOHNSON *et al.*, *Speech Handi-capped School Children*, 229–329. New York, Evanston and London: Harper & Row.

— 1967b, A open letter to the mother of a "stuttering" child. In WENDELL JOHNSON *et al.*, *Speech Handicapped School Children*, 543–54. New York, Evanston and London: Harper & Row.

KESSLER, CAROLYN & QUINN, MARY ELLEN 1982, Cognitive development in biling-ual environments. In B. HARTFORD, A. VALDMAN & R. FOSTER (eds), *Issues in International Bilingual Education: The Role of the Vernacular*, 53–79, New York: Plenum Press.

— 1987, Language minority children's linguistic and cognitive creativity. *Journal of Multilingual and Multicultural Development*, 8 (1/2), 173–86.

KIELHÖFER, BERND & JONEKEIT, SYLVIE 1983, *Zwiesprachige Kindererziehung*. Tübingen: Stauffenberg Verlag.

KLOSS, HEINZ 1966, German-American Language Maintenance Efforts. In JOSHUA FISHMAN (ed.), *Language Loyalty in the United States*. The Hague: Mouton.

KOLERS, PAUL 1968, Bilingualism and information processing. *Scientific American*, 218(3), 78–86.

KOUZMIN, LUDMILLA 1976, Some patterns and conditions of code-switching from Russian to English. *Talanya*, 3, 107–116.

KRASHEN, STEPHEN 1973, Lateralization, language learning, and the critical period: Some new evidence. *Language Learning*, 23, 63–74.

KRINGAS, P. & LEWINS, F. 1981, *Why Ethnic Schools?* Canberra: ANU Press.

KUPINSKY, BONNIE 1983, Bilingual reading instruction in kindergarten. *The Reading Teacher*, Nov., 132–37.

LADO, ROBERT 1977, Acquisition and learning in early reading. *Hispania*, 60, 533–35.

— 1987, Early reading and language development with exceptional children. *Inter-national Preschool Reading Association Journal*, 1(3), 7–10.

LAMBERT, WALLACE & ANISFIELD, ELIZABETH 1969, A note on the relationship of bilingualism and intelligence. *Canadian Journal of Behavioral Science*, 1, 123–28.

LAMBERT, WALLACE 1975, Culture and language as factors in learning and educa-tion. In WOLFGANG, A. (ed.), *Education of Immigrant Students*. Toronto: Ontario Institute for Studies in Education.

— 1977, The effects of bilingualism on the individual: Cognitive and sociocultural consequences. In HORNBY, PETER, (ed.), *Bilingualism. Psychological, Social and Educational Implications*. 15–28. New York: Academic Press.

— 1978, Some cognitive and sociocultural consequences of being bilingual. In ATLATIS, JAMES (ed.), *Georgetown University Round Table on Languages and Linguistics 1978*, pp. 214–9. Washington: Georgetown University Press.

LAPKIN, SHARON,SWAIN, MERRILL & ARGUE, VALERIE 1983, *French Immersion: The Trial Balloon That Flew*. Ontario: Ontario Institute for Studies in Education.

LENNEBERG, E. 1967, *Biological Foundations of Language*. New York: John Wiley and Sons.

LEOPOLD, WERNER 1939, *Speech Development of a Bilingual Child: A Linguist's Record*. (Vol. I): *Vocabulary growth in the first two years*. Evanston: Northwest-ern University Press.

— 1947, *Speech Development of a Bilingual Child: A Linguist's Record*. (Vol. II): *Sound learning in the first two years*. Evanston: Northwestern University Press.

— 1949a, *Speech Development of a Bilingual Child: A Linguist's Record.* (Vol. III). *Grammar and general problems in the first two years.* Evanston: Northwestern University Press.

— 1949b, *Speech Development of a Bilingual Child: A Linguist's Record.* (Vol. IV): *Diary from age two.* Evanston: Northwestern University Press.

— 1957–8, American children can learn their German mother tongue. *The American-German Review,* 24, 4–6

LIEDTKE, W. & NELSON, L. 1968, Concept formation and bilingualism. *Alberta Journal of Educational Research,* 24, 4–6.

LOWIE, ROBERT 1945, A case of bilingualism. *Word,* 1, 249–59.

MACNAMARA, JOHN 1966, *Bilingualism and Primary Education.* Edinburgh: Edinburgh University Press.

— 1967, The bilingual's linguistic performance — a psychological overview. *Journal of Social Issues,* 23, 58–77.

— 1971, Linguistic independence of bilinguals. *Journal of Verbal Learning and Verbal Behavior,* 10, 480–7.

MAGNESS, ANGELA 1987, A British-style education overseas. *The Bilingual Family Newsletter,* 4(1), 3–4.

MCGILL, GRAHAM 1980, Bilingual Education in the Northern Territory. In Lê, THAO & MCCAUSLAND, MICHAEL (eds), *Proceedings of the Conference Child Language Development: Theory into Practice, September 1980,* 195–205. Launceston: Launceston Teachers Centre.

MCGREGOR, CRAIG 1987, Class in Australia. *Good Weekend,* 9 Oct. 1987, 36–67.

MCKIRNAN, DAVID & HAMAYAN, ELSE 1984, Speech attitudes towards outgroup members: A test of a model in a bicultural context. *Journal of Language and Social Psychology,* 1, 21–38.

MCLAUGHLIN, BARRY 1978, *Second-Language Acquisition in Childhood.* Hillsdale, N.J.: Lawrence Erlbaum Associates.

MEIJERS, J. A. 1969, *De taal van het kind.* Utrecht/Antwerpen: Uitgeverij Het Spectrum.

MEISEL, JÜRGEN 1986, Word order and case marking in early child language. Evidence from simultaneous acquisition of two languages. *Linguistics,* 24(1), 123–83.

— 1987, Early differentiation of languages in bilingual children. To appear in HYLTENSTAM, KENNETH & OBLER, LORAINE (eds), *Bilingualism across the lifespan: In health and pathology.*

MENYUK, P. 1971, *The Acquisition and Development of Language.* Englewood Cliffs, N.J. Prentice-Hall.

MÉTRAUX, R. 1964, A study of bilingualism among U.S.–French parents. *The French Review,* 38, 650–5.

MONTERO, ANA 1985 (in progress). Relation of Preschool Literacy to Oral Language Development Among Spanish-English Bilinguals: Spanish Pronunciation. Ph.D. dissertation. Washington: Georgetown University.

MORRISON, J. 1958, Bilingualism: Some psychological aspects. *The Advancement of Science,* 56, 287–90.

NEUSTUPNY, JIRI 1985, Problems in Australian-Japanese contact situations. In PRIDE, JOHN (ed.), *Cross-Cultural Encounters. Communication and Mis-Communication,* 44–64. Melbourne: River Seine Publications.

NORDBERG, B. 1976, Sociolinguistic research in Sweden and Finland. *International Journal of the Sociology of Language,* 10, 5–16.

NYGREN-JUNKIN, L. 1977, *The interaction between French and English in the speech of four bilingual children.* Master's thesis, Ontario Institute for Studies in Education, Toronto.

OKSAAR, ELS 1971, Zum Spracherwerb des Kindes in zweisprachiger Umgebung. *Folia Linguistica,* 4, 330–58.

— 1973, Implications of language contact for bilingual language acquisition. Paper presented to the IXth International Congress of Anthropological and Ethnological Sciences in Chicago, Aug. 28–Sept. 8 1973.

— 1976, Code switching as an interactional strategy for developing bilingual competence. *Word,* 27.

— 1977, On becoming trilingual. A case study. In MALONEY, CAROL, (ed.), *Deutsch im Kontakt mit anderen Sprachen,* 296–306. Kronberg: Scriptor Verlag.

O'SULLIVAN, EMER & RÖSLER, DIETMAR 1983 *I like you – und du?* Reinbek bei Hamburg: Rowohlt.

PADILLA, AMADO & LIEBMANN, E. 1975, Language acquisition in the bilingual child. *The Bilingual Review,* 2, 34–5.

PARISH, PEGGY 1976, *Ootahs Glückstag,* trans. BAHN, URSULA. Reinbek bei Hamburg: Carlsen Verlag.

PAST, AL 1976, *Preschool Reading in Two Languages as a Factor in Bilingualism.* Ph.D. thesis, University of Texas at Austin.

PAST, KAY 1976, A case of preschool reading and speaking acquisition in two languages. In LADO, ROBERT & ANDERSSON, THEODORE (eds), *Georgetown University Papers on Languages and Linguistics,* 58–73. Washington: Georgetown University Press.

PAST, AL & PAST, KAY 1978, Early childhood: the best time to become bilingual and biliterate. *Childhood Education,* 54(3), 155–61.

PAULSTON, CHRISTINA BRATT 1975, Ethnic relations and bilingual education: accounting for contradictory data. *Working Papers on Bilingualism,* 6.

PAUWELS, ANNE 1980, *The Effects of Mixed Marriages on Language Shift in the Dutch Community in Australia.* M.A. thesis, Monash University, Melbourne.

PEAL, ELIZABETH & LAMBERT, WALLACE 1962, Relation of bilingualism to intelligence. *Psychological Monographs,* 76, 1–23.

PEÑA, A. & BERNAL, E. 1978, Malpractices in language assessment for Hispanic children. In *Occasional Papers on Linguistics No. 3,* 102–116. Southern Illinois University at Carbondale.

PENFIELD, W. & ROBERTS, L. 1959, *Speech and Brian Mechanisms.* Princeton: Princeton University Press.

PERRIN, GEOFFREY 1982, Divergences between spoken and written language – their implications for the classroom. *The British Journal of Language Teaching,* 20(1), 55–57.

POLITZER, ROBERT 1978, Errors of English speakers of German as perceived and evaluated by German natives. *The Modern Language Journal,* LXII, 253–261.

PORSCHÉ, DONALD 1983, *Die Zweisprachigkeit während des primären Spracherwerbs.* Tübingen: Gunter Narr Verlag.

PRICE, C. & PYNE, P. 1977, The immigrants. In A. DAVIES *et al.,* (eds), *Australian Society. A Sociological Introduction,* 331–55. Melbourne: Longman Cheshire.

PRIESTLY, T. 1980, Homonymy in child phonology. *Journal of Child Language,* 7, 413–27.

REHBEIN, JOCHEN 1985, Diskurs und Verstehen. Zur Rolle der Muttersprache bei der Textverarbeitung. *Arbeiten zur Mehrsprachigkeit 1,* Hamburg: Universität

Hamburg, Germanisches Seminar/Deutsch als Fremdsprache.
REITMAJER, V. 1975, Schlechte Chancen ohne Hochdeutsch. *Muttersprache*, 310–24.
REYNOLD, DE. 1928, In *Bieler Jahrbuch – Annales Biennoises II*, 105.
RICHARDS, JACK & TAY, MARY 1981, Norm and variability in language use and language learning. In L. SMITH (ed.), *English for Cross-Cultural Communication*. New York: St. Martin's.
RONDAL, J. 1980, Fathers' and mothers' speech in early language development. *Journal of Child Language*, 7, 353–69.
RONJAT, JULES 1913, *Le développement du language observé chez un enfant bilingue*. Paris: Librairie Ancienne H. Champion.
ROSIER, P. & FARELLA, M. 1976, Bilingual education at Rock Point — Some early results. *TESOL Quarterly*, 10(4), 379–88.
RŪĶE-DRAVIŅA, VELTA 1967, *Mehrsprachigkeit im Vorschulalter*. Lund: Gleerup.
SAER, D. 1923, The effect of bilingualism on intelligence. *British Journal of Psychology*, 14, 25–38.
SANTOS, PERCILIA 1984, Biliteracy and language development in low-income Spanish-speaking preschool children. Ph.D. dissertation. Washington: Georgetown University.
SAUNDERS, GEORGE 1980a, Adding a second native language in the home, *Journal of Multilingual and Multicultural Development*, 1(2), 113–44.
— 1980b, Creating bilingualism, *Australian Review of Applied Linguistics*, 3(2), 122–30.
— 1982a, Infant bilingualism: a look at some doubts and objections, *Journal of Multilingual and Multicultural Development*, 3(4), 277–92.
— 1982b, Der Erwerb einer zweiten "Muttersprache" in der Familie. In SWIFT, JAMES (ed.), *Bilinguale und multikulturelle Erziehung*, 26–33. Würzburg: Verlag Königshausen & Neumann.
— 1982c, *Bilingual Children: Guidance for the Family*. Clevedon: Multilingual Matters Ltd.
— 1984a, Creating bilingualism revisited. *Australian Review of Applied Linguistics*, Series S, No. 1, 24–35.
— 1984b, An interview with a Turkish–English bilingual. *Bilingual Family Newsletter*, 1(2), 3.
— 1984c, Mother-tongue playgroups for pre-school bilingual children. *Bilingual Family Newsletter*, 1(2), 4–5.
— 1984d, Listening to your children read can make them better readers. *Bilingual Family Newsletter*, 1 (3), 4.
— 1985a, Recognition of children's bilingualism. *Bilingual Family Newsletter*, 2(1), 4.
— 1985b, The monolingual versus the bilingual view of bilingualism as seen by François Grosjean. *Bilingual Family Newsletter*, 2(2), 2–3.
— 1986a, Video cassettes from abroad — an excellent idea for language maintenance and development — but don't forget compatibility. *Bilingual Family Newsletter*, 3(1), 3–4.
— 1986b, Health workers and bilingual families. *Bilingual Family Newsletter*, 3(1), 5–6.
— 1986c, Teaching children to read at home — a look at some of the literature. *Bilingual Family Newsletter*, 3(2), 3–4.
— 1986d, "Artificial" bilingualism. *Bilingual Family Newsletter*, 3(3), 3–4.

— 1987, The benefits of community language instruction: Recent research. *Migration Monitor*, Year 2, No. 4, Jan., 9–10.

SAVILLE, MURIEL & TROIKE, RUDOLPH 1971, *A Handbook of Bilingual Education*. Washington: TESOL.

SCHAEFER FU, GAIL 1986, In defence of the monolingual mother. *Bilingual Family Newsletter*, 3(4), 3–4.

SCHLIEMANN, HEINRICH 1881, Autobiography of the author. In *Ilias, the City and Country of the Trojans*. Reprinted New York: Benjamin Bloom, 1968.

SCHMIDT, ANNETTE 1985, *Young People's Dyirbal. An Example of Language Death from Australia*. Cambridge: CUP.

SCHNITZER, M. 1978, Cerebral lateralization and plasticity: Their relevance to language acquisition. In MICHEL PARADIS, (ed.), *Aspects of Bilingualism*, pp. 149–55. Columbia: Hornbeam Press.

SCOTT, S. 1973, The relation of divergent thinking to bilingualism: cause or effect? Unpublished research report, McGill University.

SCOVEL, T. 1969, Foreign accents, language acquisition, and cerebral dominance. *Language Learning*, 245–53.

SEGALOWITZ, NORMAN 1977, Psychological perspectives on bilingual education. In SPOLSKY, BERNARD & COOPER, ROBERT, (eds), *Frontiers of Bilingual Education*, 119–58. Massachusetts: Newbury House.

SHARP, DERRICK 1973, *Language in Bilingual Communities*. London: Edward Arnold.

SKUTNABB-KANGAS, TOVE 1984, *Bilingualism or Not. The Education of Minorities*. Clevedon: Multilingual Matters Ltd.

— & PHILLIPSON, ROBERT 1985, Support for bilingualism in the family. *Sproglæreren*, Dec.

SMOLICZ, J. J. 1979, *Culture and Education in a Plural Society*. Canberra. Curriculum Development Centre.

— & HARRIS, R. 1976, Ethnic languages and immigrant youth. In CLYNE, MICHAEL, (ed.), *Australia Talks*, pp. 131–73. Canberra: ANU.

— & HARRIS, R. 1977, Ethnic languages in Australia. *International Journal of the Sociology of Language*, 14, 89–108.

SØNDERGAARD, BENT 1981, Decline and fall of an individual bilingualism. *Journal of Multilingual and Multicultural Development*, 2(4), 297–302.

STEPHENS, K. 1952, Reader's letter. *The Linguist*, Nov., 307.

STOFFEL, GERTRAUT 1983/84, Veränderungen und semantische Konflikte im Anredeverhalten Deutschsprachiger in Neuseeland. *Muttersprache*, 94, 185–93.

STOLT, BIRGIT 1964, *Die Sprachmischung in Luthers Tischreden: Studien zum Problem der Zweisprachigkeit*. Stockholm: Stockholmer Germanistische Forschungen.

SWAIN, MERRILL 1972, *Bilingualism as a First Language*. Ph.D. thesis, University of California at Irvine.

— & LAPKIN, SHARON & ANDREW, C. 1981, Early immersion later on. *Journal of Multilingual and Multicultural Development*, 2, 1–24.

TAESCHNER-FRANCESE, TRAUTE 1978, Zwei Sprachen als Muttersprache. *Umschau in Wissenschaft und Technik*, 23, 738.

TAESCHNER, TRAUTE 1982, *The Sun is Feminine. A Study on Language Acquisition in Bilingual Children*. Berlin: Springer-Verlag.

TAYLOR, L. J., DE LACEY, P. & NURCOMBE, B. 1972, An assessment of the reliability of the Peabody Picture Vocabulary Test. *Australian Psychologist*, 7(3), 167–9.

THIÉRY, CHRISTOPHER 1976, Le bilinguisme vrai. *Études de Linguistique Appliquée*, 24, 52–63.

THOMAS, JENNY 1983, Cross-cultural pragmatic failure. *Applied Linguistics*, 4(2), 91–112.

THOMPSON, STEFANIE 1980, *Australia Through Italian Eyes*. Melbourne: OUP.

TIMM, LENORA 1975, Spanish-English code-switching: El Porqué y How-Not-To. *Romance Philosophy*, 14, 473–82.

TIZARD, J., SCHOFIELD, W. & HEWISON, J. 1982, Collaboration between teachers and parents in assisting children's reading. *British Journal of Educational Psychology*, 52, 1–15.

TOLL, C. 1977, Frühe Zweisprachigkeit im Unterricht und die deutschen Auslandsschulen. *Zielsprache Deutsch*, 2, 15–24.

TRELEASE, JIM 1984, *The Read-Aloud Handbook*. Hammondsworth: Penguin.

VENT, HENRIETTE 1958, Letter to the editor. *The American-German Review*, Jan., 39–40.

VIHMAN, MARILYN MAY 1985, Language differentiation by the bilingual infant. *Journal of Child Language*, 12, 297–324.

VOLTERRA, VIRGINIA & TAESCHNER, TRAUTE 1978. The acquisition and development of language by bilingual children. *Journal of Child Language*, 5, 311–26.

VON RAFFLER-ENGEL, WALBURGA 1965, Del bilinguismo infantile. *Archivo Glottologica Italiano*, 50, 175–80.

— 1970, The concept of sets in a bilingual child. In *Actes du Xe Congrès International des Linguistes*. Vol. III. Bucharest: Romanian Academy Press.

WEIGT, MICHAEL 1985, Bilingualer Fachunterricht. Möglichkeiten sonderpädagogischer und sprachpädagogischer Förderung türkischer Schüler in einer 6. Klasse der Schule für Lernbehinderte. *Arbeiten zur Mehrsprachigkeit, 4*. Universität Hamburg, Germanisches Seminar/Deutsch als Fremdsprache.

WEIL, LISL 1976, *Even for a Mouse*. New York: Scholastic Book Services.

WEINREICH, URIEL 1953, *Languages in Contact*. New York (8th printing, The Hague: Mouton, 1974.)

WEISGERBER, LEO 1953, Zweisprachigkeit. *Schaffen und Schauen*, 9.

— 1966, Vorteile und Gefahren der Zweisprachigkeit. *Wirkendes Wort*, 16(2), 73–89.

WILIAM, U. 1971, The construction of standardized tests for Welsh-speaking children. *Educational Research*, 14(1), 29–34.

WILKINSON, ANDREW 1971, *The Foundation of Language*. London: OUP.

WODE, HENNING 1974, Natürliche Zweitsprachigkeit: Probleme, Aufgaben, Perspektiven. *Linguistische Berichte*, 32, 15–36.

— 1978, Developmental sequences in naturalistic L2 acquisition. In HATCH, EVELYN (ed.), *Second Language Acquisition. A Book of Readings*, 101–7. Massachusetts: Newbury House.

ZEHETNER, L. 1977, *Bairisch. (Dialekt/Hochsprache — kontrastiv 2)*. Düsseldorf: Pädagogischer Verlag Schwann.

ZIERER, ERNESTO 1977, Experiences in the bilingual education of a child of pre-school age. *International Review of Applied Linguistics*, XV/2, 143–9.

Author Index

Subject Index